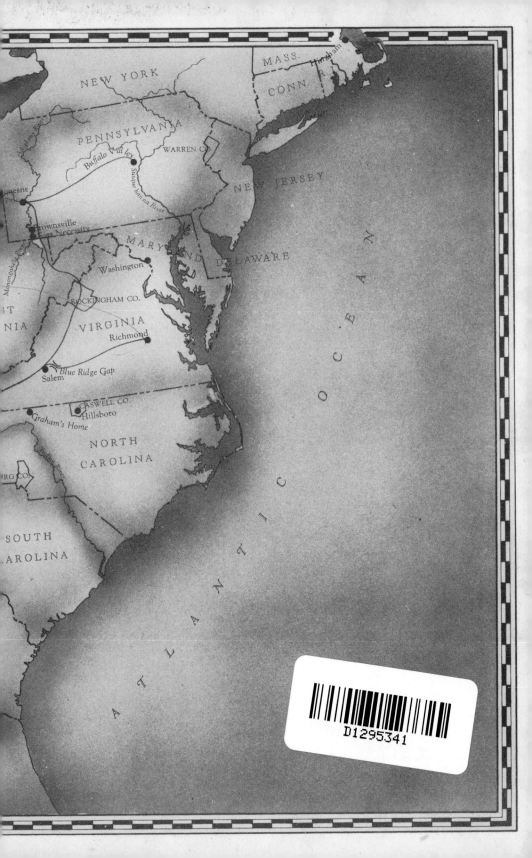

Mentor Graham

The man who taught Lincoln

GRAHAM AT THE TIME HE TAUGHT LINCOLN

KUNIGUNDE DUNCAN and D. F. NICKOLS

Mentor Graham

The man who taught Lincoln

University of Chicago Press · Chicago

THE UNIVERSITY OF CHICAGO COMMITTEE ON PUBLICATIONS
IN THE HISTORY OF THOUGHT AND CULTURE

JOSEPH A. BRANDT STANLEY PARGELLIS

RICHARD P. McKEON JACOB VINER

JOHN T. McNEILL   GEORGE WILLIAMSON

NAPIER WILT

Drawing for title-page by Edmund Giesbert
Jacket design by Kathleen King

University of Chicago Press · Chicago 37

Agent: Cambridge University Press · London

To the American Teacher

TWO FOREWORDS

I

*T*HE PURPOSE of this book is to render a measure of justice to a worthy pioneer schoolmaster who, somehow, has been overlooked for three-quarters of a century.

Who was Mentor Graham? What sort of man was he? Just what did he do? Such questions have been asked repeatedly since the early biographies of Abraham Lincoln were written. That he was the village schoolmaster who taught Lincoln grammar and surveying is reported by historians and biographers. And that is all.

Having myself been identified with the teaching profession for more than forty years in Logan County, Illinois, in the very heart of the Lincoln country, next door to New Salem, my interest was stimulated, a full generation ago, in this unusual man. It was heightened upon learning that Miss Flora Graham, one of my teachers, was a granddaughter of Lincoln's teacher and that her distinguished grandsire had lived for a time in my own city of Lincoln.

When the restoration of Lincoln's New Salem was begun, a movement was also started to return the remains of Mentor Graham from Blunt, South Dakota, to Illinois; but for various reasons the venture failed. Later, to the credit of another of Graham's granddaughters, Mrs. Mary Graham Bradley, of Greenview, Illinois, the reinterment was finally consummated, in Farmers' Point Cemetery, near New Salem. In these reburial rites I was privileged to take part, as well as in the erection of the memorial which was later placed at the grave by the Illinois Education Association.

For many years Graham's biography had seemed to me merely

a desirable thing that should be done; but on summing my notes for the reburial address, the project began to assume the form of a definite, personal responsibility that I must not shirk. I had the local research somewhat in hand, but I had learned nothing of Graham's early life.

A chance conversation with Kunigunde Duncan ended in my asking her to undertake the task with me. Immediately our quest went from local to nation-wide. For five years Miss Duncan and I have sifted libraries over the country; and each of us has made many excursions into the South and about Illinois, searching out the facts of Mentor Graham's life. The result is this volume.

In the light of all that happened at New Salem, it is clear that that village was the turning-point in the life of Abraham Lincoln. It was the springboard of a career unparalleled in secular history. This book is presented in justice to the forgotten man who did more for Lincoln than all others. The familiar metaphor which speaks of New Salem as "Lincoln's Alma Mater" should be completed by adding: "The faculty was Mentor Graham."

D. F. Nickols

Lincoln, Illinois
August 1944

II

WHEN a humble schoolmaster has been dead for more than a half-century; when fire has destroyed his books and papers, including his own carefully kept record of his daily affairs; when there is little to be found concerning him in public prints, since he figured only rarely and modestly in any public capacity—can his biography be written? Few would concede that it could be: the task would seem to be an impossible one; yet that is the task that has been undertaken here.

In the beginning we had literally nothing but faith to proceed upon—faith in two dependable, if idealistic, principles. The one, that there is a fate that keeps alive in the world, after he is dead, the influence of a good man; a fate that *records him in others*. The second, that no man is of himself, alone. Quickening of wit and will, of bodily form, of temperament, of mental and spiritual stance—all elements of him—are traceable in large degree to things and people outside himself: his ancestors, his associates, the kind of world through which he passed. Upon these beliefs we proceeded.

Not more than twenty statements have been written about Mentor Graham, and those are duplicative. To this meager portrait we added a few elements gleaned in our quest covering places where he and his forebears once lived. We searched decaying headstone, crumbling record, local history, newspapers. We paged his ancestors and his associates and the kind of world through which he passed. In spite of this, Mentor Graham failed to come alive.

But accidental discovery of distant kinship led to adoption by the Graham "clan." They were amply able to supply the lacking and essential essence. In many scores of men and women fate had kept alive the memory and influence of this good man. We found him, *recorded in others*. They could catalogue the chief experiences of his life, the details of his childhood, manhood, old age. They gave us his letters. But more, they had seen his hurried, rangy stride, his piercingly keen eyes. They had heard his kindly words—and fearless.

It has been my challenging privilege to attempt to extract from more than two hundred living sources those truly biographical elements—events, people, experience, *words*—that molded Mentor Graham into the man that he was. I can put down with certainty that only a few incidents, and those quite commonplace, were the turning-points in his eighty-six years. In this, again, another cherished theory has proved out. Biography is neither dates nor achievements. It is those bright words that slip through every-dayness, to be lived by forever; and hardship of blank years, with yet some little glint of purpose and reason of life shining through; and midnight friends; and the soul becoming certain of life as death nears. Writing a biography of this kind is following a soul-quest, so that the reader receives that impact—implicit, electric, in inanimate words set down. That I have fallen far short of this I am deeply conscious. Even so, these pages are offered with a degree of satisfaction, for I believe Mr. Nickols and I have made an exhaustive search of Graham's visitations, blank years, and midnight friends; and I have recorded our findings with the utmost integrity and sympathy of which I am capable.

To annotate each statement would have doubled the volume, without great gain. However, our informants' names are included in the text *whenever their family traits serve to make the man Graham more seeable;* for the Grahams are not a clan for nothing: their characteristics are unfailing and identical, generation upon generation. The signatures of four generations of William Grahams are scarcely distinguishable.

Yet, like the biography of Lincoln, this biography must rest chiefly upon what others knew of, saw in, and heard about Graham, not upon what he revealed about himself. Doubtless it is distorted by human myopia, as all such appraisals inevitably are. Yet through it Graham becomes less lost an identity than he would have been had he remained as defined by the twenty statements through which history until now has known him.

And, as Mentor Graham was not of himself, alone, so, too, the recorder of his life: no one person ever writes a book—nor two nor three—though their names appear in the authors' place upon the binding. Every writer leans upon all that has gone before: thought, writing, research, record. To that past I give deep and grateful acknowledgment. And I must acknowledge an even greater debt as a writer.

The coldly columned list of informants to be found in the Appendix is indeed small recognition of the part all these kindly and generous folk had in bringing together the big and little puzzle-pieces that, fitted in place, turned into the likeness of Mentor Graham. Data have been sent from across the length and breadth of the United States, hunted from trunk and drawer, attic and memory. Records have been deciphered overseas and forwarded. And all of it out of pure good will and interest. A poor best, indeed, this type-gesture of thanks, in a columned list.

The story of how and from whom material was assembled would, of itself, compose a volume larger than this and perhaps little less interesting as a human document. Our letter count stands at 2,241 and represents coverage of every library and historical association in this country and individuals over eleven states.

Our travel, by train, automobile, bus, mule cart, and afoot, totals seven thousand miles in three states during the last five years.

Though the reader will necessarily judge these pages in the light of their title and decide for himself whether or not Graham could and did teach Lincoln, *may he find here also a man who— had he never known Lincoln—would deserve this recognition for his royally played part in the spiritual story of America.*

KUNIGUNDE DUNCAN

WICHITA, KANSAS
August 1944

TABLE OF CONTENTS

Beginning his story with the birth of a man in no wise accounts for him. He reaches back into what his forebears thought, believed, and were. After weighing all the evidence, it seems clear enough that Lang Willie of the Border, the Regulators, the Long Hunters, Baptist church history, Benjamin Lynn, and Johnson Graham—and much more—were definite elements in Mentor Graham's equipment when he was born. Upon this premise we offer

A PROLOGUE

—K. D.

PROLOGUE
1603–1787

*E*NGLAMOURED by legend is the figure of Lang Willie Graeme, Scotch clansman, who had no rein on his tongue, no sheath to his sword, and no fear of kings in his heart. Genes of eloquence, courage, and adherence to principle seem to have come down, little altered through fourteen generations, from the redheaded borderer, Lang Willie, to the redheaded backwoods schoolmaster, William Mentor Graham, of the American frontier days in Kentucky and Illinois.

Lang Willie's sept ruffled King James of England. They talked back. They kept up a continual ruckus with other clans on the border, always honoring the method of their founder, Lang Willie, in dealing with things to which they objected. If Lang Willie's own son disgraced him by marrying a girl from that Armstrong clan, the son found himself in a dungeon.

Because the Graemes did such things, they were, one hundred and forty strong, unceremoniously deported, packed off by ship one foggy morning in 1603, from Workingham, England. They were deposited, a little farther from uneasy royal slumber, upon lands the king had confiscated at Roscommon, Ulster.

Thus began the drama, enacted through many centuries, in whose climax William Mentor Graham was to play a difficult, pivotal part. Its scenes were to unfold slowly at first, but with increasing rapidity and tension, leading up to one of the greatest leaders of the modern world. The tragic nature of the drama was foretraced in the simple words of John Rolfe, secretary of the Virginia Colony, when he wrote in his record, after the Scotch deportees had been some sixteen years in Ireland: "About the last of August came in a Dutch man-of-warre that sold us twenty negars."

If anything, King James's deportation only served to strengthen the Graeme clan. Those transplanted Ulster folk—Scotch-Irish, as they were to be forever after called—were naturally hated by the Irish upon whose lands they had been dumped. Many a William Graeme, keeping his sword unsheathed, had had to fight it out. For a hundred years the English kings, set on persecuting Catholics, inevitably stirred up counterpersecution of deported Baptists and Presbyterians by Catholics; yet the north-of-Ireland generations of Graemes only grew more staunch in their faith. Though England curtailed flax and looms and flocks in Erin, the Graemes —spelled Graham, now—managed to pasture sheep, grow flax, and spin and weave, and, doing so, waxed mightily.

Even in England, weaving was likely to net a meager livelihood. Many a weaver's apprentice, like Samuel Lincoln, had left for the New World before La Salle canoed down the Mississippi. And, when the cruel years came, when the kings sought to starve Ireland; when Ireland became a lawless land of smugglers of linens and woolens to other ports than England's; when dire poverty was the common lot and there seemed little hope of anything better—a certain youngish William Graham and his family, along with other Scotch-Irish folk, among them a Mr. and Mistress Andrew Lynn, set sail one foggy morning, in the year 1701, for the fabulous land of America where a man might hope to be a man.

Brawny, ignorant, the two young men, William and Andrew, were friends. La Salle and his Fort Crèvecoeur, near the spot where a great scene in the slavery drama would take place, were not even names to them. They knew nothing of Marquette's camp, pitched upon the site where an Illinois capital, Vandalia, would rise. Nor of a Mississippi River, which had now been proved not to flow into a western ocean. It lacked but a few years of being the one-hundredth anniversary of that other foggy-morning sailing at a king's command—but this sailing was commanded by the voyagers' own vision. They said farewell forever to an Old World and went forth to a New, with courage and in fear of no man. Their ship headed out for Massachusetts Bay, bearing men and women bent upon inheriting a new kind of world; who would furnish some of the battle-blood that would make the hopefully named New World a world worthy to inherit.

Like the weaver's apprentice Samuel Lincoln, who had come to America three generations before, William and Andrew knew flax and looms and linen. By what twist of destiny was it that they, like Samuel, landed at Massachusetts Bay, passed through Hingham, where the lad Samuel had worked as an apprentice, and went on to settle in Warren County, New Jersey, near the place where Samuel's descendants then lived? For these weavers themselves were to become the warp and woof of a glowing New World moral fabric, patterned with the dignity and worth of common men and their right to govern themselves. And after many harsh years these same men of vision, in the blood of their descendants, would empower a great emancipator. In Britain the Lincolns and those Scotch deportees had lived one hundred and fifty miles apart. Now the hand of the Great Weaver converged his living threads, preparatory to the pattern. In the New World the Lincolns and the Grahams were frontiersmen together. Free men!

But there came another ship sailing to these new shores, and its cargo was five hundred black men. To work the mines for the white's profit; to pay with life if they killed a deer; to receive the white's eighty lashes; to rise in the night, fearfully, to visit their kind. . . . . Whose affair was it why or how a master killed his slave?

At first Andrew and William knew nothing of all this. Like most newcomers, they had been content to settle near shore, where earning a living for growing families and the zest of free enterprise was enough to use up energies and to satisfy. Inland risks, southern plantation slaves, the mystery of what lay beyond the mountains, did not intrigue them. They *owned* land. Some of the Lincolns were very extensive landowners in the Schuylkill Valley.

Within a decade, as the Lynns and Grahams increased and flourished, a fourth weaver came into their midst—a George Boone, from Columpton, near Essex, England. He settled near neighbor to the Lincolns. One son, Squire, was to sire that Daniel who would follow, by a few months, the Grahams and Lynns in exploring the wilderness where the Great Emancipator would be born. Squire remained a weaver only a short time. Like the Lincolns, Lynns, and Grahams, he heard the call that comes to men—but not of them—and answered it.

Marvelous tales these weavers heard of men who had "crossed" and found Frenchmen beyond the mountains. Strange words they heard: "buffalo," "the Illinois," "Indians," "Big Bone Lick," "Great Meadows," "the Wilderness." These horizons were to challenge all the weavers, their children, their children's children.

By the early 1750's the Scotch-Irish Lynns and Grahams had children living in Buffalo Valley, one hundred miles to the west, in what is now Northumberland County, Pennsylvania; and the Lincolns, forty miles away, were known to them. In a petition signed by Lynns and Grahams, Buffalo Valley asked Gouverneur Morris for ammunition to keep off the Indians; but the Six Nations outfought the whites and the west-heading tide was driven back eastward. But it soon surged up and west again, to that gateway which led "beyond the mountaings," the Monongahela country, where Fort Pitt would rise upon the ashes of the French Fort, Duquesne.

For a decade or more Buffalo Valley prospered. Perhaps many of the pattern's threads, left untraced, are to be found here. Something more than coincidence, it would seem, included in the list of these settlers names that were duplicated, after almost another hundred years, in a log-cabin village called New Salem on the banks of the Sangamon River in the Illinois country—a village which, itself, flourished but a decade. In Buffalo Valley, as in New Salem, there were Lukinses, Potters, Camerons, Armstrongs, Duncans, Onstots, and Grahams. The fact that Hawkins Boone brought news to Buffalo Valley from the Lincolns in Berks County, completed the pattern-to-be.

But the big trek was still unmade. It beckoned out Monongahela way and south, with an insistence not to be resisted. Farms might be richer than any known in the Old World; yet the beguiling dream of ever richer lands that might be elsewhere, might be "over the mountaings," drew the human tide on like a triple moon-magnet. Slowly the great movement began, gathered momentum: west, down the Ohio waterway; south, following the mountains through

Virginia to Carolina. Lynns, Lincolns, Boones, Grahams, went with the rest. Squire Boone left in 1750, and soon after came Hawkins Boone with his six sons, the youngest, Daniel, just turned sixteen. The Boones had followed John Lincoln—who was to be the Emancipator's great-grandfather. Lincolns and Lynns went as far as Rockingham County, Virginia; but the Boones went on south—farther, farther.

Third Colonial generations of Lynns and Grahams were big landowners in Franklin County, Pennsylvania, by 1769; and some of them had already gone on west to the Monongahela. Here an Andrew Lynn, son of the first Andrew, had a thriving family. Three of his children—William, Benjamin, and Nancy Elizabeth—were destined to take part in the slavery drama. Meanwhile, one branch of Grahams had gone south into Virginia; and to the head of this family—who was yet another William Graham—was born a redheaded son, who was named William, of course. This child grew up to become a landowner in North Carolina, a soldier for the Colonies, and the great-grandfather of the redheaded backwoods schoolmaster, William Mentor Graham.

How long these Virginia Grahams remained in Virginia is not clear. But certain it is that the redheaded William born there in 1750 wed none other than Nancy Elizabeth Lynn, whose giant brothers, William and Benjamin, were destined to out-Boone Daniel Boone in Kentucky. These Lynns were grandchildren of that Andrew Lynn who had set sail from Ireland in 1701; and Nancy Elizabeth Lynn's husband, William Graham, was a grandson of Weaver William of the same voyage.

Evidently the Virginia Grahams joined the 1754 exodus of Baptists from New England and Virginia. Refusing the confession of faith as outlined by a Philadelphia Baptist convention, they rose up almost to a man, went south, and wrote their own confession. Most of them settled on Sandy Creek in North Carolina; and the "plantation" grew until it reached the Yadkin River, forty miles to the west. Early in 1760 the Grahams were settled on Hogan's Creek, Hillsborough District, of what is now Caswell County, North Carolina.

Few frontiersmen could not boast of at least six sons and as many daughters. Marriage was early; and if childbirth and hardship killed a first wife, a second often supplanted her within a year.

Thus it is not strange that, while Andrew Lynn was growing old on his rich Monongahela lands, with a young second wife and a young family, his eldest daughter by his first wife, Nancy Elizabeth, was married to the itch-footed William Graham, down in the Yadkin country.

Yadkin folks were hearing tales told them by Indians who wore French ornaments. The burden of these tales was that there was going to be a fight. The Ohio, the Illinois, the Wilderness, were not going to be had simply by going into them and settling. Even in the 1740's, Thomas Walker, following the Warrior's Trace (see endpaper map) had ventured through the Gap (Cumberland). Some time later, Christopher Gist had rafted down the Ohio River and by way of the Kentucky River had arrived at the Yadkin, where some of the Boones, Lincolns, and Grahams then lived. Gist told the bewondered Yadkinites of an Ohio country and of a "mighty fine broadenin' of the Ohio River they called 'the Falls.'" Ohio country belonged to the French. Homesteaders like Andrew Lynn, who had pressed out Monongahela way, had found a French fort, Duquesne, at the confluence of the Allegheny, Ohio, and Monongahela rivers.

When the trouble came to a head, the Yadkin folk were in the thick of it. Sandy Creek men and Hogan's Creek men rallied round, gave cattle and wagons, and found themselves under a young commander named George Washington, in Braddock's British army, with Thomas Walker and Christopher Gist as guides. Daniel Boone and a man named John Findley were wagoners. But Fort Duquesne did not fall; and the wagoners and patrols, escaping on the backs of their draft horses, made it home as best they could, with plenty of time to speculate upon fortunes that might be made "yon side." These Baptists had heard Washington read Episcopal prayers at Fort Necessity—not their kind of religion.

Daniel Boone returned to hunting in his "dooryard"—the Clinch, the Holsten, the Big Sandy and Wautauga rivers, and often as far as the Cumberland. Here he met the Grahams, out on like business. The Grahams were again hot under the collar because of the antics of a king. The last proclamation had prohibited settling upon any lands but those watered by streams flowing into the Atlantic Ocean. *What? Not cross the mountaings?*

It might as well have ordered them west. In effect, it amounted to that. North Carolinians were ready to move on, for Governor Tyron had been levying upon cabinfolk for fifteen thousand pounds with which to build himself a mansion. Land officials charged exorbitant fees for deeds and wills. This was a combination those Scotch-Irish couldn't and didn't tolerate. They organized militia called "The Regulators," wrote and sang a hymn of hate, burned a few barns, and mobbed a judge or two. But they lost, in the end. Governor Tyron got his mansion, and the land men their fees.

Well, there was still that country "yon side." Let anybody try to stop a man from crossing! With the mountains a perpetual challenge, these men who lived against the mountains thought more of what lay beyond them than they did of kings' edicts. They could, by their own wit and muscle, maintain themselves out of sight and hearing of royal governors. Though less than ten years had elapsed since the debacle of Fort Duquesne, and even if the mother-country now thought to control the Ohio, the Illinois, and the Wilderness, to the Yadkinites that made little difference. Their minds were set on "yon side," no matter who owned it.

Did not the frontier promise fulfilment of that dream of peace, plenty, and perfection in which men must forever believe? More. The sport of persecuting Baptists, which had run such a high fire in Virginia, had now caught in Carolina. Something akin to the urge that beset William, the weaver, back in 1701, now beset the Grahams of Hogan's Creek, Hillsborough District, Caswell County, North Carolina. It was only natural. The Long Rangers, John Findley and George Crogan, brought back reports that fitted "The Dream": tusks of animals, tusks as tall as a man, found at Big Bone Lick; trees, ten feet through; peas and cane, which would fatten cattle, growing wild. And game was so plentiful a hunter could stand still and kill more in five minutes than he could eat in a month. Ready-made traces (natural roads) had been stamped hard and wide by migrating herds of buffalo, animals with marvelous fur and fat and forequarters.

Not yet poised for flight, the hunting Boones and Grahams nevertheless ranged farther west each season. More and more frequently travelers brought word of folks who were rafting it down the Ohio, down to "Kan-tuck-ee," place of fabulous green meadows. "Land of tomorrow," the Indians called it; but little did the venturing hunters weigh the words of Iroquois or Cherokee Indian. They saw no grim specter haunting The Dream. Indian fighting was their second calling. They scorned Indians almost as much as they disdained the tidewater folk, squires, and "silk-stockings," whose doings as colonists were far from exemplary. Their lure was "the West."

Thus it happened that petite Nancy Elizabeth (Lynn) Graham, patient and full of courage, waited in her cabin on Hogan's Creek, in the year 1769, for the return of her William who had gone through The Gap with other hunters into a wilderness they called "Kaintuck," with a man named Knox as their leader. After a while Nancy Elizabeth went to stay with her man's kinfolks. She bore her absent hunter a son, a redheaded, strong-willed little William who was running about when his pappy got back. Grandpap had gone, too; but the womenfolks didn't mind. They were in the midst of the Graham "plantation"—the families of Edward, George, John, and Peter Graham were settled on land all about. Nancy Elizabeth's William had land, too, well cultivated; ordinarily he did not prefer hunting. The old folks' home was here also; and as their daughters—Lena, Polly, and Charity Ann—had not married yet, it made five women to keep things going and to spoil baby William. Seventy-five miles to the south, Rebecca Boone was staying with Daniel's kinfolks, waiting his return.

Daniel was in cahoots with a townsman, Richard Henderson, who had rigged him out for a long hunt over the mountaings into Kaintuck. In return, Daniel was to keep an eye out for more than game: firstcomers, managers, might make a fortune out of the land. When John Findley had come back from Indian trading, he had fired Daniel anew with the "wilderness fever," and he had offered himself as guide. So Boone's party had followed Findley off, one fine spring morning.

More than twenty men made up the hunting party of Nancy Elizabeth's William. Known to history as the "Long Hunters," these men who started a few weeks before Boone exceeded his time away by five months. Their trip took twenty-seven months; Boone's, twenty-two. William had mighty tales to tell of the pack horses half-buried in peltries, stumbling along under their weight. They had made bullboats of buffalo hide, filled them with melted fat, and paddled them down the Cumberland River to the lower settlements. Fat and pelts had brought good profit, some of the pelts selling as high as twenty shillings each. They had ranged far to the west of Boone's party,[1] as far west as the Green River country, and thence south into Tennessee.

Nancy Elizabeth's brother, Ben,[2] had been along. He was the brother who had left home when seventeen to live with Indians. He had hunted with them as far south as Natchez. He knew the Wilderness well enough to find his way anywhere in it. He had been the guide of the party, taking them, at the suggestion of Indian friends encountered on Dick's River, to the "Land of Beech-woods," as the Indian's poetic name described Kentucky's Green River country.

When the hunters were all in camp one night, after having hunted in separate parties during the day, Lynn failed to rendezvous at the appointed knoll. One of the wits, missing Lynn, said: "Well, here's the knoll, alright; but no Lynn!" Then and there the stream upon which they were camping, later to become famous as the birthplace of Abraham Lincoln, was named No-Lynn. They searched for Lynn; and when they found him camped alone a few miles off, they called the near-by brook Lynn Camp Creek; after all, it had been quite an effort to go hunting a hunter after dark.

The spot where they found Lynn was three miles from where Mentor Graham was later born. The lives of the Lynns, Grahams, and Lincolns were soon to be intimately affected by the very soil and streams where these Long Hunters pitched their Green River country camps and stored their great weight of peltries, too heavy to carry home all at once.

The Long Hunters would have to come back for their skins and furs, back to the spot that has come down to us as Camp Knox,[3] Kentucky. It must have been a magnificent spot before the "clarin'" of the settlers thinned the great beeches. These settlers, coming a little later, saw the possibilities of a certain broad-topped knoll as an Indian lookout and planted Mount Gilead Baptist Church on the very spot where the No-Lynn jest originated. The Long Hunters, themselves, had had no lack of good, sound "doctrinin'." Ben Lynn and Skaggs and two or three other Long Hunters had already been "called" and had preached in the cabins of the settlements, "amongst their kin."

The Boston Massacre took place the year they left the Yadkin. While they were roaming the western reaches of what is now Kentucky, the same George Washington under whom the Boones and Grahams and Findley had marched against Fort Duquesne had gone down the Ohio to the mouth of the Great Kanawha and filed upon five thousand acres of land in Kentucky County of Virginia. All young men went west—if they could. The Long Hunters had left behind many fortunes in deerskins. Any patient wife could see that they would have to go back for them.

This time the party was larger—perhaps as many as forty—with the first expedition men acting as guides back over the trails to the Green River country. Killing as they came, they at last neared their cache of pelts, salted down and skilfully hidden in a rock cave on Skinhouse Creek, as they named the stream whose banks were all but impassable with wild cane tangles—it is still so called. They shot buffalo, elk, white-tailed deer, wild turkeys, black bear—"turning up stones to get at the insects," as they themselves related. They had struggles with wildcats, already nicknamed "mountain lions." They had had splendid hunting on the Barrens, the name they gave to the almost unforested, great, grassy meadows where buffalo, unused to men, stood in mild interest, easy targets to be shot down.

Yet the fortunes in deerskins were never made. The pelts had rotted. Returning home, the hunters now talked only of fortunes to be made, of deep soil, big trees, good hunting—a place where a man might hope to be a man. They left the Green River country—now known as "the Lincoln Country"—resounding with their hunts. Besides Nolyn River[4] and Lynn Camp Creek, there are Caney Creek; Russell and Skaggs creeks and Camp Knox, named for their three leaders; the Barrens; and Little and Big Barrens rivers. But the river they named the "Louisa" became the "Kentucky" River. Until fifty years ago a jackknife-carved legend cut by one of them in the bark of a giant beech tree was still legible: "2300 deerskin rotted, ruination, by God."

Like Rebecca Boone, Nancy Elizabeth Graham listened to the stories of the first Long Hunt. Unlike Rebecca, she also heard the tales of a second Long Hunt, something like those she had heard in her father's cabin on the Monongahela about a paradisial place called Caroliny. She knew what such stories meant: eventually she would be going to Kaintuck, just as she had come to Caroliny. A good wife never crossed her husband. Besides, she had a hankering to go where her own blood-brothers were, William and Benjamin, Nathan and James and David.

But the Boston Massacre had had its sequel. As the 1770's wore on, William Graham volunteered to fight the Red Coats; and it happened that lithe, patient little Nancy Elizabeth was to grow old and knotted—at thirty-five—with seven living children and four dead—before she and William would go homesteading through Cumberland Gap.

But she would go. The French, settled in the Illinois, at Kaskaskia, Cahokia, and Prairie du Rocher, living indolent lives with a slave for every three whites, knew nothing of the coming encroachments of red-blooded people like the Carolinians, of hardship-toughened women like Nancy Elizabeth Graham and Rebecca Boone. Their ease was soon to be rudely shattered, for the frontiersmen—men who could wrest a living from the wilderness by their own wit and muscle, men whose wives, unlike the French, would go with them—the frontiersmen were coming. Soon Cumberland Gap would be witnessing a procession, headed northwest, unparalleled in the annals of the New World.

Lexington, Concord, Ticonderoga, Crown Point, Bunker Hill— all occurred while Nancy Elizabeth waited for the homecoming of her William who had gone to war. Back and forth before her cabin went the roused, fighting-mad Carolinians, who finally, in near-by Mecklenburg County, proclaimed a Declaration of Independence. Just as the Assembly was on the point of adjourning, George Rogers Clark arrived from a two-hundred-mile foot journey through the Kentucky wilderness to beg gunpowder. The Indians were going to have to be driven out. That was in May. By December, 1775, Clark had gotten his gunpowder as far as Limestone (Maysville, Kentucky).

Nancy Elizabeth, tending her children, scanning the blue haze to the west that to her was the "Blue Ledge Mountaings," could only wait and wonder. At first, after the Long Hunts, news of her brothers had trickled back through The Gap to Hogan's Creek, with even a promise of a visit on their way back to Old Redstone Fort on the Monongahela, near which their father, Andrew Lynn, still lived. From there you could raft it down the Ohio to the Falls and so be within walking distance of the Green River country, which was the apple of the Lynn brothers' eyes. But now no news had come from them for many months.

Nancy might have tingled with pride could she have known that they were playing a vital part in the birth of a nation. For Ben, hearing from French traders in the Ozark that Colony troops were trying to drive the French from the Ohio and the Mississippi, had set out on foot for the Monongahela, where the troops were being organized. Tramping a "cutoff trail" through the wilderness, he had come upon Harrod's Fort and had been welcomed for his knowledge of Shawnee, Delaware, Maumee, and Kickapoo Indian tongues, his rifle skill, his acquaintance with Indian and hunters' traces far to the south, west, and north. It was in January, 1777, that James Harrod, commander of the fort, named Ben Lynn, among others, to fetch Clark's gunpowder from Limestone for the fort's defense. Thus it happened that Clark named Lynn as a "spye of the Illinois" at the time when he named James Harrod and John Todd his captains. Todd's descendant, a certain Mary Todd, was destined to play her own dreary part in the slavery drama, whose scenes now quickened.

When the gunpowder had been safely delivered to the fort, Lynn and his companion "spye," Samuel Moore (More), set out for the French settlements in the Illinois. On foot and by stolen canoe they made it, evading the Indians, obtaining the information sought, and, having been warned by a trader friend of Lynn's, at Kaskaskia, escaping just in time, running like deer at the moment when the Indian council was deciding upon their capture and torture. In the light of a full moon they fled across the Illinois prairies, slipping down buffalo traces, charting their course by salt licks, and coming in, amid cheers, at Fort Harrod, to give George Rogers Clark "all the information I could reasonably expect."[5]

William Lynn had done even greater deeds for the cause of liberty. He was one of an intrepid party that in 1776–77 conveyed nine thousand pounds of gunpowder upstream, in barges rowed by forty men, from New Orleans to Wheeling and Fort Pitt.[6] After long months of poling and after wintering at Arkansas Post, they succeeded in reaching Wheeling and Fort Pitt—not Fort Duquesne any longer—in an exploit that may have saved the Colonies. William reported back to Clark, was made colonel, went through the

entire Illinois campaign, and completed his service by accompany-
ing home the Kentucky three-month volunteers and by strengthening the fort on Corn Island (Louisville).

But to Hogan's Creek news of all this had not come. News of the
Philadelphia Declaration of Independence had been slow in coming in 1776, as had that of the new flag in 1777. But William Graham had gone, leaving his books and his plow to Nancy and the
children. And when, at last, he came home, alone and on foot, wan
from a long camp illness, he would not go to bed until he had gotten Neighbor Hobbs to go back in his stead. All that winter he lay,
fighting death, ignorant of Valley Forge, of the Virginia John Lincoln's son, Abraham, captaining Shenandoah militia and acting
as military judge; ignorant of the great treks Nancy's brothers had
made for gunpowder and "as spye."

The winter of '79 was long remembered in North Carolina for
its protracted cold. Game was scarce, and cabin folk froze to
death. Little wonder that Nancy Elizabeth "talked Kaintuck,"
especially after Ben Lynn's message saying the last place he had
settled was the best spot on God's green earth. His cabin was on
Beech Fork, just a few miles from Skinhouse Creek, where the
twenty-three hundred pelts had rotted. William, strengthening,
wondered if they wouldn't do better if they went to Kaintuck, too.
Carolina slaves were causing trouble, and the Baptist Grahams
were against this slave business. And now that Virginia's new law
permitted anyone with a land warrant to survey and pre-empt
land anywhere he pleased in Kentucky County, the Grahams decided they would join Ben Lynn. He had bounty land of thousands of acres. His part of the country was Baptist. Lewis Craig's
persecuted Baptists from Virginia had arrived in a body, hymn-
singing through the wilderness out to the "blue-grass country."[7]
Ben, himself, at Phillip's Fort (Hodgenville, Kentucky), had
planted a Baptist church (Phillip's Fort Church) on the South
Fork of the No-Lynn (Nolyn, Nolynn, Nolin). Despite the bloody
tales that drifted back over the Wilderness Road which Daniel
Boone had marked, Baptists were going through The Gap, over
the mountains, away from uppity tidewater silk-stockings, who
beat—even killed—their slaves.

The terrible near-by battles of Cowpens and Guilford Courthouse had brought the Revolutionary War into the Grahams' very

dooryard, but the surrender of Cornwallis set Carolina wild with joy. A free world at last! A great West, to be inherited! But William Graham's illness did not mend; and time passed while Nancy plowed and fed the soldiers who straggled by, and kept her family fed and clad.

Over in Kentucky County, by 1781, Thomas Lincoln, father-to-be of the Emancipator, was living not far from Severn's Valley Church, a Baptist church that had been named for the family from which Ben Lynn's wife came—the Severns. Here a score or so of whites had constituted a worship place under the trees. Mark, Hannah, and Dye—Negroes, the church record reveals—stood with the rest "under a green sugar-tree" to vow their faith. The men, standing guard with ready rifle and tomahawk, might have been Indians as far as appearance went, for they wore moccasins, leggings, and breechclouts and their headgear was made of buffalo wool. They stood where the village of Elizabethtown now stands, black and white together, there in June, 1781—a few miles from the spot where Abraham Lincoln was to be born—and after service returned to their half-faced camps and round-log cabins.

Two months before, William and Benjamin Lynn, attempting to found a settlement in the Beargrass (near Louisville), had been overpowered by Indians. All in the party escaped except William, who was killed, fighting till the very last even when both legs were shot to shreds under him. For the Indians, remembering his prowess under Clark, had counted on taking him alive for torture.

Even this news did not swerve William and Nancy from their intention of going to Kentucky. Their thread in the weaving was needed for the design: the urge to go was insistent, not to be denied. So, while Ben Lynn was preaching antislavery in his Green River circuit of Baptist churches, they made ready for the long journey. While a baby, Peter Cartwright, was learning to toddle in Virginia and Preacher Elkin and Preacher Lynn "laid on hands" and denounced slavery in the Kentucky cabin meetings, William and Nancy and their children were setting out toward The Gap, setting out for the country where a man might hope to be a man.

They were going to be "backwoods, wild Kentucians"; yet, strangely enough, they were going to the most enlightened section of the new country. It had taken several years for William to recover his health and sell his land, and during that time many

events had culminated to make their destination the seed bed of
Negro emancipation. John Bradford, of Lexington, was putting
out his *Kentucky Gazette*[8] and sending it by postriders to Brush
Creek and many other budding settlements. The paper carried national and European news; Bradford himself wrote the copy,
worked the hand press, and never missed an issue. By this time
Congress had prohibited slavery in the Northwest Territory; and
the new preacher at Severn's Valley Church refused to admit
slaveholders into his congregation. Thus the fuse of the Civil War
was already lit when, sometime during these hurrying events, the
Grahams came through Cumberland Gap.

Challenges of a new world that had come to the ears of weaver
William and weaver Andrew and weaver Boone nearly ninety
years before were being answered by their children and their children's children: buffalo, Indians, the French, the Illinois, Big
Bone Lick, the Wilderness. Slavery's wide wing-sweeps are lifted
into place, and now unrolls the somber backdrop of travelers on
Boone's muddy Wilderness Road. We hear the thub-glub of
William Graham's pack train; he is at its head, and behind him,
holding on for dear life, is little Jerry, aged six, the father-to-be
of Mentor Graham. They are heading northwest, to the Green
River country, now known as the birthplace of Abraham Lincoln.

I

BRUSH CREEK SETTLERS

1787–1800

THE Wilderness Trail was no longer dim, but stood out plainly ahead, worn by thousands who had preceded Nancy and William Graham and their children. They were plodding along with a stream of settlers, patiently, hopefully snailing through the heavy mud with a kind of distance-infatuation drawing them on: shrining pilgrims, the light of a West-enchantment in their eyes.

The Graham cavalcade was a thrifty one, the family, nine strong, all being mounted. The older boys brought up the rear, where they kept the milk cows and pack horses moving forward. Up, up, over an ever roughening trail, and so, two hundred long miles, to within sight of The Gap.

Baby Elizabeth rode in one of the panniers on her mother's mare. The older brothers—Johnson, Garrison, and Robert—herding the cattle, each had his own mount. The smaller children, Nancy and Lynn, rode the same horse; and little Jerry, six, or thereabouts, hung on tight behind his pappy. Weary days they plodded on, days slowly multiplying; and, even when at last they stood at The Gap and looked across the new-green forest, rolling endlessly beyond, they knew that they had come not much more than a good halfway.

Showers and heavy rainfall beset them night and day as with painful slowness they approached The Gap. For days it had been in sight, yet never seeming any nearer when, by nightfall, the slow pace at which they had had to travel had brought them only another ten or a dozen miles. Their spasmodic sleep at night was rarely refreshing, broken as it was by the memory of Indian horror-tales, once calmly listened to in the safety of Hogan's Creek, North Carolina, but now nervously remembered. Through the chomping of the cattle and horses tethered near they listened, tensed, in dripping camp sites, for the coming of Indians who— more luckily for them than for many a caravan—were never seen or heard.

Bits of the story of the Wilderness journey were kept clearly in the memory of a man of ninety-three, having been told to him by his grandmother, and to her by hers. They were related by Fielding Vaughn Graham in his Brush Creek cabin in the late summer of 1941, a few weeks before his death—by a man awaiting death in extreme pain and as a good Baptist awaits it, a man whose schooling had ended with "log-school larnin' " at nine.

Part of the trail was a buffalo trace, a wide roadway sunk deep below the surface by centuries of thudding hooves of migrating buffaloes. Once the party was stopped by such a herd of deer as not even Daniel Boone could tell of. They watched the animals crowd around a spot where greedy tongues fought to lap at a salt lick. Once they passed a stomping ground—a wide opening, a "slash" in the ever present forests, with not a trace of vegetation upon it. The earth was hard and smooth from the tramping of numberless herds of buffalo and was a little frightening, even to the travelers' hardihood. What if the "varmints" that made it should be met in this deep trace as the deer had been met?

At last the weather "broke away fair," cabins began to appear, and the travelers saw "men sottin' in to clar fer corn and 'baccy, little gals a-milkin', little boys a-herdin' pigs and workin' the well-sweep—and it heartened 'em. They figgered they mought be comin' nigh onto Crab Orchard. The sluttish weather was over and done, they'd had most of the endurin' time. They'd ought to be, iffen they'd counted right. Benjie had sent, sayin' he'd come so far to show 'em on. That Crab Orchard[1] was right smart of a place— yes—*shorely*—that was hit—crabs, there, them sweet wild crabs was in bloom, everywheres nearabouts, enough to make a body want to shout A-min!"

"They almost disremembered one another, Benjie that husked in skin clothes, and Nancy that wore out with wifin'; but they all honed to Benjie, seein' as he a-knowed all they hain't about Kaintuck."

Thus the relator, in language scarcely altered from their day, told of William and Nancy's coming to Kentucky. His eyes, a marvelous deep blue, lighted with precious memories as he spoke. His snowy hair, uncut his lifelong out of respect for a Bible rule as he interpreted it, swept down about his shoulders and haloed his clear-cut, mobile, delicately sensitive features. His face glowed with pride that "any tale I recollect—think on it!—bein' put into a readin' book!"

Shortly after leaving Crab Orchard, the cavalcade emerged from the perpetual gloom of forests into a region of sunny, open meadowlands, with frequent, heavily timbered watercourses. Here they saw "men harrying fer flax with tree brush" in patches of already plowed land, and "took a heap of notice of them thar canebrakes that's plumb gone now, fur as I know—fearful big tanglesome stuff, run up all of twenty foot and a-goin' on fer miles and miles and lookin' like ye best stay away from. O, they was catamounts, never you worrit, enough to make any man a-feared, and none so many as in the cane lands of Kaintuck."

"Come Sat'd'y, Benjie was all fer holdin' meetin' next day. So they stopped at the next cabin and after the regular askin', 'What mought yer name be? War ye be bound fer?' was made right welcome. As soon as Benjie made knowed he was a preacher, they was all fer ridin' out fer neighbors and right smart of forty fin'ly set. Benjie, I reckon, was exhortin' with the best, nor did y' hear preachin', them days, except after long spells by them as was itineratin'. Benjie was one a them bear-men, never sick a day in his life, and only onct not up to road-fixin'.'"

Thus, through oral tradition maintained for four generations, appears that Sabbath, somewhere in the wilderness northwest of Crab Orchard in the late 1780's. Nancy must have been proud of her giant brother who was being received "loud in the a-mins" by total strangers, and it probably was she herself who first told the tale. For the raconteur in 1941 added simply: "And Nancy shouted 'Glory to God!' at havin' her livin'-born safe and all, and Pappy William, and almost to settlin' agin."

Little Nancy had milked during the trip, as that work was "too galish" for boys, and she had had to help her mammy with baby Elizabeth, "fer her mammy had another baby to get borned soon." The small sons, Lynn and Jeremiah, had ground corn in the hand mill for the eternal campfire pones, and once they "ketched a whole tuckin' of fish." Pappy William had "headed out from Caroliny with a gun across his saddle horn, come Indians, and a blue-glass bottle of whiskey in the bosom of his huntin' shirt, come sickness."

Other glowing fragments were revealed by the old man's tiring voice, almost whispered as his breath came hard. Always wistfully woven into the story, the "smell of sweet gum and yellow jassamine" recurred often. At clear pools, every day or two, Nancy had overseen the children's baths, scrubbing the wild-strawberry stain from little faces and hands and feet, smoothing out their "taggy heads" with the one family comb.

When the cavalcade finally drew up before Lynn's door on Beech Fork, "there was a heap sight huggin' and kissin' and un-laborin' pack beasts and rubbin' cramped arms and legs. Benjie's cabin was plain kivered with peltries, front, sides and back, tacked up, stretched to dry, y' know, fer he was as good at huntin' as at preachin'—b'ars, hedgehogs, possums, deer, buffaloes." It took the three women (Hannah—Lynn's wife—and her mother, and Nancy) to turn enough pones for them all for "Lynn had a big fambly of childer." Even before they had all tumbled off their horses, Hannah had whisked long-handled frying pans to the tripods above the coals and the air was "mighty nigh not enduringable with the good smell of sausage." She made wonders (doughnuts) to delight the tired children; and, as she poured them big gourds of milk, she curdled their blood by telling them: "My mammy cain't speak nary a word on account of Indians slitting her tongue."

We must leave the Grahams and Lynns with this glimpse, for the relator ended here, worn out with his painful effort. Yet imagination begs to add the buckeye backlog flickering away the chill of a spring night, the candle-lighted faces about the long planked table, the shaggy head of Benjamin Lynn bowed above pewter bowl and spoon for a long, hearty blessing, expressing the grateful joy of "them as had got clean to Kaintuck, safe and whole."

Graham and Lynn soon went prospecting into a land of abounding springs, where Green River flowed swiftly between precipitous banks, darkened by hardwood timber. They decided against Russell and Skinhouse creeks in favor of land farther north, on Brush Creek, a tributary small replica of Green River, with its beetling banks and big-boled trees. A dozen springs fed it, and its fifteen-foot fall promised power that would soon be turning spools in a spinning factory. Close at hand was a salt lick. For ages annual floods had enriched the soil. There would be incredible crops, once the clearing was done. In later years Pappy William was fond of telling his children how it all looked when he first saw it, before he and the clan had sprinkled it with patches of tobacco and flax, corn and barley, hemp and cotton. Lynn, who had roved this wilderness for years, always referred to Brush Creek country as "the Promised Land." Pittman's Station on Pittman's Creek, Phillip's Fort (Hodgenville), and Skaggs's Station to the north, with Gray's Station (Greenburg) to the south, made a community that could band together strongly against Indians. Two other stations are said to have stood near by, one on the present site of Summerville and the other ten miles south of Greensburg.

William Graham built the loopholed cabin that some local historians refer to as "Graham's Station." It must have been well built, for the chimney still stands, its stones solidly cemented. This bit of Wilderness which he and Nancy and their children tamed is farmed today by one of their descendants, James Graham, a blue-eyed, direct-spoken, licking-good farmer. His daughter, Dorothea, jitneyed the family car thirty miles and back every day to junior college at Campbellsville, earning her way by taking other passengers. In the summer of 1941 she was a thin slip of a girl, who, taking her bearings, pushed aside the brambles before me and disclosed the headstones of the graves of Johnson Graham and his wife, Cassandra—her great- great- great-grandparents. Johnson Graham was William and Nancy's eldest son. Near the graves the old chimney still stands, choked with wild-grape vines, and the forest is returning there. Trees crowd closely about the hearth, trees whose trunks will one day not far distant wrest the mortar apart.

About this hearth William and Nancy's children worked and worshiped—and played when their duties were completed. Here they were wed, or went forth to woo. Little Jerry who had ridden behind his pappy when he came to Kaintuck grew up here to win his girl Mary and become the father of William Mentor Graham. It is a spot to linger in when the hush of a Kentucky spring twilight is broken only by the woods-dimmed cry of the whippoorwill. The man who piled these stones and the woman who spun and brewed and baked here are long dead. Their bones lie unmarked in some forgotten Brush Creek burying ground, for they were humble folk; not public figures like Nancy's brother Benjamin Lynn, nor even like their own son, Johnson,[2] the preacher, and his wife, Cassandra, the fine weaver. All things connected with their obscure existence have long since decayed. But their daily lives of honesty and toil, of doing the best they could for their children, their insistence upon conscience-heeding, their simple piety, and their intellectual awareness—these things, handed down through their son, Jeremiah, to his son, Mentor, bore fruit for the ages.

As far as can be told from land records, the Grahams probably arrived in the spring of 1787. They were well established there by the time the Brush Creek community, known as Graham's Station, had its forge, its furnace, its tannery, its spinning factory, and its church. Its gristmill had to wait, for that took money and a long journey to the quarter-sessions court to obtain permission. But nothing had stood in the way of "planting a church."

The first record book of Brush Creek Church, stained with red mud and fingerprints and time, still has one cover of what must have been a deerskin binding, with the hair left on. Mr. and Mrs. C. E. Graham, of the clan, Greensburg, Kentucky, lent it to me. The recital begins under the date 1791, and its painfully perfect handwriting, a fine stroke in ink still bright, carries back into vanished time. The very scene rises up out of the words: "Constituted under a red oak tree on Brush Creek, by Rev. Benjamin Lynn and Elder William Graham, and including the families of Elder Graham, James Gordon, John Duncan and Edward Lewis." Below this entry, in different penmanship and ink, there appears in large and intricately curlicued capitals the heading: "Rules of the Church." Nothing could possibly yield a better picture of the kind of a world into which Mentor Graham was soon to be born than these rules, quoted here in their entirety:

No member shall have the privilege of laughing during the sitting of this church, nor of whispering in time of public speech.

No person shall abruptly break off or absent himself from this church without liberty obtained from it.

When any male member misses any two consecutive meetings, he shall give satisfaction to the church for so doing, before he takes his seat.

Members of this church who stay longer than their necessary business requires at places where drunkenness, frolicing or revelling are carried on, they shall be dealt with as transgressors.

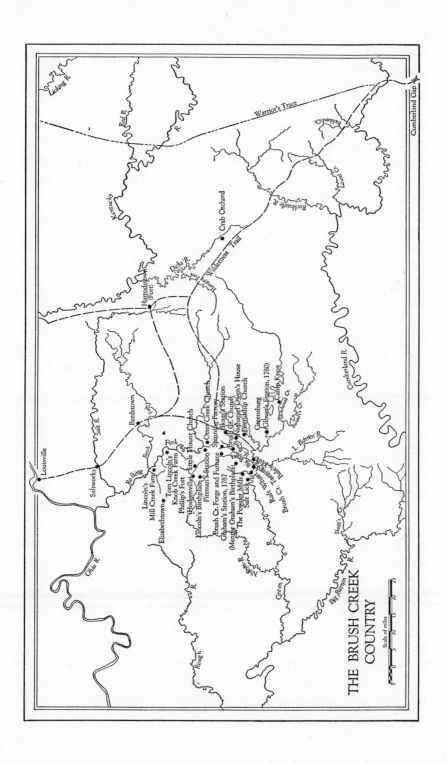

THE BRUSH CREEK COUNTRY

Scale of miles

This church condemns the practice of its members carrying unlawful weapons such as pistols, dirks, etc.—unless travelling at a distance—such being contrary to the spirit of the Gospel, and any member of this church carrying such weapons shall be dealt with as though he were guilty of criminal conduct, as the church may think fit.

The Reverend Benjamin Lynn was taught to write by his wife after his marriage, but Elder William Graham was addicted to books. Thus it is fairly evident that Graham, rather than Lynn, composed these rules. In the William Graham cabin hung a shelf of books—well-thumbed, well-meditated volumes.

The church grew to a hundred members. Charges were brought against a sister for dancing, against one who falsified. A brother was dealt with for directing a fist fight from the side lines, after which a rule against such conduct was added, as well as a rule prohibiting betting on presidential or other elections. Berry Skaggs was suspended for drunkenness. But these were only the straws that showed the direction of the high wind of their righteousness; for, in an hour when a world crisis was approaching, the first alarm was sounded in Baptist yearly meetings when Brush Creek and many another congregation meeting in the wildwood asked: "Is it lawful in the sight of God to keep a fellow-creature in perpetual slavery?"

By coming to America the Grahams had not left tyranny behind. By migrating to Virginia they had won persecution for their religion. By moving on to North Carolina they had gained little, though they had seen a law passed prohibiting a master from killing his slave. But in Kentucky they helped strike the first blow against slavery.

Backwoods folk though they were, they had read and seconded the petition to the general assembly begging that the "yoke of slavery be made more tolerable"; and they knew why it was being deferred, session after session. Itinerating parsons like Lynn came across many currents of American thought and moral direction in their far-flung circuit rides, and Lynn's stopping at the Graham cabin always meant much news from the world. Fireside talk on Brush Creek was always serious. Religious liberty and perpetual slavery were the common topics for debate at home, at church, and even at the tavern. Lynn always lent excitement to the Grahams' conversation by telling of the ideas and doings of men beyond their little world of planting and weaving and hunting and the eternal struggle to make both ends meet. In simple humanity the Grahams weighed human issues, humbly seeking to better their own lot and the world's by so doing.

Like Lang Willie of the Border, theirs was a perpetually unsheathed sword—though a spiritual, not a physical one. The very August that little Brush Creek Church was constituted under its red oak tree, its members joined the Elkhorn Association and set their names to a memorial asking the Kentucky Constitutional Assembly to strike perpetual slavery from its decisions. Though this went unheeded, the following month Elkhorn Association, to which Brush Creek Church belonged, met with other Baptist associations at the Great Crossings and drafted and passed resolutions against perpetual slavery. Other denominations at once answered by resolutions condemning the Baptist stand.

When he had attended the convention three years before, Lynn had brought Brush Creek news of the Richmond Resolution: "Slavery is a violent deprivation of the rights of nature and inconsistent with a republican form of government and we therefore recommend it to our brethren to use every legal measure to extirpate this horrid evil from the land, and pray God Almighty that our legislature may have it in its power to proclaim the Great Jubilee....." De Yeah ob Jubilee was long in the awakening hope of the Negro before it crept into his songs. Ben Lynn, exhorting under the red-oak tree, roared out these things to a small—but how mighty—assembly that went off through the darkened forest aisles to talk them through, again and again, around their hearths.

Luckily, many slaveholding whites settled only temporarily. The feeling that the next frontier would be the perfect one was stronger than pride in possession. A feverish unrest and a willing infatuation whenever a "new location" was mentioned goaded settlers up and on. Even while they were clearing and planting, they talked of the Illinois and "Down South"—any unknown place. The Ohio River was jammed with keelboats and arks, broadhorns and bateaux and flatboats, filled with families on the move. The wharf at Louisville was noisy with cackling geese, crying and shouting children, and the gross oaths of river hands. The Louisiana was the latest fever.

Yet after roads had multiplied, the Indian danger been overcome, and the silk-stockings had arrived with their slaves, enough

of them remained so that the 1790 Kentucky census showed that a
fifth of the population was Negro. But the Baptists yielded no
fraction of an inch. Their decision upon slavery was unalterable.
They read the *Kentucky Gazette*, the precipitate that settled mid-
west Kentucky and kept it settled for a free-state constitution.

Several generations of pulling up stakes left many like the Grahams hungry for books and an intellectual life—so James Graham,
William's cousin, opened a seminary and a bookstore in Lexington.
He taught languages, history, mathematics, and astronomy and
sold such books as *Spirit of Law, Rise and Fall of the Roman Empire, History of Kentucky, Defense of the American Constitution,*
hymnbooks, the Bible, Euclid, Greek and Latin grammars and
dictionaries, Marshall's *Life of Washington, Universal History,* and
copies of the English *Spectator.* Though it was months late, the
Gazette carried the details of the storming of the Bastille and the
execution of Louis XIV. Bradford's resounding editorials on human liberty were read aloud and discussed in the cabins of the
Grahams and many other Brush Creek families.

Through Lynn, who was a "marryin' preacher" now and was
called away often, the Grahams had a good idea of other settlements far and wide and what went on in them. Mississippi commerce was the main topic in Louisville, a town of almost a hundred
houses that was becoming more prominent than Judge Symme's
settlement, halfway on up the river to Cincinnati. But Louisville
was a scandalous place: there women played billiards in public
with men and men held all-night eggnog parties. Both men and
women attended the "travelling dances" where, for a fee, stranger
danced with stranger, the money thus obtained being spent on
"river tootin'." The Louisville wharf was a kaleidoscope of prospecting travelers and settlers and nervous new Kentucky mer-
chants launching their flatboats of tobacco, whiskey, and livestock,
ingratiating themselves shamelessly with the copperfaces, who for
a tawdry trinket rowed the heavy cargoes upstream. Innkeepers
did a hustling business. Lynn's solution to the times was to found
more churches. He had seen the Devil at work in Richmond, Fort
Pitt, Cincinnati, Louisville, and Fort Massac—once his old hunting grounds—and with increased zeal he went out and founded
Level Woods Church.

At Phillip's Fort, "up north a piece" from the Grahams, Robert

Hodgen had built a gristmill, had been elected to the general assembly, and had opened an "ordinary" to help support his family. By this time the Mississippi question had begun to seethe; and with nine roads leading into Lexington a man like William Graham could canter in once in a while to hear what was being said.

Living was not so hard come by in these days, for now you could buy salt and real calico, plowshares and saddles, books and paper and ink, and there was more time for religion and law. Yet both religion and law were all too often steeped in superstition. When William Skaggs murdered Martin Frazier and was found not guilty, lightning struck dead both the defending attorney and the judge. It was the hand of God—who could doubt it? Everybody knew that Skaggs, the Long Hunter, had killed Frazier, the Long Hunter. Likewise, when William Bledsoe, another Long Hunter, who like Lynn had turned preacher, displayed to his congregation an egg inscribed "Repent, for the day of judgment is at hand," it precipitated a stampede of twenty black sheep to the altar. Though the Day failed to appear, faith in egg inscriptions did not flag.

True to form, the Grahams had become a sizable clan, having been increased by William's four brothers and their families from Caswell County, North Carolina, and two or three families of Elmore kinfolks. William's eldest son, Johnson, married now and constable of Greensburg, was kept busy with rum-drinkers, pig-stealers, and fisticuffers. William, something of a surveyor, helped lay out the boundaries between old Green and new Hardin counties, while his newly arrived neighbors, Nathaniel Owens and James Goldsby, listed the landowners to tax for the survey. William bought two hundred additional acres, for spot cash. Ben Lynn came to live on Brush Creek, since the one church was now large enough to support his family.

Graham's Station on Brush Creek, with its proud weavery, tan-yard, furnace, and powder mill—and its new church—had lost the county-seat fight to Gray's Station, renamed Greensburg for the Revolutionary War hero. But Brush Creek still had hopes for the future and welcomed Jacob Bale, who put up a fulling mill and a gristmill. At least now housewives would be free of the hard labor of fulling their homespun and farm lads need no longer tote a pack of corn clear up to Hodgen's mill.

One by one, however, Greensburg licensed five taverns. Intemperance began a steady climb until Johnson Graham had to have an assistant constable. Against the rising tide of opposition, Brush Creek Baptists continued to suspend their topers, Jeremiah Graham among them. Although his brother, the constable and a man who had had a "call" to preach, had to do the informing, and although his father was an elder and his uncle the preacher of the church, Jeremiah was suspended. He just would drink—a little.

The congregation, now meeting in a fine twenty-four-foot-long log church, was made up of the very people who, a few years later, composed the little village of New Salem in Illinois when Lincoln lived there: the Abells, Watkinses, Armstrongs, Bales, Owenses, Todds, Yateses, Conovers, Whites, Lukinses, Onstots, Duncans, Grahams. The logs of their church are still doing service, rebuilt into a barn. But before the church had been built, these people had worshiped many years under the red oak in summer, around a rousing fire in frosty weather, and in their cabins in winter.

Now, in their new church, they denounced Greensburg's new dancing-master. They denounced Silas Burk, who had come down as the town's "very successful professional gambler and horse-racer." They denounced William Tyman, who remains on record as having ridden in from Big Barrens for the sole purpose of discovering if he could lick Greensburg's strongest man. Brush Creek Church did not approve of the fisticuff code, of settling business or social affairs by matching muscles—the order which prevailed. Into this order Mentor Graham was born, his parents members of the church that disapproved of it. And the order endured and was carried over intact to New Salem nearly twenty years later.

When the new stone courthouse at Greensburg was almost completed, stocks and a pillory and a whipping post were put up in the village square—Old England come to Green County, punishments, quarter-sessions courts, and all. The separate clerk's room and the courthouse still stand, the first west of the Alleghenies. The old building is dignified, beautiful, and spacious, its rude stair and ruder courtroom floor and elevated platform much worn by use. Its fireplaces still function. The criminal's dungeon opens down underground through the debtor's prison by a trap door, ten inches thick. How anticlimactic it was to be directed "one squah ovah and two up" to the new courthouse—already much older looking than the old—and to find men loafing on its squat, unkempt porch. The old records had been dumped into a room in the new courthouse.

In 1800, men, women, and children used whiskey in daily "bitters," and many drank it as a beverage; but Graves's Tavern dispensed rum and peach brandy, and we read between the lines that it was here Jeremiah Graham learned to love the bottle too well. The frolics were held in this tavern (which still stands); and rough and backwoods they must have been, judging from descriptions given by descendants of Greensburg pioneers. The superior young-blood could, without missing a beat, click his heels together three times in mid-air and go on with the dance. The calico- and deerskin-clad dancers were always ready to throw out bodily any "vacant top story who was brash enough to come to a frolic in store-clothes."

But this was only during court week. Greensburg may have been gay during court week, but education was its hobby. The rest of the time religion and books claimed its first attention. Greensburg had its own merchant in books now and its own sprouting "academy," just as many other towns had. The school was held in the clerk's room and displayed the high-sounding name New Athens Academy. Less than a dozen young men struggled with Latin and Greek here under the able tutelage of Lawyer Howe.

Everybody knew the Bible, of course; and many could repeat the whole of the New Testament. Among the candlesticks and dirks, the pelts and calico, at the village store, room was made for books. Among them were Tom Paine's *Age of Reason*, Volney's *Ruins*, Gibbon's *Roman Empire*, French grammars, and Kentucky laws. The frontier folk could now buy schoolbooks and a history of Kentucky. They had their frolics on court days, but the rest of the year they had their classical school in the clerk's room. Up in Lexington, Pisgah Academy had become Transylvania College, the first west of the Alleghenies. Thus by the year 1800 the church, the court, and the school had come to Green River country; and a young man could obtain as fine an education right there as he could anywhere.

It is not hard to picture the mental outlook of the Grahams who rode into Lexington to hear Henry Clay orate on states' rights and who came back to horrify Brush Creekers with the proved fact that Preacher Moore, president of Transylvania, played the flute! Folks speculated wildly about unusually long skeletons found in the little-explored caves, and about the regular mason-made stone wall, like a fortress, a little above Greensburg. And who couldn't repeat at least some of Tom Johnson, the handsome reprobate poet who had come and gone by the "co'n likka" route, leaving profane verses as his memorial. Published in Danville, they made even the most godly smile:

> Strange things of Orpheus poets tell
> How for a wife he went to hell:
> Hudson, a wiser man, no doubt,
> Would go to hell to be without!

Sometime during the last of the 1790's southern Indians marauding north gave Brush Creek a real Indian scare. Pappy William got down his gun, and he and his sons—even the gangling Jeremiah—joined the forces of William Whitley and marched south. Jeremiah, silent as a boy and silent as a man about personal exploits, was heard to speak of this occasion only once. There were still one hundred stations in Kentucky, and Brush Creek defenders gathered in at Graham's and marched off in double-quick time.

They were away some weeks. When they returned, they found that Squire Shelby, up Lexington way, was the new governor; that the president's White House was completed; that the Mississippi waterway furor was fever high. The Baptists had fought the good fight and lost; Kentucky had not adopted a free-state constitution. But all Kentucky was united on the question of using the Mississippi, and not a man on Brush Creek but would have gone at the first call to fight for possession of it. The *Gazette*'s warning that "Genêt has just come to get us into war" went unheeded, and Kentucky remained hotheaded even after President Jefferson warned the state. Clark had his two thousand men ready to march on the lower settlements.

But Genêt was recalled in time to prevent disruption. Lexington, a little town of less than one thousand, burned John Jay in effigy when that gentleman sailed from England. Brush Creek was loud and loquacious about white-livered folks, for Kentucky was a state now and proud, with France her idol. The president's insistence on neutrality roused her new statehood power to angry denunciation. Every good Democrat in Lexington and elsewhere knew that the Mississippi should be unceremoniously demanded from Spain.

As the century closed, Kentucky conversation bristled with questions. Slavery? Drunkenness? Education? Transportation? Along with the slow news of mob rule in Paris came the faster news that a Crab Orchard parson had dropped a male member for dancing. That the parson's daughter ran off with the sinner only added to the pros and cons. Patriotic pride grew under the stimulus of a new state constitution and the new mailboats and the new White House. Now, for only three muskrat pelts, you could send a letter clear back to the Monongahela. Green County celebrated independence with feats and feasting and toasts, and in the village square raised the flag to fifty volleys fired by a deerskin-clad and moccasined militia.

That year, fifty wolf bounties were paid off at one time. Cattle, sheep, swine, and goats were judged "unseemly in a village street." The first stagecoach rumbled into Greensburg; and Johnson Graham helped lay out a road over Muldraugh Hill, a bit of driving that is still difficult even with modern pavement. Frontier Kentucky found a little time on its hands, time that was no longer claimed by vital necessity, time to pull strings of pike from the streams, to go visiting by horseback and skiff.

The last records of the century in Green River country also reveal less peaceful moments. One reads with an inner tremor: "Slave brand this day registered by James Goldsby: crop off the right ear; two under bibs on the left."

Jeremiah and his Mary lived in their new little cabin on land that cornered with James Goldsby's. Their daughters would one day marry Goldsby boys—one sister going north, one south. John Chisholm, who would soon marry a daughter of Benjamin Lynn, was now, as sheriff, "jerking up cruel and careless slave-owners."

Boone's silver thread of the weaving ends with his Wilderness Road. Never to be cured of the "itch-foot," he moves on, farther west. The Lincolns and the Grahams, drawn through The Gap at about the same time, seem settled for good. Thomas Lincoln, just back from a short stay with a slaveholding uncle on the Wautauga in Tennessee, is working diligently at the carpenter's bench, buying land near Brush Creek—a well-thought-of young man, riding his high-stepping mare to the Baptist church on Sabbaths.

As the century passed with the death of Washington, William Mentor Graham was born down in the little new cabin on Brush Creek, built by Jeremiah for his Mary, on land that cornered with the slave-holding Goldsbys'. Jeremiah was ensign of the militia of which James Goldsby was captain.

II

DUTIES

1800–1806

*T*HE GLORY of late autumn lay upon the Kentucky Wilderness
the morning Mentor Graham was born. From the steep, spring-
watered banks of Big Brush Creek, away to the east over rolling
hills that swept ever higher and higher toward the Cumberland
Mountains, the forests were still brilliant with the last, late color.
Where the Graham cabin stood in its quiet clearing, within hearing
of the creek, the very air was lighted with the glow of tulip tree
and sweet gum, shellbark hickory and oak. In 1800 these vast
timberlands had been only nibbled by man's little ax; and in
the more open Green River Country, many villages lay within a
twenty-mile radius of the Graham cabin, whose blue wood-smoke
curled above the painted treetops with the smoke of neighboring
hearths. Peace was newly earned: on Brush Creek there was no
fear of Indians.

In the cabin, on a rude corner pole-bed lay Mary Graham, her
first-born son in her arms. The hand-woven "kiverlid" was pulled
snugly about them, against the frosty early-morning air that came
in through the open-top half-door. Jeremiah, as skilled at women's
work as Mary was at man's, turned the johnnycakes expertly, sizzled the bear bacon, and brewed the herb tea while his wife and
the baby slept. Minerva, a year old, slept in the trundle bed.

Faintly hearing the blue jays that called and scolded near the
cabin, Mary stirred and woke. She thought of squirrels, scouting
for the fattest nuts that were falling everywhere—as she could
hear—on a thickening carpet of leaves. Through half-closed eyes
she saw, as in a dream, the last flames of the woods: scarlet,
tawny gold, wine-red, with now and then a slender tongue of or-
ange sassafras or a cardinal frond of sumac. Mary loved trees.

Straight from Ireland, she was a poet at heart, though untaught. Her prayers for her new son surged through her mind—like so many more bright-colored autumn trees—for this little new life she held in her arms, with such solemn blue eyes and such curly, red, upstanding hair.

When the food was ready, Jeremiah came to the bedside, the puncheons rattling dully under his moccasined tread. He lifted the coverlet and touched the baby's hair. It was heavy and deeply waved and stood up in a comical pompadour. At his touch the baby squirmed, stretched, yawned, opened his deep blue eyes, puckered his thin little face, and wailed. Minerva, wakened, joined in.

"Hush, Minerva," Jeremiah said. "Hush and have a look at your borned brother," and he lifted the bundle and displayed it proudly. Jeremiah was almost twenty. "I made breakfrus fer y', Mary."

But Mary said, smiling, "I don't aim to contrary y', Jerry, but I be only wantin' the least gourd of milk."

"Don't be fer gittin' up. I'll fotch hit."

Jeremiah brought the milk and Mary drank, her eyes constantly upon the door. "How purty hit is out. Mis' Bale comin' back?"

Mrs. Bale came back shortly to tend the two babies and the mother of a first son. "I left Bet with ourn," she told Jeremiah. "She's better nor a growd woman with 'em. Never you fret, Mr. Graham, I'm aimin' to stay till darkenin'."

Jeremiah took his flintlock and went out to bring down a grouse or squirrel for Mary's soup. As he left he said, "Mebbe I kin fotch down a deer, Mary, to make more moccasins," and they both laughed. Mary watched him turn at the edge of the woods and look back, then disappear among the thickly set beech trunks.

He was going to town to mail a letter to her people in Ireland; he had written for her days before, only waiting till the baby should be born to add that news. She had let them know how Cassie Stone had first worked in the weavery on Big Brush, back of the church on the falls, how Cassie had met and married Jerry's brother, Johnson, and now was "wantin' for nothin' "; how wolves were scarcer and some folks even raising sheep; and about the flax she had ready to haeckle. Jeremiah had added the news about the baby, and she had X-ed her name.[2]

Jeremiah delivered the precious letter to the postmaster, ate hominy and honey with him, did his errands, and started home. His hunting luck was good, and he got three squirrels and a doe.

Toward evening Mrs. Bale hushed Minerva to sleep and set out to walk the two miles through the woods to relieve Bet. The cabin was awesomely still as the sun set and Jeremiah did not come. Try as she would, Mary could not drive the thought of little Johnny Trabue out of her mind. Johnny, coming home from the mill with a little bag of flour for which he had been sent, had been killed by the "terrible Harpes," two white men and a woman "gone Indian," who had been lurking in canebrakes and murdering and thieving without hindrance. Long after the search for Johnny had ended, someone found his skeleton where it had been hurled, deep in the cane. Mary lay, praying as she waited, until her fears subsided and she began to think more cheerfully.

Now that the baby was born, she could go to meeting again. She had missed meeting, especially since neighbors had reported that the Methodist "jerks" had even gotten into the Nolynn church. She was eager to witness these doings. It would be hard to wait for the next preaching day—nearly a month. She wished Brush Creek had a "weekday" oftener—a meeting held on a weekday, not the Sabbath.

History says this year of 1800 was one of religious stress and clash. At the time, most doctrinal emphasis was placed upon getting the soul saved for a happy and eternal hereafter; and with this the Green River Baptists broke off, believing that what men did here and now—like the lashing and breeding of slaves—was the thing to be made right. Of strong significance and of shining texture is this thread of the weaving. The newborn baby in his mother's arm was to grow up to teach the unflinching doctrine of "here and now." Brush Creek Church and Little Mount Church, the church of which Thomas and Nancy Lincoln were to become members, belonged to an association commonly referred to as "those emancipation Baptists." Every one of their preachers preached openly against slavery. Benjamin Lynn and Johnson Graham had been "messengers" when this association had been formed, and their stand against slavery had all but divided the Brush Creek congregation. When they reported back against slavery from the association convention, it became necessary to add still another to the church rules: "No member of this church shall speak while another is speaking."

Teachers in the blab schools—which were held in the solemnity of log meeting-houses—taught good Baptist doctrine along with the *a-b—abs*. Public prints were a veritable tempest of debate about right and wrong, heaven and hell, truth and justice. Religionists questioned statesmen. Atheists ridiculed religionists. The reading of Tom Paine and Volney seems to have been very nearly universal, even in such backwoods communities as that in which Mary Graham now lay, pondering such of these things as had reached her, wondering what should be withheld, what taught, to the new little son.

For herself, Mary believed in a devil-in-person. That is what she made out of all the hot church talk and the hotter home talk when Lynn stopped in. Although he preached regularly at Brush Creek, his itinerating trips into the Ohio, the Illinois, the Arkansas, netted arguments throughout a wide area. His own decision was against slavery—and camp meetings. He had been to witness camp meetings. He knew. And if the Baptists, the Lord's anointed, did not make a stand against the Devil, who would?

Through him Mary had heard of the shrieking, hullabalooing, and throwing of fits that the camp meetings called religion. Mary could only side with Lynn and Jeremiah: anybody who "got religion at a camp meeting and kept on breeding niggers for sale had just got orders from the Devil"—a doctrine Mentor Graham was to absorb from his earliest hours.

Jeremiah, reaching the clearing at last, saw a lighted candle in the doorway. The pup, Jower, came with his awkward hound gallop to meet him. He shook the leaves from his moccasins after he had thrown his load of meat inside the door. "How be y' and the boy, Mary?"

Minerva, still sucking a finger, was asleep. The baby slept, too. Mary had dressed herself and sat up now on the edge of the bed, trying to twist her hair properly into a matron's knot, trying to make the back comb steady with a hand that shook uncontrollably. It was she who had set the candle in the doorway; but it was Jeremiah who had to help her with her hair. Mary had heavy black hair, twisted in coils.

After Jeremiah had "rightly skinned the squirrels and set them bilin'," they talked of a name for the baby. Recalling his father's tales of his grandfather's college learning, remembering the swinging shelf of books in the cabin which his father had read from kiver to kiver, knowing how he had longed for but had had little of such things—Jeremiah "wanted that his boy should be a teacher." Mary, who had only heard of such things, agreed that "Mentor"—which Jeremiah said was a fancy name for "teacher"—sounded like a good name. So the baby was named that night—"William for his grandpap, and Mentor for hisself."

Mary worried as days slipped by. Her Catholic forebears had christened babies and got the Lord's blessing on them before they were a month old, and no later. Before Minerva was born, she had made a fine dress with no other thought than that it should be a christening robe. But her Baptist husband said that Baptists did not christen, and so she had to be content with a public prayer for her child. Lynn would pray for Mentor as he had prayed for Minerva. It would be nearly the same as a christening. But the month was almost gone and Lynn was still off, itinerating. What if the Devil should fill her little one with evil before he was protected by the man-of-God? Even Jeremiah grew anxious.

When Lynn finally returned, news went round that the baby would wear "that fine dress." Spun and woven by her own hands from the choicest flax in the little corner patch Mary had tended with a hand hoe, the cloth had been bleached through one entire summer until it was dazzling white. Mary's finest stitching had gone into it. But what the women were agog to see was its frill of handmade lace from overseas. The men looked forward to turning rude jests about a youth of nineteen begetting a son and to the social moment when the bottle would go the rounds, after meeting when they were untying the horses and leading them round to the mounting stump.

Through the chill air they came, on foot and horseback, folks from Brush Creek and down Friendship and Otter Creek ways, even from Greensburg. The women were in gray or brown or deep plum-purple linsey-woolsey, with white neckerchiefs; the men in buckskin pants and long, blue, red-fringed hunting shirts. Children clung to their mothers' ample skirts; and young lads, as blushing and self-conscious as the maids, gave strict but snatch-glanced attention to all Preacher Lynn said of the Devil, slavery, camp meetings. On their stick-leg puncheon pew the young parents sat, through the long prayers, longer slow-drawled songs, and three-hour sermon; they, like the other worshipers, scarcely moved a muscle. Every now and then someone dipped snuff or softly knocked the ashes from a pipe. Mary put her own hand upon the baby's head when during the final prayer Lynn, as she had requested, pled for the grace of God to fall upon William Mentor Graham, infant son of Jeremiah and Mary Graham. Jeremiah had long been restored to church membership.

In the hubbub after meeting, folks pressed round to see the baby, who waked and yelled lustily; and many a woman contrived to caress the lace frill before Mary swaddled Mentor in the long, brown, hand-knitted comforter until he was like a big cocoon. The child slept all the way home in his mother's glad young arms, as she sat on the pillion behind Jeremiah, who had Minerva up front. Mentor, their man-child, their teacher-to-be, was safe from the Devil.

From the child's earliest months until he was three years old, the hotly belabored question of "bodily exercises" at camp meetings took the center of the Brush Creek stage. Lynn went to Caneridge and reported thousands "falling together as if the breath of God had mowed them down." He had seen fallers laid out in rows, with frantic relatives trying to "bring them to." He had heard children, revived by vinegar, "preach like inspired angels" to crowds that stood spellbound, unconscious of heavy rain streaming down, the fallers among them lying face-down in the mud where they fell. Lynn had to concede that this was nothing short of God's intervention. Lynn, too, believed. His report filled the Graham cabin with abject horror: he was no longer their friend, adviser, relative—for Mary and Jeremiah had decided to hold with little Brush Creek Church's rules.

Lynn, who had given Brush Creek hearty and vital spiritual food, was now offering nothing less than insult. He told how, at Caneridge camp meetings, for seven days and seven nights, Presbyterian, Methodist—even Baptist—preachers stood on stumps keeping up a continuous exhortation, with the auditory (audience) moving from preacher to preacher at will; how there were processions of fervent singers and how bugle calls summoned sinners at all hours so that sleep was impossible in the candle-lighted forest; how, in a wild pandemonium of sights and sounds, ten thousand people shrieked, prayed, preached, sang psalms, danced, jerked, whined, even barked. Little Brush Creek Church had written as its last rule: "No member of this church shall speak while another is speaking." It decided to hold to rules. Because ten thousand barked and whined did not make it right for real worshipers to do so.

Lynn, after twenty years of converting sinners to be good Baptists, was himself converted to the New Lights, who held for "hell-fire redemption." Saddened, an aging man, he was dismissed from the church he had constituted under the red-oak tree; and William Matthews, a good Baptist direct from Culpeper County, Virginia, replaced him. He became an elder in near-by Pittman Creek Church and helped write into their articles of faith: "No Christian shall be finally lost." The Emancipation Baptists, however, broke completely with such faith. They wrote a new tenet: antirevival. Certainly no good Baptist believed that a sinner, once in hell, could be freed from it. This was the doctrine Mentor absorbed as a toddler, in the kind but letter-strict discipline of his parents.

Listening to differences of opinion, Jeremiah and Mary "held with their own." Still, privately, Jeremiah was a mild hell-scoffer. Thus it is quite likely that Mentor heard his father, chinning on the square, say that the Lord, if he was worthy, wouldn't pick out only the Baptists for his anointed. Certainly his father said that often when Mentor was older. Jeremiah, who had been churched for mild drinking by the strict rule of the Hard-Shell Baptist church, found spiritual food at the courthouse. His favorite theme for derision—out of church circles—was the hymn:

> Laugh, ye profane, and swell and burst
> With bold impiety:
> Yet shall ye live forever cursed
> And seek in vain to die.
>
> For ye shall stand upon a dreadful slope
> And all beneath is Hell:
> Your weighty guilt will sink you deep
> Where the old serpent fell.
>
> And you'll confess the frightful names,
> And plagues you scorned before
> No more shall look like idle dreams,
> Like foolish tales, no more.

Jeremiah enjoyed court week. He liked to hear the law in action, dealing out justice. He enjoyed standing with the rest while some loudly efficient reader stood on a stump in the courthouse yard and read the latest *Gazette*, from the first word to the last. Jeremiah did not always go with the crowd when they cheered or hooted; but he found it vastly good to listen with them, though he did his own thinking.

As a very young child, Mentor listened, too, for he had formed the habit of going to the courthouse to listen to trials with his father. He retained the habit during his entire life. Back home again, these cases were reviewed by Jeremiah, with his own comments as to the justness of the decisions. Nathaniel Owens, the judge, was a wealthy slaveowner who had married Jeremiah's sister, Nancy.

At court week also there was hoss-tradin', with all that jovial term implies, pursued with about the same zest as "getting the works" at camp meetings. Like Old England, Green County had her cockfights and horse races and her inebriated yokels circling a fist fight that had been precipitated by too many ticklers of whiskey. Young men, bragging of their prowess, vied with each other at throwing the sledge, heaving the bar, shooting at a mark, and wrestling, neighborhoods sending in their champions on Saturday to establish a best man.

Greensburg Square was noisy with geese, pigs, calves, and sheep brought in to market, and often a slave auction went on. Like other farmers, Jeremiah spent Saturday in town; and, tripping to town with his father, Mentor's childish gaze fell upon these things. His bartering over, Jeremiah listened in at court, drank his bit—though certainly not as much as most—and, with his little son, went out to the horse races, watched a town-square fisticuff or dog fight. But he was never known to lay a bet. He sold his pigs and tobacco, flax and whiskey, at Greensburg; or, if there were going to be better races there, at Elizabethtown.

As Greensburg grew, Brush Creek Church's congregation of a boasted "round hundred" fell away, by action of its members who continued to drop slaveowners, topers, and camp-meeting attenders. It withstood the popular heresy that pointed to Isaac Hodgen, who, though sheriff, had in a drunken spree smashed the contents of a store at Bardstown—and who, saved at Severn's Valley

Church revival, was now a more powerful preacher than Lynn had been or Matthews was. Its membership dwindled to thirty, and two of the thirty were Jeremiah and Mary.

More and more learners, nowadays, were trekking into Greensburg to attend John Howe's classical school, the New Athens Academy, held now in the jury-room of the courthouse. Among them was a James McElroy, destined to become the tutor of Mentor Graham. The school often had to disband, for the law had increasing business and Nathaniel Owens needed the jury-room more often. Many cases concerned runaway slaves: brutality was becoming worse. The slave constable, Christopher Bush, finding his duties too demanding, was given young Thomas Lincoln as his assistant patroller. Both men were *against* slavery, but both were *for* law: and the law provided that runaway slaves should be returned to their masters. In their cabins, the slaves were even then singing:

> Run, Niggah, run! De pateroller'l git y'!
> Run, Niggah, run! De Debbil cotch y' shoah!

And now, the land trouble that had caught up with Boone was catching up with Green County Grahams. Peter, Edward, George, Johnson, Jeremiah, and their father all lost land, by "bad title." Lynn also lost his land and went to live with his daughter, Mrs. John Chisholm, in Alabama (where he died in 1814 at the age of seventy-six). Yet, on the whole, the Graham plantation prospered, for they still owned enough land. Freeholders like Jeremiah could increase income by jury duty, road overseeing, surveying; and Jeremiah seems to have prospered more than the others, since his regular attendance upon court resulted in his being appointed guard-escort of prisoners to Elizabethtown or Bardstown—where he often met Tom Lincoln on similar duty. He began to trade and "dicker" in land, with some success.

Jeremiah and all his brothers and uncles also belonged to the militia, and Mentor went with his father to militia muster. As an aged man, living with Mentor, Jeremiah told his grandchildren (and they later told theirs) how they all walked into town or rode horseback, or paddled in in summer, wearing their "everydays"—deerskin pants and homespun shirt, with skin coats and yarn mufflers in winter. They carried any gun they happened to own—flintlock, musket, or blunderbuss—dirks and even "cuttoes," and

stepped briskly to the captain's "O yes, O yes, All you who belong
to this company, fall into ranks and *Pā'rade!*" Jeremiah was ensign—standard-bearer—and his young son tended to idolize him
for his place—the best place of all, carrying the flag of whose history Mentor, even as a very young child, knew the main facts.
Militia drill, thus executed, was a lasting experience, remembered
and thrilled to always. Dimmed into insignificance were the duel
of Hamilton and Burr and Napoleon's doings in Paris, though the
boy knew of these things, too. Proud little Greensburg was wrest-
ing a place for herself in the sun. Her own young man, Ninian Edwards, was presidential elector.

Meanwhile, in the cabin that now had a new room added,
Mary's hands flew faster and faster: spinning, weaving, carding,
churning, soap-making, sewing, gardening, raising fowl, milking,
brewing, baking, candlemaking, keeping stomachs filled. Jeremiah had sinewed and matured in body, from clearing more acres
and going farther and farther to hunt. In due time the ladder of
pegs was driven into the cabin wall, and Mentor and his little
brother, Robert, climbed it at night to their featherbed on the
attic floor, where they tucked themselves in with bearskin and
buffalo robe and a blanket from Mary's loom.

Jeremiah and Mary had become solid and respected citizens.
Theirs was a household strict in courtesy, economy, obedience,
and thrift, with a spicing of merriment and a great deal of argument and discussion, and only a slight and rare "family jar."
Warmly hospitable, they welcomed any and all who came to their
door.

At five, Mentor had duties. He must rock the baby, feed the
ducks, run to the spring whenever his mother bade him fetch fresh
water in his little gourd. He must straighten her linen, bleaching on
the grass, whenever the wind ruffled it. He must watch for pigs in
the garden and help chase them across the creek. But he played,
too, with Minerva and Robert—games of their own making, there
among the big trees by the spring. As a man, Mentor Graham almost worshiped trees. His childhood must have been spent in a forest of primeval grandeur, judging from Brush Creek woods today,
even though they have been logged off for nearly a century and a
half since then.

Never in his long life, it is certain, did Mentor forget the hubbub of wild turkeys flocking in at night to roost in the tall trees along the creek; nor the hoot-owl's cry; nor the catamount's terrifying shriek, heard as he lay snug in bed with Robert. As an aged man, Graham recalled that before Robert's birth he had slept with Minerva in the trundle bed and that, when timber wolves howled up to the very door in the middle of the night, his mother had held out a reassuring hand; his father had gotten up in the dark with gun and dog to rout them from cattle and pig and sheep runs and from the ducks and geese and chickens roosting in the saplings along the creek.

The word Mentor heard most often was "wicked." It was wicked to waste food, to tear your clothing, to let the ducks go hungry, not to want to rock the baby, to disregard either parent's slightest suggestion or wish or command, to lie, to "cuss," to be lazy—that is, not to want to watch for pigs or straighten linen. Strong lessons for a child of five or six; yet how steeled they made the man. His gods—his father and mother—agreed that their God—someone whom no one could see, yet who could see all, and who made all things—their God had so said. Theirs were solemn faces; but if there were switchings to enforce duties, Graham, as an old man, did not choose to relate it or had forgotten them. Mary was very sober, but she was kind; Jeremiah "required" of his oldest son up to the boy's very wedding morning, but he likewise was kind.

On the ears of six-year-old Mentor fell the grown-ups' talk of "wicked slavers"—at home and at church. William Hickman, however, was dismissed by his congregation over on Elk River for antislavery preaching. When, in 1808, David Barrow was ousted for a like offense, Barrow struck back by organizing an emancipation association. Nine Baptist churches answered his call, among them Brush Creek. Most of these congregations came from the Licking and Locust River settlements, and because of that the organization came down in history as the Licking Locust Friends of Humanity Association. Little Mount Church, which Thomas and Nancy Lincoln and little Sarah and Abe would soon be attending, also joined. How vital a part in the drama of slavery this little section of Kentucky would come to play! Its spiritual dam was to hold against the swirling, rising tide of the slaveholder's greed.

As a little child, Mentor knew about manumitted slaves, as some near-by planters practiced this course as a solution for slavery. His uncles owned slaves. He saw slaves auctioned from the block in Greensburg and "E-town" (Elizabethtown). But every Sabbath he also heard Preacher Matthews say that slavemongers went to an unequivocally endless hell.

III

BLAB SCHOOL AND THREE-DAY PREACHING

1806–10

*W*HEN OTHER boys in the neighborhood longed for Barlow knives and bear traps of their own, Mentor longed for books; for although, like other boys, he had learned to trap and shoot at a very early age, he did not enjoy it. Like all the other children, he learned to read a little of the Bible before he started to school; and since its words had been constantly in his ears since babyhood, learning to read was somehow easily accomplished. He and Minerva went to the Brush Creek meeting-house to school, two miles through woods that housed panthers and bears and other furry but friendlier creatures. At the age of seven Mentor took his turn carrying the heavy gun, which both of them knew how to shoot, as hand in hand they followed the creek, passed two cabins and the tannery, and came to the church. If they studied hard, they might be sent to the new log academy at E-town.

According to oral tradition, their schoolmaster was Frederick Borun. Little has been preserved about him except his surliness and irritability and his dependence upon the birch cane as a means of inducting learning into childish heads. He bawled out his commands, and as likely as not cuffed the youngster off his feet just when he was trying hardest, if the answer was not prompt enough. Mentor was both shy and sensitive, even though it did take a good deal to make him cry; and he was eager to learn, so he bent to his tasks. He doubtless took his share of thrashings, however, and from early childhood was completely deaf in one ear, whether from freezing it so often or from Master Borun's whacks is a matter for conjecture.

To save candles, he and Minerva studied by firelight. After school they collected brush to pile high on the backlog, where it would catch slowly and burn longer, making enough light to see—

in not too interrupted flashes—the ciphering they did on the split, white side of wood heaped in the chimney corner against early-morning needs. We are told that Mentor applied himself with great faithfulness and soon left Minerva far behind. Her schooling stopped after a few years; but the boy, acting upon his parents' pronouncement that he mûst be a teacher, just as he acted upon their other "musts," went ahead rapidly.

His school world was even more serious than his home world. At sunup he tiptoed into the meeting-house, doffed his cap, and offered a respectful "I wish you good morning, Sir" to Master Borun. Wearing a scowl meant to intimidate the older boys, that worthy opened school by bellowing his rules. All the children lugged to school the flitches of bear bacon, or pig hams, jerked venison, lard, peltries, whiskey, pot metal, or ground corn that was the master's pay. Mentor and Minerva once led a calf to the Brush Creek meeting-house as the price of their term's tuition.

Most of the pupils tried earnestly to learn, for they knew how hard these "quarterings" were to obtain and to carry to school. With harsh school rules, a master's angry palm, a promise of hell-fire both at home and at church, few had the temerity not to stick to business. Not in Master Borun's, but in some near-by schools, big boys sometimes ganged up on the teacher and threw him out if he refused a politely requested half-holiday or had thrashed a little too often or too thoroughly. Up north, neighbor boys had smoked out their teacher and ridden off to Elizabethtown, several to the horse, to see an elephant. They took a licking apiece the next day. But in Brush Creek, a parental licking always followed a thrashing at school. The culprit got licked for getting licked.

Big, gawky boys and girls who had had no "chanct afore" stood up to spell against little lads like Mentor and took their seats before his superior ability. But it was they who could catch a black snake, barehanded, break its back with a twist, and freeze Mentor's blood by chasing him with it at play-spell. With awed faces the little group finally stood about the flung-down snake while some oldster proclaimed the familiar truth that "she cain't die against sundown." The passing of an oxcart or horse-back-rider might break the spell, for then every one of them must go running to the roadside to doff cap and curtsy and chorus: "I wish you good day, Sir."

The one time Master Borun "treated" his school, he followed the accepted fashion of rolling apples on the floor and letting the best scramblers obtain the most apples. If the babies cried, the big girls divided theirs with them. As scholarship prizes the gals and the galish boys were allowed to make goose-quill pens, and the big scholars were given a choice between a "chaw of terbacker and a nip of whiskey."

Mentor learned to make pens. He took immense pains with his writing; and on a certain proud day he came home to find that his Uncle Robert had been by and left him a pot of sumac ink and a pound of paper and a sander, in celebration of his evenly "joined hand" and brave capitals. Uncle Robert, the doctor, had no children. Just as it was at home, so at school it was charcoal and split wood for ciphering. There was little precious paper. On it, the learner, duly impressed with its cost, finally wrote his own name, an achievement usually arrived at after one or two terms.

At school there was the baseborn (illegitimate) boy, Charley, who never played when, with sham Indian war dance and battle, the other boys went howling through the woods at play-spell, gobbling like wild turkeys, throwing the tomahawk, wrestling, shooting wooden guns. They had "hated him out," taunted him with "Baseborn Charley! Baseborn Charley!" and he stayed in the meeting-house while they played and shouted and gouged at each other in fierce imitation of grown-up market-day goings-on. Mentor excelled at throwing the tomahawk, making it spin dizzily in air on the way to hit the mark charcoaled upon the tree trunk.

In summer term the children studied out of doors, sitting about on logs, the big boys gladly taking time out from study to chase snakes and crack their heads with rocks. After-harvest school was held indoors, where young eyes strained to see by the half-light from the small hinged windows that stood open except in the coldest weather. Then the light from the fireplace or a candle or two had to do for all of them, though the big boys were sometimes herded out of doors with a "chunk o' fire" to start their own new one and "figger digits" on wood they split then and there.

Mentor skipped the hornbook, a hand-mirror-shaped contrivance that held removable disks printed with letters and simple words, which a chubby hand could turn this way and that to catch the light. He became a "blabber" and joined in the ener-

getic uproar that went on until nearly sundown, the accepted time
for dismissal. Short, slight, with a heavy mop of bright-red hair,
Mentor added his high, shrilling voice to the hubbub of Master
Borun's blab school, where the loudmouthed endeavored to drown
out the meek.

During the day, in the order of arrival at school, each pupil
stood before Master Borun to be praised or rulered, according as
he had or had not mastered the lesson assigned him. A few owned
a Dillworth's *Speller or New Guide to the English Tongue*, but the
majority studied from copied lessons, "set" by the master.
Through the noise of the lesser learners' *ba, be, bi, bo, bu*, as they
studied out loud, rang the older ones' voices, reeling off geography
answers or multiplication tables while the master made or mended
goose-quill pens, kept up the fire, smacked down wrigglers and of-
fenders—and sometimes made a hasty trip to his saddle-bagged
steed outside, to taste of the cup that cheers.

Advanced scholars memorized set answers to set questions in a
subject called "geography," which included a brief history of each
nation and the astronomy of the solar system. Woe to the unlucky
one who stuttered or forgot! But arithmetic was the Armageddon.
The child not only must learn to write and mentally juggle figures
but must word his own answers in his own inadequate vocabulary.
"Intellectual arithmetic" brought more beatings than correct answers in Master Borun's school. In this, as in much later time,
"the rule of three"—that is, ratio and proportion—was the pin-
nacle of backwoods pedagogy. Few scholars ever got so far, and
few masters could teach it.

The blab school's vocal hubbub was brought to order four times
a day: twice for singing, Bible reading, and a lecture on morals;
twice for a spelldown. If the best speller used up Dillworth, the
master switched to pronouncing words from the Bible, if he did
not possess a dictionary. It was a method that lasted a hundred
years and produced rare spellers. The smallest child heard hundreds of words spelled every day, saw the downed one take his
seat, disgraced, and the smart one receive Master Borun's curt
nod of approval. Since "giving out" words included their definitions by the pedagogue, a spelldown taught much more than
spelling.

Whipping girls was taboo, but they might be stood in the corner with their hands stretched high above their heads. The boy who had earned a flogging was himself sent to cut the stick with which he would be beaten. He must stand before them all and take his medicine. His refusal even to wince, much less cry, and the size of the stick he brought in were his weapons with which to win the place of the hero among his fellows. Through them he could show utter contempt for the master. If he nursed his stripes in private, that was his own affair.

But Brush Creek School had its rich compensations; and thrashings were soon forgotten in the zest of a game of fox and geese, or fox and hounds, in the level snow before the meeting-house, or of prisoner's base in good weather. In season there was wild fruit, free for the seeking—wild grapes, pawpaws, persimmons, wild crab apples, and plums—and sweeter nuts than were ever bought over a counter. A grapevine swing dangled above the creek, offering the thrill of traveling from bank to bank over the falls by the weavery; and every smooth-boled tree was a challenge to be answered. After the long hour and a half play-spell came the jangle of the master's bell from the doorway, and the unwilling roamers gathered in to his severe "Books! Books!" until sundown.

The thrashings brought a question to the earnest mind of Mentor Graham, teacher's pet. He seems always to have possessed a logic that was precision itself, a mind that died trying to make illogical elements in life fit each other. He had heard, had been required to memorize, a "suffer-little-children" doctrine at home and at church. But everybody whipped little children. Perhaps it was in Master Borun's school that Graham, as a child, developed his lifelong philosophy, one that has made him remembered—by friend and foe alike—as being utterly gentle, patient, and kind to little children.

Clear in his memory when he was eighty-five years old were many details of his childhood. These we have from his school-teaching granddaughter, the late Mrs. Flora Graham Seller of rural Lincoln, Illinois, who heard them when she was a child and he lived in the home of her parents. Most vividly recalled was the spring bath. After a bathless winter, at last the welcome, warm day would come when Mary would say: "Children, change today." Each child in turn carried the wooden keeler of water, which had been warmed in a big iron pot over the dooryard fire, up the wall-peg ladder to the privacy of the attic. Here winter clothing was discarded, and a boy came forth from his wooden-tub bath with soft soap, feeling, in his flimsy summer tow-cloth clothes, like a butterfly divested of its cocoon.

The autumn scene was one in which the children were lined up before the fire or on the doorstep in the sun, with pieces of wetted leather tied about their feet, sitting patiently until Mary decided that the leather was dry enough. The wait was a good time to barber heads, too—the last haircut until spring. Mary removed the pieces of dried leather, molded to the shape of each foot, slit the top edges with openings large enough to admit deerskin thongs —and the children's winter footgear was provided. The day came when Mentor caught one of his shoepacks between floor puncheons in the meeting-house and, awkwardly half-hopping home that night through the snow, froze the shoeless foot.

Often there was preaching at the Graham cabin, especially after the slavery question waxed hot, for the abolitionists had to keep themselves bolstered up. For long hours children sat listening to terrifying hell-torment predictions for slaveowners. Mentor, delegated to turn the spit over the dooryard fire—for there was much more and much better food on such occasions—could hear it all through the open door. For that matter, he could have heard it as easily with the door closed, as could anyone for some distance in any direction. Voice volume, explosiveness of delivery, and facial contortion must be expended in direct proportion to the number and blackness of souls to be saved. It was a poor excuse of a preacher who could not wring tears and groans from his auditory.

Mentor, turning the spit outside, indulged in fearfully wicked thoughts. Perhaps those in the flaming oils of hell became the feast for the Devil and his minions, even as the mouth-watering carcass sputtering lusciously over his fire would soon be the congregation's feast. He laughed heartily at that, as an old man; but as an eight-year-old he turned the meat with utmost care, unwilling either to tempt God or call forth Mary's rebuke. Eating the burned portion was the punishment for such carelessness. He kept his thoughts to himself and concentrated his whole attention upon the meat, knowing by experience that glorious relief was on the way and, after the last hymn, the feast would follow.

One of the favorite hymns was:

> No foot of land do I possess,
> No cabin in the wilderness,
> A poor, wayfaring man.
> I lodge a while in tents below
> And gladly wander to and fro
> Till I my Canaan gain.

Now that was a real puzzler for a logically minded boy. Almost every singer owned acres and acres of land and had a perfectly good two-, three-, or even six-room cabin in the wilderness. *Tents?*

But all such questions were soon forgotten in the splendid uproar of neighbors unpacking roast possum, turkey, squirrel, pigeon, pig, and deer from hickory-withe creels on pack horses tethered about the dooryard, their shadows dancing like imps in the flicker of Mentor's fire. Then came the delicious clatter of wooden piggin and bowl and trencher on planked-out tables, the slicing of good (wheat) bread, the dipping-out of honey and maple sugar—with children clamorously running and fetching and the odors of food becoming almost unbearable—till at last, having waited through the long, long, blessing, he fell to like the healthy little animal that he was and gorged himself.

Afterward came the scrambling off upstairs to bed with brothers and sisters and the neighbors' children, rolling up in blankets and buffalo and bearskins, packing the attic floor tight, giggling and tickling, and finally going off to sleep to the sound of the winter wind. It was perfect, and might have remained so had not the elders held a second session downstairs and a hell-proclaiming voice pierced the attic floor and boomed among the rafters, waking Mentor and setting him to reviewing carefully how well he had performed his duties for that day. Somehow he drifted off to sleep again, to wake up in the bitter cold and dress and hustle down to help with preparations for another day of religion.

Summer church in the woods was not so terrorizing. Like Mary, his mother, Graham seems always to have been a near-worshiper of trees. In later life he went to the haven of the woods when troubled, just as he did as a young boy. Many parts of the Baptist religion were, even then, untenable to him. Early in life, walking alone in the woods, he concluded that his mother's belief in witch-persons, together with the preacher's eternal tortures, were wrong.

Against his will, he was, however, spellbound by his mother's witch-tales, especially the one about their neighbor, the first Jacob Bale. Mary had a way of mimicking that froze the boy's spine.

This tale you can hear today in the cabins on Brush Creek. Jacob Bale found it necessary to go back to the "Old Country" (Holland) for grindstones for his mill. He was gone six, eight, ten, eleven months. Folks began to say he was gone for good. But his second-sighted wife met all their sallies—and offers of marriage—with: "No. Jake'll be back. He'll come." Goggle-eyed, the neighborhood came to her "invitin' in" on the last day of the twelfth month. They were all seated at "the high-noon feast when the door opens and in walks Jake.

" 'You've been sick, Jake,' says she, before he can speak.

" 'Yes, wife, sick and like to die,' says Jake; and pale enough he looked.

" 'I a-knowed it, I a-knowed it, I a-knowed it,' says she, three times, a-fingerin' her witch-charm. And from then she was skithered around, one of them thar hard wimmen, with powers."

Mentor—shy, diligent, thoughtful, rarely "contrarious"—became ever more meditative. He worked without talking and finished first at his home tasks while the others dawdled and gallivanted off to play. He had the application of a man when it came to filling the gourd with berries or wild grapes or nuts. Duties done, he rambled off into the woods, alone, and loved nothing better than to get soaked with rain.

Sitting before the fire, listening to his parents talk, he heard much that didn't fit. He spent hours trying to make it fit. Court-day trips with his father brought the worst puzzles. He thought court-week games bully, loved to watch them, and came home to teach them to the children; but then there were those ticklers of whiskey and those "flips of blackstrap" against which the preacher railed. Within the courtroom, sitting in the shadow of his tall father's great hunting coat, he watched the frowning judge, Nathaniel Owens, his uncle, in dun-colored leggings, broadcloth pantaloons, triple-caped overcoat, and high fur hat, mount the bench and accuse culprits of "profane swairing," "travelling on the Sabbath," and "not paying heed in meeting." Outside he saw women publicly whipped for pig-stealing, and men and women in pillory and stocks being badgered by a lackadaisical crowd while

they fulfilled sentence for gossiping or gouging. And yet when the
market-day crowd set upon a man and hated him out for not joining up with the militia, and the man took to his heels, with the
crowd following and hooting and gouging and "profanely swairing," nobody interfered. He saw men flinching under the forty
strokes for burglary, and slaves being taken off under the lash by
men who had just bought them. What men taught in the church
and what they did outside the church did not—emphatically did
not—fit.

Mentor was always glad to come home to quiet little Brush
Creek after being all day in the noisy Greensburg square with its
threats and lashings, bets and bickerings, and its roistering young-
bloods, bragging the inimitable Kentucky brag that they could
lick their weight in wildcats. All the men carried tomahawks at
their belts, he was used to that; but many of the wildest ones in
town, who referred to themselves as "red hawses," carried dirks
and those long, deadly knives to which they jokingly referred as
"Arkansas toothpicks." Mentor lingered thoughtfully over many
of their words. What was a "loony," a "stop-hell," a "too-good"?

Returned home, he could forget all these things in his books, a
world apart, one of pure joy, where living was divested of all questions and where he could revel in the names of things he knew and
loved: "wide-dale," "woodside," "tallhill," "hazelgrove." He rarely read long at a time, for the book was always asked to wait on
work: the eternal woodpile, the tater patch, milking. Or reading
might be interrupted by the excitement of Jeremiah's going off
with other hunters on a bear or wolf hunt. Stirring the mush pot
after supper in preparation for tomorrow's breakfast was not so
bad, for then you could think to yourself and perhaps ask a question or two. There was, of course, always a baby to be tended and
rocked to sleep; and big boys, past eight, got up early to fetch the
day's greens from the truck patch before breakfast and afterward
returned with a hoe to cultivate the interminable rows in the tater,
corn, squash, bean, or cabbage patch.

With chickens and geese and ducks foraging through the woods,
hunting eggs was a delightful, time-consuming job where a boy
could trot up fast to see what stirred the grass, or walk slowly and
whistle—just as he pleased, for a change. And there was always
Nigger, his black colt, to fondle and curry and save sugar for, and

ride when he fetched a jug of buttermilk to the men in the field. On spring days the red maples were tapped and the syrup hauled in on homemade sleds. When it had been boiled down, it was stored in gourds—soft, runny, delicious sugar.

Time spent on duty was doubly fruitful for the Graham clan— and there were twenty-two first cousins by now—for they were set to memorizing pieces out of poetry books, the Bible, or other books on the shelf that now held the position of honor over the fireplace in Jeremiah's, as well as in many another cabin. Off they went for nuts, jackets fastened with locust thorns against frost, bobbing along to the rhythm of "When I consider thy heavens," always with some oldster who had already committed it to prompt a forgetter. At home the children sliced cork to be covered for buttons, tended rye coffee to see that it did not boil over, stirred the mush pot, and minded the baby while they were committing to memory gems from *Family Poetry Collection*.

At nine Mentor could handle ax, adz, auger, and saw. He could plait shoe mats, horse collars, and ropes from cornhusks. He could sing "Barbara Allen" and a dozen other ballads his mother taught the children. And there was one homemade ballad, composed by little, work-brittle grandmother Nancy Elizabeth:

> A couple lived on the River Yadkin
> In the state of North Caroliny. . . .

By the fire Mentor shivered at night, listening to his Granny tell how Jack Armstrong fought the Devil. "He fit the Devil all night, he did," and came out winner, though he had to crawl home. Folks passing that way saw where the fences were "tied in knots and the timber splintered flat—three hundred poles and more square," where the fight had been.

"Long comes Granny Jewell, cacklin,' cacklin', cacklin'.

" 'What ye be laughin' at?' they says.

" 'O, I jes' passed Jack Armstrong's cabin,' says she, flappin' her bony arms, 'and hearin' shrieks and rattlin' chains I looks in, jest in time to see the Devil jerkin' Jack down between the puncheons' —and she's gone in a whirlwind!' "

Mary was a singer and knew all the ballads of the British Isles. Her favorite was the ballad of "Jim Beams and Tempe Creason" —a wife-stealing and elopement. She sang to them of Goodpenny, who was hung for murdering his wife, a Brush Creek favorite that was performed in its most terrifying manner when "fiddlin' Jim" made the rounds of the cabins with his violin, imitating the march to the gallows and the death-shrieks of Goodpenny.

In fact, many a Brush Creek youth more gullible than Mentor was "skeered clean outen his hide that he mought be a-meetin'" of wild cattle in the woods." If the boy ran back home, he'd "catch it." If he went way round and was late to school, he'd be even worse off. In this predicament, little wonder that many a boy chose to go fishing instead, sitting way back under the rocks of some cave where neither wild cattle—"them as is hanted by human sperits"—nor irate parent or schoolmaster could "scrubble down into." Besides, there was all that gold hidden somewhere on Brush by robbers, that a feller might grub up, if he hunted enough. But none of this for Mentor.

Uncle Robert came by one evening and talked half the night with Mary and Jeremiah. Master Borun had been telling around that Mentor was the smartest scholar in Brush Creek. Jeremiah did not doubt it. He knew how far his little son could outwrite and outfigger his pappy. Robert, the doctor, had two cases of books. In his childless household he and his wife, Frances, would care for Mentor with devotion. Robert would teach him in spare time and take him along when he rode his doctor's circuit, to study as they went. The boy would get ahead faster. Thus Robert, who had had an education, persuaded Jeremiah, who had had a smattering, and Mary, who had had none, to let him tutor the smartest scholar in Brush Creek school. The parents gave up their prided little son that he might live with his uncle, twenty miles away, where he would "git larnin' quicker than t' hum."

Mentor begged not to go. He had rarely seen Uncle Robert, who seemed kind but was so big and so positive. When the child clung to his mother, she smiled down at him and told him he *must* go and make her proud of him. So Mentor Graham went from home, fearfully but obediently, chiefly because he saw that his mother's faith in his ability was complete, but also because he hoped her faith was changing over from witches to wisdom. That smile Mary Graham gave her little son was one of the greatest influences in his life. His mother *knew* he would get ahead faster; he did.

The evening before Robert came for him, his mother returned

from a horseback trip she had made alone to Elizabethtown to buy Mentor his first store coat. She had news. The South Fork Nolynn church had split over slavery; and most of the members— the antis—had left it, among them Jessie and Mary Friend and Tom and Nancy Lincoln. She had stopped by the Lincoln place, coming home, to warm her foot mantle. They'd had a boy born last Sabbath. They reckoned they'd call him Abraham, after his grandpap, killed by the Indians.

Tom Lincoln[1] had moved to his farm on the Nolynn a little before this, combining farming with a trade, as most had to do. His cabin was almost ten miles northeast of Jeremiah's. He and his young wife, Nancy, belonged to the Little Mount Baptist Church, whose preacher was that same Elkin who had brought an entire congregation of persecuted Virginia Baptists hymn-singing through the wilderness to Kentucky in the early days. He often preached at Greensburg and exhorted during the three-day preachings held at both the Lincoln and the Graham cabins.

When Tom's father had first come to Kentucky in 1779, he had pre-empted eight hundred acres of land south of Green River and had attended Long Run Baptist Church, where Ben Lynn often preached. After his murder by Indians, his family, who then owned two thousand acres in the Green River country, moved north into Washington County. Lynn had preached to them there at the time when William and Nancy Graham were settling on Brush Creek. Lynns and Lincolns had tomahawked land rights near each other in the Beargrass, near the Falls.

Thus, with the birth of Abraham Lincoln in the cabin on the Nolynn, the shape of the design grows more distinct. Near neighbors, of the same faith, and further unified by a common hatred of slavery, the Lincolns and the Grahams "lived clost," in both a physical and a spiritual sense. And Christopher Bush, the slave patroller, lived "on up a piece."

IV

HORSEBACK SCHOOL

1810-11

*I*T WAS NO new world into which Mentor rode behind his Uncle Robert. He found the same milk-mixed, sweetened whiskey, administered every morning by Aunt Frances just as his mother had administered it, "to keep you healthy." Uncle Robert had the same wide-swinging door, the same hospitable welcome for all who knocked. The boy must still wield the ax at the woodpile and follow after with sickle when Robert cradled wheat or rye; flail flax; hunt cows by their bells; stack fodder and straw; help earmark little pigs and spoon gruel into sick lambs before the dooryard fire; and do his share of milking into the big gourds.

But his bed was no longer in the cockloft. Now he slept, all alone, in the "second-best" room. When he went to do his chores, he wore a pair of Aunt Frances' old stockings, not for extra warmth, but to keep his brand new copper-toed boots shiny. Aunt Frances cooked bean and corn ashcakes and fried mush and hominy, as his mother had; and gave him bear's grease to try to smooth down his hair. But there was one big difference: Uncle Robert saw no harm in roaming the woods alone, doing nothing. Mentor could even pick strawberries on a Sabbath afternoon. Or whittle.

Where Jeremiah "chawed terbacker," Robert "lighted segars." Mentor was used to seeing mammies and grannies smoking corncob pipes, and he had hoed plenty of tobacco in the field. He had even tried chewing it; but he had never smoked a pipe or cigar. When Robert one day left an unfinished cigar lying in the cowshed, Mentor decided to try it. The canebrake beyond the last cornfield seemed a private enough place, so he took "segar" and flint and went on down to make the trial. But it was much nearer dark than Mentor realized, and canebrakes have outwitted far more experienced woodsmen than the boy. He was lost. Up at the house they rang the dinner bell and shot off the gun—and by midnight neighbors were out thrashing the brush up and down the creek ten miles from the spot where Mentor, crying a little now and then but struggling on, was making his way straight through the brake. He finally came out on the farther side, and toward morning limped in under his own steam; but that was his first and last cigar. As an old man, he is said to have smoked an occasional pipe, but cigars were not for him.

When Mentor first came to live with his uncle, Robert was preparing for a round of the circuit that he covered four times a year. Each day, prompted by the portly man's kind voice, the child recited his lessons, sentence by sentence, in the utter quiet of the "best room." His one deaf ear, evidently, had been handicapping him in the hubbub of the blab school, for now he progressed surprisingly. As a reward, just before they started on the circuit, Robert and Frances took him for a few days' visit at home. Those few days were among the happiest of his life, for his family feasted him and "made over him"; and when he rode away behind Robert, his store coat bulged with the first book he had ever owned. In the common phrasing of the times, Jeremiah had written in all the other books on the shelf:

> Bought this ——— day of ———, 18——,
> by Jeremiah Graham
> For the advancement of his family
> and himself

But this book—*Aesop's Fables*—bore the fabulous inscription:

> William Mentor Graham
> from
> his Father and Mother
> For good Behavior and Lessons

Robert was busy measuring herbs and filling capsules, sharpening lancets and counting his calomel pills. Mentor watched, listened, asked questions, learned. When the day to start came, he scrambled up behind Robert, his legs held far out by the doctor's fat saddlebags, and off they went for what turned out to be almost the equivalent of a liberal college education.

As they rode, Mentor recited or listened earnestly to Robert's answers to questions such as "Why do they call it the 'rule of three?' " or "Why does the sun go down?" Mentor's schooling on horseback seems to have surpassed all plans, classic or modern, for results. His laboratory, nature, was ever at hand, furnishing examples for any puzzle's answer. And here was a good, honest, capable, strong man to answer his questions—a man whose muscle and wisdom would take them safely five hundred miles through forests and across rivers, providing food and shelter for himself and the redheaded boy on the pillion. Riding thus through the primeval woods, its unwithholding wisdom was theirs to tap at will. And they possessed an element rarely included by theories of the ideal school—they loved each other.

Among the towns through which they passed were Elizabethtown, Springfield, Harrodsburg, Leitchfield, and Bowling Green. They did not stop in the towns, for Robert treated the ailments of rural folk and their animals: horse galls, proud-flesh cattle knees resulting from wolf attacks, decayed human teeth, chilblaines, bear-claw wounds, rheumatism, windlessness, dislocated fingers and broken ribs, dimming vision, snakebites, lung fever, cholera, carbuncles, childbirth. . . . . From loving, Mentor grew to idolizing his Uncle Robert, whose very appearance seemed to help the waiting sufferers. Proudly he clambered up after each stop, to ride on again, jog trotting. To that rhythm, and compelled by a heroic pride in such an uncle, the boy learned the conjugations and declensions and how to use them in speaking, multiplication tables up to eighteen, mensuration tables, and the history of the United States.

Few ten-year-olds could answer as quickly as he when Robert, smiling encouragingly back at him, would propound some such problem as this: "If one deerskin is worth two and a half beaver, how much will a store coat cost in beaver skins if it is priced at one and a half deerskins?" It was a practical problem in their day, when money was rarely seen—Robert was paid for his lancings and leechings, poultices and pills, in deer and badger and otter skins. The boy earned a story after ten such problems had been correctly solved in his head, and stories from books Robert doubtless told him. But the ones that clung to the memory of an old man were ones from his grandsires' lives: the fight at Alamance, Regulators who objected to being overtaxed for a king's palace; the mighty

Long Hunts and the fortunes in rotted deerskins; the spy on the
Illinois; William Lynn sneaking gunpowder fifteen hundred miles
through the wilderness by pack horse and canoe; men galloping
in and out of blockhouses with bullets peppering the air about
them. All had happened near at hand, with the lad's grandparents
and great-uncles in principal roles. If Mentor squirmed in his place,
it was from thrilling pride and not because both legs had gone to
sleep from dangling so long.

Robert hurried, when necessary, in order to get to the next
cabin at the regular mealtime and not make extra trouble. The
lad had fine practice in holding on then, and this may account for
his expert horsemanship later. He rode, and rode well, until he
was eighty-five. But his chief joy came when his idolized uncle announced that they would have to camp for the night, for then they
would sit side by side on a log while the grouse sizzled above the
campfire. Then Mentor would hear about women and children
who brought water to Bryant's Station (Lexington), right in the
face of the Indians, to save the fort from thirst during a siege; how
they laughed and joked and did not run, not even the last steps
coming back, with their filled keelers. Or he would be carried out
of time and place by his uncle's low voice, reading from one of the
books in his saddlebags, words whose entire import was healing
the sick.

Then they would eat and lie down together under the sheltering
trees with the stars peeping at them and talk themselves to sleep
about hell-fire and the Mississippi River, getting tipsy, warts, and
witches. Robert didn't much believe in hell-fire and witches; but
he knew tipsying, lying, cussing, fighting, and stealing were wicked
—and he could cure warts. He cured Mentor's on that first trip—
"and I had both hands full," Mentor later said.

From his tenth until his twelfth year Mentor lived with Robert
and Frances and went itinerating four times a year. He learned an
amazing amount of literature, religion, medicine, and history;
about birds, animals of the woods, and English grammar. He
stretched out and plumped up and became much, much more
freckled—the freckles all but touched. He lost his habit of trying
to make things fit, for Uncle Robert's world had few misfits in it
—and as a result he became a boy who laughed easily and loved to
play tricks.

One night a storm broke when they were almost home, and they were obliged to stop at the cabin of Thomas Lincoln. Mentor played with little Sarah and read to her out of his *Aesop's Fables*, which made every trip with him. The little brother, Abe, listened too, and their parents; but the tale was interrupted by a third storm-bound traveler bursting in. It was Christopher Columbus Graham—Mentor's cousin, if records are not faulty, though Mentor did not know it then or ever. With such large families as were then common, second cousins were likely to be strangers. Christopher was thought to be a queerish fellow, for he was always "traipsin' round after yarbs and peculiarish stones and animal bones and suchlike." He said you "might be able to make out what used to be in Kaintuck," that way. He had been a guest at the Lincolns' before, and Abe and Sarah were permitted by their parents to go with him as he hunted stones over their farm. The Lincolns slept on the earthen floor this night and gave their own bed to their three guests.

Mentor, on these rounds, became acquainted with itinerant peddlers from as far away as Boston, clacking their wares, amazing cabin folks with such wonders as tin cups and milk-strainers. He and Robert sometimes stopped to listen in at a court held under some greenwood tree, and the streams they forded were laden with raftloads of peltries, tobacco, and whiskey, heading for the Ohio or the Mississippi. Kentucky was growing up, and Dr. Graham decided to open an office at Leitchfield.

Returned home, Mentor found a new and larger house, pewter on the board, and his mother and the little girls wearing fine store-bought shoes and mantles. With him he brought his dog, Salem, and considerable pocket money given him by his uncle, together with three books of his own and a satchelful of new clothing. Once he had dreaded having to become a "bound boy"; now that dread passed. Since Mentor pitched in to help with the farm work— cellaring potatoes, chopping mincemeat with an ax, scraping hair from pig carcasses, and keeping the wood box filled—Jeremiah said he couldn't spare such a son, and Mary found welcome release in Mentor's entertaining the children for hours on end with his fund of information and experiences. The parents, listening, beamed with pride: why, the boy could almost outtalk the preacher! Jeremiah vouched for all the stories Mentor had had from

Robert; and he himself told a story of how, when he was a boy, there had come a cautious thump on the door and the low word, "Indians." They had all risen and dressed in the dark to sneak the women and children down to Gray's Station, everybody laden with as many flitches of bacon as could be grabbed down hastily from the rafters. Arriving at Gray's Station, the men—he and father William among them—deposited the women in its comparative safety and went on south to join with other companies. They had harried the Indians, had driven them "clean to Arkansas, and after that had no more rippets and ructions."

Few could have guessed that the blue-eyed boy they had grown used to seeing behind Dr. Graham had a better conception of the world and man's place in it then they; of the history of America and Kentucky, and the part this section played in it; of the human body, its ills and care. A thousand things besides had been included in his horseback college. Jeremiah and Mary listened spellbound as the boy feverishly related what he had done and seen and learned. His education had, indeed, been hastened. Yet he was quivering with eagerness to learn more.

That winter Mentor went to "invitings in" on Brush Creek, very sleek of hair except where it just would curl. But he did not shine socially, for the hero here was the lad who could tell how he killed the snake whose skin was wound about his cap. Mentor could not bleat like a fawn, in preparation for the proud day when he would seduce and slay a doe. But he could and did join in the old kissing games, handed down intact from Scotland. Innocently enough, the children enacted as they sang it some such jingle as this:[1]

> O sister Phoebe how merry were we
> The night we sat under the juniper tree—
> The juniper tree, Hi Ho!
> Take his hat on your head to keep your head warm
> And take his sweet kiss—it will do you no harm—
> But a great deal of good, I know, I know,
> But a great deal of good, I know.

Not a child gave a thought to the biting wind when, going home, they slid on the smooth ice of the coves of Brush Creek and made fine pictures of themselves, coontail cap and all, in the soft depth of wavy snowbanks.

The latest Graham baby, Nancy, was a year-old toddler.

Minerva was a tall girl, nearing thirteen, strong for her age, and in between these two were Mentor and Robert and Rachel and Benjamin. The children drew charcoal pictures of witches on the firewood and shot them with wooden toy guns. Mary's fine gilt-framed looking glass was turned to the wall most of the time because it could be looked into so many wrong ways and thus make evil things happen. Mary had persuaded Jeremiah to singe the foreheads of his farm animals to ward off spells; and she went borrowing salt from Granny Skaggs—when she had a keg of it herself —to break any possible spell the old lady might have cast.

These things worried Mentor, fresh from his Uncle Robert's matter-of-fact tutelage. Mentor quoted Robert to his mother: Crops wither not from a withering-witch but because there is too little water in the ground, and so stopping suddenly in the center of a field and clapping your hands couldn't possibly do any good. Neither could tapping on a green-barked tree as you whistled bring rain, because it rained only when the sun had drawn enough water into the air to be heavy enough to fall. She was amazed at the boy's knowledge—but only partially convinced. Under her influence Mentor dropped back into some old superstitious practices and would not turn back for a forgotten book, lest bad luck befall him.

However, he did not lose his eagerness to learn—and it was soon rewarded. Judge Owens brought his family over for a Sabbath visit, a rare event, for although his wife was Jeremiah's sister, the two families were not very cordial. There were two reasons: Uncle Natty was a very wealthy man and lived in great style in one of the finest houses in Green County; and, even worse, he was a slave-driver. On this day, however, things went smoothly, and the judge was so impressed by Mentor's speech and intelligence that he made Jeremiah and Mary promise to send Mentor to Brush Creek Academy, which Owens was soon to open at his home with James McElroy (one-time student at Howe's New Athens Academy) as tutor. He was asking in other neighbor children—in fact, that was the purpose of his visit. The Grahams, of course, were to pay the tuition.

Owens was an enormous, placid, kindly, highly educated man. His wife Nancy, Jeremiah's sister, had learned books from him since her marriage. She was a tiny woman, but a dynamo of energy and housewifeliness. Mentor would be going into a household of culture and luxury.

One recorded description of Brush Creek at this time has come to light. While Mentor was learning from his Uncle Robert at the age of eleven, an English traveler named Cummins paddled up Brush Creek. He wrote in his diary: "About eight miles from the salt lick we passed on the left a fine settlement of several large farms and good farm houses, called Graham's Station, on Kennedy's Bottoms; and three miles farther, on the right, a new town of Adamsville with one very good house and three or four small ones, finely situated near the mouth of Brush Creek which is a charming little river about thirty-five yards wide."

The "very good" house last described was Nathaniel Owens'. It is still standing, a three-story red-brick Georgian building with a deep wing and many outbuildings and slaves' quarters—so many that the traveler took it for a town. Almost forgotten, it now sleeps in a thickening grove, the new forest that has supplanted the clearings of the pioneer. With eyes half-closed, I stood before it, in 1941, trying to restore its sagging shutters to their once trim white paint, to rebuild the fifty-foot sweep of the front veranda with its three-story white columns.

It was not hard to imagine the lad, Mentor, meticulous even now in dress, crossing Brush Creek on the steppingstones which country lads today still use, trotting over the wide lawn-sweep to the drive and up to the house, hugging his books. He slips through the carved double front door and up to the twenty-by-twenty south "fireplace room" on the second floor where Brush Creek Academy is in session. A bright fire crackles, slave tended; and a row of west, unshuttered windows lights the room. He greets a neat, kind, and very smart young man, James McElroy, who looks him straight in the eye, ready with answers to the battery of questions last night's study has fermented in the boy's mind. He has studied hard: if he succeeds here, he is to go to the new brick academy at Elizabethtown and find out about such mysteries as fluxions and gauging, astronomy and navigation, dialing and trigonometry, as the handbill from that institution promises. This handbill, in larger type, rules out "cards, gambling, cussing, and unseemly language."

V

BRUSH CREEK ACADEMY
AND LATIN

1811–13

MENTOR WAS "twelve goin' on thirteen." No one had to tell him what that meant, for in those days a boy turned fourteen was counted a man, expected to do a man's work. He applied himself with keener diligence than ever, revolving in his young mind many an adult problem as he hugged his books and hurried through the January snow, long miles to Uncle Nat's big house with its roomful of books and many newspapers on the library table. Aunt Nancy gave him the newspapers as they accumulated, and he bore them home gratefully.

He sat late by the fire to learn from them of Burr's conspiracy, Henry Clay's notion of making Kentucky all-powerful by Kentucky people buying Kentucky products. He read of the French boatmen, the *voyageurs*, singing in their sixteen-oar trapper's boats on the upper Mississippi; of the new mail route three hundred miles by horse-post north through the wilderness; of the fact that "white work" was no longer to be had on the rivers. He read of the new kind of boat that could push itself upstream faster than the barges like "Lady Washington" and "Mary Jane" went down.

His Uncle Nat knew Audubon, now storekeeping in Louisville, who had come to America to paint birds and was now accumulating iron pots and calico to buy the good will of savages west of Arkansas Post when he went there to paint. Everything his uncle said to the boy opened toward new worlds of knowledge and spurred him to read faster. There was going to be another war, his uncle said. Why? All the boy's teaching had been that hating and fighting were wicked. But now the big boys in the neighborhood, drilling to fight and kill, were being called noble.

He now read avidly, stirred to his depths to know a part of the world beyond Brush Creek. And as he walked back and forth to Brush Creek Academy, he imagined himself a man, talking with men—he actually made up speeches and spoke them aloud. Audubon's horseback trip from Louisville by way of Nashville to Richmond and Philadelphia was a trip he pretended to take. He *was* Audubon. People in Louisville, E-town, Frankfort, and Lexington whom he followed in print were actual acquaintances of his. He pretended to talk to them.

He got work as an ash-boy in Fairthorn's furnace, pig iron from which had long been shipped by ox sled and river barge to New Orleans and on to England. But now, with England at war with America, a rafter's wharf had sprung up at the place where Lynn Camp Creek joined Green River and cannon were being floated down to New Orleans. Men were scarce, and the older boys had gone to war. Lads of Mentor's age worked like men. Sometimes he ground leatherwood or saltpeter. If England thought she could bully us, let her try it! The boy worked furiously with his hands, carrying ashes, grinding, and gouging, while in his imagination he fired the cannon at sea. At twelve Mentor made powder and helped make cannon that won the battle of New Orleans. He was steeped in the Kentucky brand of courage and never, in his long life, ran away from a fight.

But he could be frightened. One night, on the way home from work, he met Christopher Columbus Graham with collecting bag and stone hammer out looking for specimens along Brush Creek.[1] They met after sundown, and the boy was startled out of his wits by the enormous man in his fringed deerskins who strode suddenly out from behind the trees. All Mentor had heard said about Christopher rushed through his mind: "kin to witches," "strong yarbs," "always mumbling." Christopher's innocent bag seemed bulging with mysterious horrors. He lifted a piece of saltpeter from the bag and said: "Seen anything like this around here, sonny?"

The boy worked with the stuff every day, but all he could manage was a wavering "No Sir" as he fled, the Brush Creek gossip ringing in his ears: "close to crazy," "holds talk with the Devil," "never seen in town." That sack—Mentor had taken no chances. He ran without looking back and burst breathless into the warmth and security of his own firelit cabin. When he explained his haste to his mother, she, half-laughing, half-concerned, told him:

"Christopher is some of your kinfolks, whether he be Satan's help-meet or no."

Yet, even if he had been sure that Christopher was the Devil's servant, Mentor would have risked meeting him every night for the precious joy of journeying through the woods, when work slackened, to Aunt Nancy's house—and the kindly, intelligent, quiet-voiced young man who was now hearing the boy's belated and postponed lessons. If they finished early—and well—Mentor was rewarded, at Uncle Nat's suggestion, by his choice of books to take home to read. Later he would sit like a stone, devouring them, page after page, his spirit winged with the magic of words. Words were the power and the glory; he, too, would master words.

His cousin, William Owens, was fourteen; Elizabeth was seven; and little Mary—the Mary whom Abraham Lincoln would one day court—was three. William and Mentor and Thomas Nance had their lessons together, with one or two other neighbor boys. Mentor is said to have finished first, usually, especially in lessons from the *New American Rational Spelling Book* and the *Columbian Orator*. Figures were not so easy for him. Cousin Sam, ten, didn't approve of this tutoring business and loitered with his work so that he wouldn't have to read any more. Cousin Nancy, fifteen, being a girl, already had learned much of what a girl needed to know, and her lessons were attended to after the boys finished—if any time was left. Mentor sometimes read aloud to her as she sat knitting or caring for little Mary. Aunt Nancy was always busy, looking after the clothing and food of her household. It was a large one, and the slave quarters were filled. Slaves did the candle-dipping and meat-curing, brewing, baking, and tending farmyard fowl; but Nancy superintended it all.

To Mentor, her house was another world—so many big rooms, each larger than the "best room" in Jeremiah's cabin, which was tucked low behind steep banks of the creek. The house, set among tall beeches, was grand looking with the wide curving drive sweeping up to it. Fire snapped in many fireplaces, and there were store-bought velvet carpets and velvet chairs and wonderful spoons, many more than one for each person. People said that Mentor's uncle was the smartest and the richest man in Green County. To the boy he was certainly the most wonderful, for a deep affection, one that lasted their lives out, had sprung up between placid, kindly Nathaniel Owens, who owned so many books, and nervous, eager-tongued Mentor, who was reading greedily. It was stiff reading for a lad of twelve going on thirteen: *Plutarch's Lives*, European history, the English poets, Craddock's *Life of Washington*. He found a book on surveying and set himself to puzzle that out, alone. He hurried. There were so many books in that room, so little time to read in. He looked forward to summer, when he promised himself he would work harder and buy himself two or three of these books that he most wanted.

Uncle Johnson, staying over at Jeremiah's cabin one night because of heavy snow, reported that Nolynn church had been dropped from the association. He and his brother sat talking late into the night about it. Johnson was of the opinion that this had started something that was going to be hard to stop. Nolynn church had been suspended because it had dropped all members owning slaves. As the talkers' voices rose and fell, Mentor, straining his good ear to hear from his pallet bed in the loft, listened, tensed. The conclusion his elders reached was that hell was the place every slaveowner would go, sooner or later. Dear Uncle Natty—would *he?*

For weeks cabin talk had had it that something terrible was about to happen. Every cabin had had sufficient "sign" in broken crocks and burned pones. Everybody knew the Devil had gotten into the Skaggs cabin and made them forget to turn the mirror to the wall in the room where Sophie Skaggs had been laid out, and everybody at the funeral had looked into it, before they thought.

As weeks passed, the tension grew. Mentor's appetite failed, and he tossed to sleep or woke fitfully, his mind harassed with the thought of the danger hanging over his Uncle Nat. All up and down Green River, churches were holding revivals with the wrongness of slavery as their theme. Itinerant preachers were, one and all, consigning slaveowners to hell. The boy watched his uncle closely—he *seemed* so good. But when *all* the preachers agreed that purgatory was scarcely a fearful enough place for men who "sold their black brothers in bondage and drove them like work-beasts," Mentor understood why Great-aunt Mary and Great-uncle Peter had given away their rich bottom farmland for two hundred dollars and had driven away in a snowstorm. They "aimed to miss the trouble that was brewin'."

All that summer Mentor cut brush and carried surveyor's chains, for overlapping claims were making boundary trouble galore. With that small portion of the money he earned which his father said he might use as he liked he bought, at Uncle Johnson's advice, a dictionary and Goldsmith's *Greece*. Under the circumstances, he thought it safer to ask Uncle Johnson, who was now a preacher, than to ask Uncle Nat.

Early in December the worst predictions came true. Mentor was reading at his Uncle Nat's, and the rest were still at their lessons. Aunt Nancy was in the kitchen, superintending the roasting of a brace of turkeys, and little Nancy was spinning. Suddenly there came an ominous roar like a tornado, and the house swayed horridly. The frenzied children, heedless of McElroy's command, ran screaming to their mother. Into Mentor's logical mind came the idea that probably only the slaveowner's houses were being treated like this by God. He made his desperate way home as the earth rolled and swelled under his feet; yet he felt a sense of inner gratitude, for he found his mother outside, little Elizabeth in her arms and the other children clinging, terrified, to her skirts. Seeing them thus, Mentor knew that his mother was praying. The earthquake was awful—yes—but it had come to *everybody!*

The petrifying thing did not pass. Almost every day the sky would darken, the rumbling would swell into a horrid crescendo, and the earth would begin to rise and fall in waves like water. After the first few days, when it still persisted and no one was killed and only a few crocks and jars were broken, Brush Creek folk went back to their usual routine, talking of their end and expecting it hourly, yet preparing to live on. Not until St. Patrick's Day was the last tremor felt. To the Irish Catholics that meant the saint had heard their prayer for deliverance—but the Brush Creek Baptists thought with Preacher Johnson Graham that it wasn't much of a saint that would keep them waiting that long.

In early March, Allan Montgomery set out to raft peltries and tobacco to New Orleans and hired Mentor as pole-boy. Mentor was tall now, but lean; and he well knew how to handle sickle, grubbing hoe, ax, adz, hammer and saw, plow and hay fork, brick mold and trowel. He had never been a raft hand, although he had heard a lot about rafting during those infrequent visits of his Uncle Joseph, who spent his life on the Mississippi.

He learned how to pole and how to shift cargo as Montgomery's raft made its chilly way up the Rolling Fork toward the Ohio. At the first big curve, where Otter Creek flows into the Ohio, the earthquake struck with redoubled force, the raft was upended, cracked in two, and the crew found their cargo gone and themselves struggling in the icy water. They managed to get ashore and to find shelter and a drying fire in a riverside cabin, and the next day started to walk home.

In Elizabethtown, Mentor read about and immediately attended "A Great Exhibition" of the Elizabethtown Academy. He bought a copy of the *Kentucky Gazette* with a bit of his pay from the interrupted raft trip. On turning a page of it, his eyes fell upon words the like of which he did not know existed: "Autumnae felix aderat grania complens. . . . ." He could not make head nor tail of them. "Felix"? That was the name of Uncle Johnson's oldest boy, and Mentor had another cousin Felix, Aunt Lizzie Greene's boy. In Greensburg lived the lawyer, Felix Grundy, for whom both had been named. But those other words? Arrived home, he raced to Uncle Nat's and laid the mysterious thing before him. His uncle listened soberly and inspected the printed enigma, then led Mentor to the library. From an upper shelf he took down six books: a Latin grammar; a Latin dictionary; Walker's *Key to Greek, Latin and Scripture Proper Names; Caesar; Cicero;* and *Virgil.* "How about a little Latin for William M.?"[2] he said, calling in James McElroy.

So it was that Mentor bent to a new and vastly absorbing task. Words became doubly wonderful to him as he saw each of them to be the story of history. "Booky," everybody called him, and he walked the woods to the grandeur of Latin conjugations. "Mentor," he read, meant a wise and faithful adviser. That was his name—what he must study to become.

In June, Greensburg square buzzed. Ninian Edwards, a Greensburg boy, had gotten to be—fabulous unreality to Mentor— "governor of the Illinois." Arriving on the square with his father and brothers that Saturday afternoon, Mentor heard all about it—and also that Governor Edwards had ordered out soldiers to destroy the Kickapoo Indians. For one steeped in Kentucky lore, that took most of the grandeur out of it all. Yet Mentor Graham was destined to walk the Edwards Trace from Springfield to Salt

Creek and to teach in a log schoolhouse beside the very path taken by these Indian-chasing soldiers.

The Grahams had come in to attend a sale. Jeremiah bid in a clavis and iron wedge but neglected to bid for the cups and saucers Mary wanted. Instead he visited the courthouse tavern and then they galloped home at a furious rate. Mary cried and Jeremiah talked loud—and they kept on using the broken cups and the old gourds. War had brought hard times; and Jeremiah, the provider, was hard pressed to make both ends meet.

The War of 1812, which had been impending, had now arrived; and it eclipsed earthquakes and grog-drinking as the worries of a thoughtful boy. His dearly loved sister Minerva was stricken by illness when Ed Goldsby left to fight. Though she was not yet fifteen, she was promised to Ed, the fine, upstanding lad on the rich plantation next to theirs. Ed, sixteen, had been in Greensburg one day watching Gabriel Slaughter drill troops; and when volunteers were called for, he spoke up. He went without telling Minerva. Mentor, at night before the cabin door, read to Minerva to keep her from crying. He brought books from Uncle Nat's that he thought might help. But she sickened in spite of it. When he brought her flowers from the woods, she cried harder.

Now there was a linsey-woolsey and yarn tithe to be taken out for the soldiers from a none-too-ample stock; and socks and mufflers must be knitted for them. Mr. McElroy, too, had gone to war; and Mentor worked early and late, longing to go to Lawyer Howe's New Athens Academy in Greensburg. Howe had recently become a near neighbor of the Graham's. His well-stocked plantation was worked by slaves. He visited the tavern oftener than most and was jovial and rotund as a consequence, though he was letter-strict, so they said, with his classical scholars. But Greensburg was eleven miles away, there was no money for tuition, and Jeremiah could not spare a riding horse. Nor could he spare his eldest son, who was fast becoming his father's right-hand man.

John Howe lent the shy, redheaded farm boy books with which he might aid himself in his interrupted task of mastering Latin; and no doubt he helped unravel many a testy construction when Mentor got stuck. Certainly, on two occasions at least, he delighted the boy by reading to him in his deep, resounding grand manner his favorite passages from Pliny and Cato.

Uncle Johnson helped Mentor get odd jobs of money-pay work. He visited at the cabin often, never failing to say a holy word about temperance for Jeremiah's benefit. War was a letdown, he said; made folks careless. Already many a waste-land school had no teacher, though the young should be taught, war or no war. Likewise, the Brush Creek congregation now numbered a scant twenty-three members; it had dropped the others mainly for tipsying, even on grape wine or sweet grog. Mentor managed to cut brush, make brick, help surveying gangs, and do a little apprentice work at the carpenter bench. By autumn he had added two more books to his growing hoard—and they were Shakespeare and Voltaire! He bought them on no one's advice, but because they were books put up to bid on at a sale. Afterward he listened to a slave sale, and watched drunken hoodlums sparring at each other. Hugging his precious treasures, he started home on what proved to be one of the most momentous evenings of his life; during that eleven-mile ride home he decided against two things, drunkenness and slavery —a boy, who would not be thirteen for a few weeks yet.

Times squeezed harder and harder as the country seemed to be losing the war. Everybody wore old clothes and went into debt. Little Granny Nancy Elizabeth had to fall back on shoepacks and turn her last year's Sabbath homespun. But, once the packs were dry and the garment turned, she was too busy helping out with her sixteen grandchildren to give new clothes a second thought. Jeremiah, however, went to King's sale and bought two coats—and a green glass-bottle.

In the stress of hard times and war, people had forgotten the earthquake. With common human frailty they had forgotten that their prediction of the end of the world had not come true. But a return of the quake in November sent them again to repenting sins in preparation for the end which was really at hand this time and had only been deferred. What else than an end, the women said, could the world be coming to when a woman like Sally Sneed died with only one blanket but with six Sabbath gowns? Jeremiah, an appraiser of Sally's estate, thought not keeping a cow had been her great sin and final undoing.

VI

MARRYIN' PLANS

1813–16

*A*FTER HIS thirteenth birthday, Mentor spent as much time as
he could at Aunt Nancy's and always went about the farm with a
book thrust into his shirt, to be readily available for any idle moment. This became a life-habit; and he once said, after his teaching
experience had reached fifty years, that it was the "bits of time
that make the profit." He was being heavily leaned upon. Not only
for the eternal wood and water and milking and barnyard chores;
but now and then—although it was much against his taste, for he
had a singularly strong revulsion to killing—he also had to go gun-
ning, if the pot was to be filled. Jeremiah, on road-overseeing,
court duty, or taking criminals to Bardstown, left his eldest son to
take his place, and he was gone oftener and oftener and for more
days at a time.

Late in January, news of the Battle of the Raisin reached the
cabin—eight hundred Kentucky boys massacred. Minerva, who
was still pale and silent but who had gone ahead with her duties
after her illness, knitted faster. She would soon be fifteen, and she
now coiled her heavy dark auburn hair and wore long dresses.
Jeremiah thought the casualty lists would be a long time in
coming.

Minerva and Mentor went to Greensburg the next day on the
pretext of seeing if their "brickle" calf was in the estray pen.
Mentor suggested it, although the calf had been missing for weeks
and they had given up hope of ever finding it. He was sure the lists
would be posted in the square, and he was right: they had been
sent down from Bardstown. He read them aloud to Minerva, rapidly, name after name. Ed's was not there. John Emerson, the
lawyer, seeing the two and guessing their mission, told them cheer-

fully that Slaughter's company was south. No, their "brickle"
calf was not in the estray pen—that is, perhaps it was not; they
forgot to go to see. That night young feet swept gaily over the ice
on Brush Creek, as they skated home through the winter dusk.

One of the Graham's neighbors these days was John Rafferty,
who had more than a dozen children. In the spring the older Raffertys had an "invitin' in" to which Mentor and Minerva were
asked. None of the lads was yet sixteen, for the older boys were all
away at war. The younger Raffertys looked on while the older ones
led off in song games on the greensward in front of their house.
They sang over and over, until every girl had been kissed at least
once:

> King William was a royal son
> And of a royal race was sprung;
> He wore a star upon his breast
> To show that he was royal-blest.
> Go, choose your east, go, choose your west,
> Go choose the one that you love best.
> If she's not here to take her part,
> Choose another with all your heart.
> Now, down on the carpet you must kneel,
> Sure as the grass grows in the fiel'—
> And salute your bride and kiss her sweet
> And then rise up, upon your feet.

Mentor had slicked his hair as well as he could, but he refused
to play because his eyes were only for one of the little Raffertys,
Sarah, who wouldn't play, either. When the first game ended, he
stood before her and led off with—

> It's raining, it's hailing, cold, stormy weather:
> In comes a farmer, drinking of his cider:
> He's going reaping and he needs a binder,—O
> He's lost his true-love and don't know where to find her.

There was plenty of laughing then—until Sarah cried and ran
away; so she told her grandchildren, fifty years later.

Felix Garris Graham and Felix Grundy Green—Mentor's cousins—were there, and little Nancy—children all, yet soon to become staid married folk. Up in Harrison County, Ann Rutledge
was a six-month-old baby. In Brandon, Vermont, Stephen Arnold
Douglas was being christened; and ten miles away, over on the
Nolynn, four-year-old Abe Lincoln was listening at his mother's
knee. Thus the design of the weaving becomes clearer as its threads

were pricked out and intertwined and drawn together a bit closer in the year 1813.

Mentor went back to studying surveying. He learned to lay brick; and, as he already knew how to make them, he now was able to get more money-pay work. He turned out a few cabinet pieces—the blue, blue eyes and the black, black hair of little Sarah Rafferty constantly before him. He worked with zeal that made Jeremiah, who praised seldom, praise him often.

How can anyone, even one who lives in the household with him, know what questions, hopes, agonies, and aspirations are in the mind of a boy of fourteen? Searching for such things—the material of true biography—more than a century later, what shall be set down as positive? We can only guess, from scant incidents that have come to light and from his own comments upon his own boyhood, what went on in the mind of Mentor Graham in the year 1814. He remembered seeing James Buchanan when he was on the point of returning to Philadelphia from Elizabethtown, where he had opened a law office but had failed to make a go of it. He worked for James Burney of Danville and certainly knew what that gentleman hoped to do about slavery.

But at this period of his life his Uncle Johnson Graham, the preacher, seems to have influenced his thinking most. Johnson was always bristling with new religious theories which gave Mentor the boy and Mentor the man the chief theme for that spiritual wrestling which marked his entire life.

Preacher Hogan had stirred up a veritable hornet's nest by demanding money of the Baptists for the saving of souls of heathens in Burma. Russell Creek Association rejected the proposal with disdain; for, as Johnson Graham reported, they replied with the "two-seed doctrine." This held that God had planted two seeds, one which sprang into good, the other into evil. Eve had been punished by having to bear both good and evil children. God meant evil to exist. Therefore, why missions?

Mentor kept silent but disagreed. Early he seems to have evolved a philosophy which stayed him through his later sorrows: the mission question, and all such questions, were not the illuminating ones. The real question was: "Why should a good God plant bad seeds?" From boyhood Mentor Graham always held—

in spite of everything—that God was wholly good and was not, therefore, the root of any evil, nor its cause.

The boy was much impressed by the auction sales, held in Greensburg Square, of the property of those who had died in debt. Each was easily read by what he had left behind. Some goods were clean, orderly, well kept; but most of the stuff put up for sale was abused and dilapidated. Very few books were offered at such sales. Books, Mentor thought, would be about the best thing a man could leave. They were what he would leave. A strange lad of fourteen, imagining his own old age and death, deciding that he would not make debts but that the many shelves of books that were to be his should be given to learning-hungry boys who longed for them. When Graham died, in his eighty-sixth year, he left no debts but hundreds of books.

He accompanied his uncle to quarterly Baptist Association meetings, where he worked at brickmaking while the session considered such questions as "What are the callings, true gifts, and qualifications of a true-gospel preacher and whence does he receive them?" The cabin answer always had been that he "must be called of God," that education had nothing to do with it; that "taught" preachers did not dispense the true gospel. That was a puzzler to Mentor, who had seen clearly how men like his Uncle Robert who knew the unfrightening truth from books were happier than hell-fire preachers who had been called. Later he publicly and completely repudiated the idea that education handicapped anyone who had something to say that needed saying. With the profit of his brickmaking he bought a Kirkham's *Grammar* and an *Intellectual Arithmetic* (i.e., mental arithmetic) the title-page of which is now too dim to make out the author's name.

After baby Simpson James arrived one night at the Graham cabin, Mary and Minerva redoubled their efforts. Minerva, hopeful now—from bits of war news that sifted in to her at church—that Ed would soon be coming home, wove and spun and cooked before the fire and laughed again. The war had been nothing but a silly man's doings to her, carried on in unimaginable places and for no reason at all, until Mentor brought home a geography and showed her where and how far and told her why. She brightened at once, and her grief that Ed had gone was now subdued by her pride that he had. She was willing now, happy to be working

doubly hard: spinning her "marryin' bolts," hand-hemming ruffles, getting her "pillow-coates true-square with the smoothing
iron."

Spring freshets were over, and the news of Napoleon at Elba
was eight months old now; but still Ed did not come and life went
on with the same old inevitability of babies being born and old
folks dying. When Preacher Matthews died, everybody went to the
funeral and wept: there had never been such a funeral on Brush
Creek, for Matthews had been a saint on earth and had boosted
Brush Creek Church back into her place in the sun by baptizing
nearly a hundred converts in the last year of his life, when he was
an old man, well beyond eighty. The procession on foot, headed by
four pallbearers with the homemade coffin slung aloft on poles,
wound down the woodway from the church to bury the beloved
dead. Mentor remembered it always; and the words "Let not your
heart be troubled" sounded at that graveside had the power to
erase, almost to the last one, the doubts and fears of his adoles-
cence. No matter about the bothering questions. He could understand, could cling to, that simple promise.

Records show that second marriage was, just then, the subject
of argument among Green River Baptists. Johnson Graham was
spokesman for Brush Creek and Nolynn churches, and he pro-
pounded the question at quarterly meeting. The answer was for
divorce and for remarriage; but Brush Creek balked. Not in their
church. Johnson, having been called, having preached in the cabins
and on invitation at other churches, was elected to fill Preacher
Matthews' place. After that, Mentor went to him with all his
spiritual wrestlings, and they talked them out together. Johnson
loaned the boy his religious books, hoping to prepare him to be
called. Johnson was famous for his library—one hundred books.
Nothing like the collection of Nat Owens, of course, but more
books than most people ever hoped to own.

Mentor circled farther and farther from home in search of work.
He did his stint of farm work feverishly in order to earn time to do
pay-work; for he thought he might be marrying in two or three
summers. He worked again for Burney at Danville—carpentering
—and had access there to Burney's newspapers. Then, with the
capitol burned and the war again going against the country, he
put aside his personal plans and came home, determined to enlist.

He stopped at Elizabethtown to attend Tom Hill's sale, thinking that he might find some books, but there were none. Tom Lincoln was there and bid in a playcart for his boy, Abe, who was now learning his *a-b–abs* from Caleb Hazel in the log schoolhouse at the fork of the Cumberland Trail and Pottenger's Creek.

Graham's parents would not give their consent to his enlistment; so he fell back into doing his father's bidding once more and eked out what time he could to puzzle over surveying and Caesar and to read from his own shelf of books which hung above his pallet bed in the cockloft.

At the sale of Preacher Matthews' estate, after everything else had been sold, the one slave Matthews had inherited from his father was put up. There were no bids. Johnson Graham said clearly: "I bid twenty dollars, not for this woman, but for the right to give her her freedom," and the hammer fell. But she refused to be manumitted; and Johnson, the "Nigger-lover," had an old Negress on his hands, a woman who insisted on a slave's place in his household.

Local news caused a ripple of unrest in Jeremiah: Tom Lincoln, having been sued for possession of his farm on bad-title evidence, had lost and was going north—Illinois or Indiana country—God's country, no slavery, no boundary trouble, where lawyers couldn't do you dirt. Neighbor Howe and Jeremiah agreed, in talking it over, that Tom was levelheaded to go. Jeremiah reckoned he'd ride up and look things over.

The regular Graham-clan December hunt that year took the "whole kit and bilin' " to Pittman's Creek, to attend the sale of old man Cook's stuff, as well as hunt. Mentor asked to go, because he hoped there would be books put up. But instead, Old Rachel was knocked down for $140; young Rachel, shrieking and protesting, for $233. The smaller children, Emmy, Camelia, Billy, and Walker Jones, were sold in a herd for $390. The old husband brought $483. After the whiskey and farm tools were bought up, the Grahams went on to hunt, talking of the Louisville cyclone, the war, their hunting plans—everything but the scene they had just witnessed that had made Mentor tremble from head to foot. He begged to go home; and when Jeremiah consented, he rode off alone. He had no books and wished to kill no game, and his soul was touched almost past endurance with the anguish of

Old Rachel and Young Rachel, the terror-stricken children, and the hopeless-eyed husband who had pulled a bit toward Old Rachel in a kind of farewell gesture and had been cut across the face with a black-snake whip.

He rode slowly, stopping at Greensburg as his mother had instructed, for the things that would brighten their lives at Christmas: bohea (tea) and "rich" candle-cord, molasses, candy, and red dyeweed. When the others arrived later with their deer and squirrels and turkeys and grouse, they found the boy sick in bed and Mary anxious, because, she said, she "couldn't make out what ailed him."

News of the Peace of Ghent had not yet arrived on Brush Creek. It had also failed to arrive in the camps of disheartened soldiers; and Ed, as Minerva learned fearfully afterward, fought in the Battle of New Orleans on the very day in January that she finished weaving her marryin' bolt—after the peace had been signed.

She and her mother listened proudly when Mentor read aloud from his *College and Academy Text Book of History, Including a History of all Nations*. The children stood by admiringly. Mentor, who had been ill, was being humored. A biographical moment, indeed, with a prideful family circling the fire and giving heed, their love for him patent in their firelit faces, their praise grateful: he could outread Uncle Johnson. The baby cooed in its cradle, deer meat sizzled above the fire, and though the winter wind howled at the door the room expanded, through the boy's eager interest, to include other times and places, other people.

Jeremiah was of the opinion that that new contraption, the steamboat, which could haul loads back upstream, was bound to change the times, ease this poverty the war had made. Now that America had won, why not go south? He was quoting his idol, Henry Clay, in this. Discussion was more than heated; and Hank Clay, back in Kentucky, running his farm, lived not far away. Mentor had often seen him; and, sitting by the fire that winter, reading of Clay, Mentor dropped back into his old imaginings, became a world-citizen, a Henry Clay.

In the last week of September, 1815, closing a summer of much study and little work for Mentor, somebody not homefolks rode pony-back past Brush Creek. Pale, thin little Jefferson Davis, accompanied by his father, rode into Springfield to enter St. Thomas'

School. As Mentor bent above his books, earnestly probing day after day, he knew nothing of the little boy, bending over his halfway between Brush Creek and Lexington. Nor, for that matter, did Henry Clay, the famous man of Lexington.

Mentor plowed that autumn and helped clear a new field, for Jeremiah had three work-teams now and went ahead with the work on a five-hundred-acre farm with almost as much profit as near-by slaveowners. Uncle Garrison, at Leitchfield, had bought two slaves; and the Negress whom Johnson had thought to liberate kept her place. Jeremiah, however, was still "dead set again' this truckin' in humans." He no longer listened without reply when Garrison or Johnson, or the new preacher, Thomas Whitman —who was elected after Johnson bought the slave—upbraided him for toping.

"Danged near safer nor your soul be mine. I'm not ownin' blacks, soul and body, like the Devil." And Mary began to speak up. She was against robbing honest folks out of their money. One hundred dollars was the sum Preacher Luther Rice had preached out of the Russell Creek Baptist Association for Burma heathen. Mary had been adamant when their church levied on Jeremiah, who had not given, and had been reprimanded as a consequence. Mary knew the two-seed doctrine was veritable truth: she had good reason to know that Eve had been punished by having to bear both good and bad children—even good and bad in the *same* child.

Mentor was deeply distressed. Uncle Johnson was all for missions; and he and the other missionary leaders—Isaac Hodgen, John Chandler, Preacher Waggoner, and Preacher Elkin—in cahoots at quarterly meeting, arranged that each preacher should preach at every other church in the association at least once a quarter. Thus, all flocks would hear what they should hear. Divided in his allegiance, Mentor no longer hung upon the words of his Uncle Johnson. He transferred his idolatry to James Burney, for whom he worked as a carpenter during the following February. Watching Burney closely, reading all he could about him, the boy concluded, as he meditated at the cabinetmaker's bench, that *men who understood and could use strong words led other men.* From afar he worshiped the handsome, well-dressed young man, James

Burney, now in the legislature, a man who knew strong words. With great relish and secret pride he read the broadsides[1] of John Pope (his great-uncle who had married a sister of Nancy Elizabeth Lynn) and Henry Clay. But—which of them was right?

In the spring he again made one of a crew on a flatboat up Green River, this time tutored by his Uncle Joseph, a Mississippi River boatman who happened by. Green River always went on a spring rampage; and Montgomery, the cargo-owner, knew that if he could manage to pole down Green the rest of the trip would not need so many hands. Most river rousters were blacks now. Blacks, Montgomery said, were tougher. Another year he'd change over. Certain it is that Mentor was very slight and not very tall; but with his Uncle Joseph's lectures on the tricks of the trade, he held his own on the heavy raft. Again he walked home by way of Louisville.

He saw that miracle, the steamboat, plowing upstream. He saw coffles of slaves, with hopeless faces and leaden eyes, southbound. He saw slaves driven under a lash to the fields by boys no older than himself. He also read in Louisville that Burney had been beaten out of his "slave-loving" and had been obliged to move to Georgia.

At the tavern where Mentor lodged for one night, another young boy sold the host a deer and a brace of wild turkey he had shot. He seemed elated over the six bits he received for them, and stayed on after his sale. He and Mentor sat together at the edge of the group of old men in the grogshop, listening to their tales of Indian scalping, Bryant's Station battles, and blockhouse life. Such tales were commonplace at home; Old Grandsir and Grandam and Great-uncle Benjamin Lynn had told them as far back as Mentor could remember. But Grandsir's tales were more about prodigious hunts and enough pelts and buffalo tallow to buy a town. The tavern talkers got on to the subject of Daniel Boone—still living, they'd heard, somewhere in Missouri. Still hunting.

When Uncle Johnson called the next time, his redheaded nephew answered back, disagreed hotly. James Burney, the boy's idol, had been beaten and had gone to Georgia—even in spite of all his brave, strong words. And all because "preachers like you collect money to save souls in places on the other side of the world, while you keep black slaves in your own dooryards!" There were now three to answer back when Johnson came, preaching temperance and missions. He came less often.

Aunt Lizzie's latest baby, a boy, arrived one spring night; and Mentor, steeped in Kentucky custom, went directly to lay his hands on the baby's head. Any new little baby ought to be made lucky, that way. At least that was Mentor's pretext for going. His real errand was to ride by the Rafferty's. Perhaps Sarah.....

Sarah must have proved out, for, by July, Mentor, with dollars in his pocket, bought surveying instruments. Sure that he could head a surveying gang, and that that, with brickmaking and bricklaying and cabinet work, would support two, he approached Jeremiah with the news that he intended to marry in one, maybe two, years. But before he put away the first dollar for himself, he bought *Family Medicine*, a very expensive leather-bound book, for Minerva's wedding gift. She and Ed, who had come back, had settled to "tie up, come fall." He also bought a volume of *Kentucky Laws*.

Soldiers were straggling home from the war, in knots and singly, ragged and weary fellows. As a matter of course they stopped at the nearest cabin at mealtime or bedtime, knowing they would be welcomed. Many, stopping at the Graham cabin, could have told afterward how closely they had been questioned by a thin-faced, nervous, redheaded farm boy as to where they had been, what they had seen—what people thought about slavery. Mary bolstered them up with cold buttermilk from the springhouse while they waited the preparation of more filling food. Then Jeremiah sent them on with his fervent "God bless you." All hands had turned in to prepare the feast they had eaten, almost like a wedding feast.

It must have been about this time, when free haying was underway on the unpre-empted barrens, that an event occurred that was later chronicled by Lincoln biographers and, as far as I can learn, was subscribed to by Graham as an old man. The story relates that halfway between Hodgenville and Elizabethtown, over by Muldraugh Hill, a knot of haymakers had gathered at the door of a cabin, drawn there by childish cries of distress. They found that the owner, in a drunken fit, had murdered his wife, who still lay across the doorsill, where she had fallen. The Grahams, Jeremiah and the oldest boys, haying that way, came up to the place just as Tom Lincoln and his small son Abe arrived. The boy is reported to have taken the little weeping girls by the hands and begged them not to cry so hard, while the self-elected posse over-powered the murderer and took him off to town. Graham had good reason to recall the incident, for Jeremiah was unusually preoc-cupied when he arrived home from town; and Mentor dated his father's almost complete abstinence from that day.

In honor of Minerva's approaching wedding, the Grahams hur-ried through the autumn cotton-picking, corn-husking, flax-flail-ing, butchering. Mary divided her store of "pillow-coates and sheates" with her daughter, who was marrying into a wealthy and slaveholding family. She hoped Ed would give up his notion of settling in Tennessee and settle north instead. The young people were going to live with the elder Goldsbys for a while, until Ed got his bearings.

Finally the morning came when Minerva, dressed in the marry-in' dress for which Jeremiah had grown the flax and cotton and which she herself had spun and stitched, her auburn hair decked with autumn woods asters, stood with Jeremiah under the tall beech by the house door, awaiting the arrival of the groom and his men. Jeremiah had supplied a small cask of whiskey, and his green-glass bottle filled with it he held high for the young men to race for. The breakneck riding was all any bride could wish.

The dooryard was crowded, for everybody had been bidden. David Elkin, unkempt as ever, was the solemnest of preachers; and Mentor, standing hand in hand with Sarah Rafferty, heard Elkin's grave voice boom out the questions and the mightily em-barrassed Ed and Minerva answer weakly. Sarah thought spring the prettiest marryin' time.

VII

GOOD SIGNS AND BAD SIGNS
1816–23

*F*OLKS WHO did not own slaves had a hard time competing with those who did, when it came to earning a living by growing corn and tobacco. Jeremiah's solution was more oxen. He dinned this into the ears of his eldest son, who had been earning cash not only by surveying, cabinetmaking, brush-cutting, brickmaking, and bricklaying but also, this winter, by teaching. Mentor bought books, often secretly, for Jeremiah had a fair idea how many parents were actually paying and how much each one paid. His son's wages were his, by custom; yet he suggested that Mentor sell half the produce paid in as tuition, for himself.

With the small amount of money-tuition Mentor received he bought books and kept them in the school chest at the church, for he had the Brush Creek school. But he also managed to mind his father's advice and, by giving a note, bought two young work-animals. By spring he had paid for them and had bought saddle and saddlebags for his riding horse, his boyhood's pride, an animal he had tended from the morning of its birth, when his father had given it to him.

Now, a young man of "lasty strength," he could ride out for odd jobs between terms. His saddle horse was black, his saddle russet red; and his store clothes set him apart from most of the Brush Creek jeans-clad youths. He looked every whit as much a gentle-man as the Goldsby boys, whose hard work was all done for them by slaves, for he was immaculate in dress and wore gauntlet riding gloves, a fine beaver hat, and, in winter, a russet-brown three-caped greatcoat. He must have cut an enviable figure when he rode—as many nights as her father would let him in—to court Sarah.

Sarah was weaving her marryin' bolts, and the two had chosen the site for their cabin—a piece of land Mentor planned to buy, come another winter. Sarah had not wanted to go as far away from home as the sinking-springs land over on Green River which Mentor would "heir" from a great-uncle when he came of age. Grandmother Nancy Elizabeth's brother David had squatted on it way back in 1772. Jeremiah, as his son's guardian, sold the land to Jacob Bale and with the money bought the wooded hillside the children had decided upon. Robert was growing fast, almost a man now and doing a man's work; so Jeremiah could spare his eldest son. Mentor's new home would be close to the Brush Creek house by the spring where he had been born; but most of the cousins who were marrying were scattering, some as far away as Little Barren's River and Pittman's Creek.

Father and son now rode out often to watch the races of the Lexington Jockey Club or lesser sprints, for Brush Creek Church permitted *watching* races, although dropping was the penalty for betting on them or donning the jockey's cap. Together father and son discussed slavery, in the light of *The Philanthropist*, which Mentor read to the family after the evening meal and after he had helped the children with their lessons. They were going to school under him at the church. Sometimes neighbor Howe or neighbor Bale joined in the discussion while the women knitted. Anyone could see that trouble was brewing fast. Even in Greensburg, when slaves were auctioned on the square, hecklers and preachers shouted their denouncements in the name of God. On the plantation next to theirs the Goldsbys were getting rich hand over fist with twenty work-teams and half a hundred slaves. Many of the oldest settlers were leaving, going up north, away from Kentucky and its slavery.

The lovers discussed their chief worry—baptism. Sarah did not know whether or not she had had "experience," but her child mind could not conceive of a married woman who did not belong to the church. Mentor was not sure, either; so they settled the matter by being baptized together. On a crisp, clear day in late March they preceded the Brush Creek congregation, singing as they filed from the church down the steep banks to the creek,

> Lord, what a wretched land is this
> That yields us no supply . . . . ;

and there, below the weavery, they were dipped by Preacher Whitman. Shivering through the long prayers before and after the immersion, they finally climbed back up the bank-path to the church, pulled dry garments over wet ones, and hurried home.

The next day Mentor cantered into Greensburg with a light heart. All was well with him and his true-love. He brought back a narrow gold ring with two large emerald settings that the gold-smith, Robert Barrett, had made to the measure of Sarah's slender finger. Two settings—symbol of a love of two that was to be for-ever alive and green. Sarah, who was only thirteen, was the hap-piest person in the world. No one she had ever heard of had such a ring. Mentor had "done noble by her." Sarah was tall and amaz-ingly white-skinned; her hair was blue-black, her eyes an amazing deep blue, so they say.

She showed the ring at her merrymaking. It was a fulling bee, where all of her own hand-weaving, her marrying bolts, were fulled. Mentor, of course, was leadsman, with his cousins and brothers and her cousins and brothers stamping themselves breathless, and the girls pouring on more soft soap between times and everybody shouting when an unlucky bare-legged young man slipped down ingloriously on the slithering cloth spread on the best-room floor. Spattered from head to foot with suds, the young men finally let go of the rope by which they had helped themselves to stand erect while they stomped the soapy cloth, and everybody fell to with a relish on the rows of meat pies and the gourds of grape wine. Now was the proper and expected time to "devil" the prospective bride and groom and, after wits were exhausted, to stay up all night, singing and dancing. As the old folks said leniently, "A person can be young only once."

The day came, late in April, when Little Ascha, as Mentor fond-ly nicknamed Sarah, pinned the wild-crab blossom—the "prettiest marryin' flower"—in her bright black hair and wore for the first time her bright-blue homespun. Standing with her father under the budding sycamores, proud and happy, she awaited the arrival of Mentor and his men. She had good reason to be proud. She had woven "two marrying' bolts for pillow-coates and a passel of sheates"—twenty yards in each. She had woven a beautiful tre-foil-patterned coverlet. Everybody marveled at the pattern, come down from Ireland and picked out perfectly—a double-woven counterpane that would last a lifetime, they predicted. They were right, it did. One side—the weekday side—was indigo blue and white in a checkerboard check. The Sabbath side had three green and white borders of plain and broken stripes that inclosed the central pattern of Irish trefoils and Irish harps.

Long afterward Sarah told her children of this day. How the young men came racing, Mentor on his black horse in the lead; how the plank-board tables in the yard swayed down in the center with their weight of roast pork, duck, deer, goose, turkey, firkins of honey, and wooden tubs of wine; how they danced all day and most of the night. The marriage had taken place "just as the sun come overhead," when the dancing had stopped and Mentor and Sarah had taken their places beneath the appointed tree. Some fathers had to marry their own daughters when a preacher was not at hand, and have the next preacher confirm it when he came by; but Mentor and Sarah were married by Preacher Harding, who wore long tails and a flowered vest and had a booming voice that satisfied the most particular.

True to custom, as the wedding feast proceeded, one of the groomsmen stole the bride's slipper, whereupon her four "waiters" —young girl friends—gave chase and scuffled until they retrieved it. Dancing went on all afternoon and by tallow dips at night, out of doors on the evenly sickled grass. Bride and groom were put to bed by their wedding party at an early hour but were refreshed at intervals during the night by platters of roast turkey and swigs from the whiskey bottle, the attendants not failing to give the toast: "Health to the groom and thumping big children to the bride."

Sarah pelted her well-wishers with her stockings, rolled into balls. In turn, she teased and drank a similar health to the girl who caught her right stocking—hose in those days were knitted as lefts and rights. Mentor threw his hose at his men. But finally all left the bridal room, and the guests who lived close enough departed. Before the sun rose, everybody was asleep.

Sarah woke, the next morning, alone in the Rafferty's best room, to find that everybody else had gone to the raisin,' leaving her behind in jest. She had to take their rude bantering as best she could when she came running through the April woods to the scene of her bridal cabin-raising.

In spite of stopping for the infare—a second wedding feast at the Graham's at noon—the many willing hands had the cabin up and ready for chinking before sundown. With a battery of chinkers under Mentor's direction mixing brick mortar for the chinking, a battery of froe-men splitting shakes for the roof, and more laying the shakes and weight-poles and paddling in the chinking, the cabin was completed the second day. And on the third the bride and groom drove to town in the oxcart Mentor had borrowed from his father and brought home a bed and two chairs, pots and crocks, a table, and a set of ten dishes.

The bridegroom set about at once making a corner cupboard, a chest, and bookshelves. Sarah's parents had given her wooden tubs, a spinning wheel, a feather bed, a loom, and a Bible. When all these things were properly set about and evening fell, the two children, thirteen and seventeen, lighted the first fire in the new fireplace and sat together to eat corn pones, fresh-laid eggs, and dandelion greens. Sarah, in telling of it, never forgot to say that the firelight shone upon the handsome red-flannel cover she had made for her Bible, which lay in the center of the fireplace shelf, awaiting its permanent place on the chest of drawers when it should be completed. It was an embroidered cover: "Sarah Rafferty Graham: Her Bible." That night no fears beset her, for she was "starting well." She had forgotten the wave of horror that had swept over her upon her wedding day when she had put on her left shoe and stocking before the right.

But the old dog from home, prowling about the cabin and howling in the middle of the night, meant trouble to her superstitious little soul. She talked about it all next day, and Mentor tried to laugh it away when he found her hugging the red-flannel-covered Bible to break the spell that might be cast. He talked of the Windsor chairs with polished deerskin seats he was going to make, and brought out the hand mill he had made to surprise her. But her hallucination held. While he was off to town, she stitched ruffles for curtains for her real glass "winders," from muslin of her marryin' bolt. She went over all the lucky things that had happened: the whiteness of her tulip-poplar cabin with its white chinking; the cornermen who had notched its logs were all fathers of husky families; nobody had tripped over the floor puncheons before they were pegged.

Still she was frightened, for Mentor had to be away so often—though she knew she could run home to pappy's in no time, if need be. Then newcomers put up a cabin near, newcomers with children, and Sarah quieted her fears by running over there every day after her own cabin was tidied.

Uncle Johnson came for an overnight visit, bringing a wedding gift of books: *The Rise and Fall of the Roman Empire* and a *Natural History*. She dusted them with pride and turned the pages wonderingly, and rejoiced with Mentor, seeing that they meant so much to him. She had hoped Johnson would give them a cow from his fine herd, so that she could make butter. Mentor, in high fettle, began to read aloud. Such strangeness of words Sarah had never heard. She was miserable, listening. Sarah could not read, except texts and the like.

By mid-July Mentor was off to his well-subscribed summer term before sunup every morning but the Sabbath, leaving Sarah to her first long, trying days alone—days that were to multiply through long years. He reveled in his work and talked of little else except when there was a vistor, which was seldom. He read to her at night, and she went with him about their fifteen-acre farm and helped with the work, except the plowing.

Preacher Cameron, caught in a violent thunderstorm, rapped at the new tulip-poplar cabin one Sunday afternoon at the same time that Johnson was visiting. Talk rose angrily between the two men of God: between Cameron, the college learned, and Graham, who had been called. It was a fearful time for the child-wife, who, not expecting a second guest, had to mix more pones. In her nervousness she burned them, which was a last straw to her peace. Left shoe and stocking, howling dog, and now, burned pones—*three* sure signs of bad luck in the first *three* months of her marriage. Sarah burst into tears and ran out into the rain, leaving the pones to their fate. After Mentor rescued her by carrying her back into the house against her will, he mixed and baked more pones. The three men ate in silence, and Cameron soon left, both storms having abated.

Aunt Elizabeth had cautioned Mentor that he must take good care of Sarah, who was not quite fourteen, for she would be a mother before spring. Not knowing what else to do, he began teaching her from books. She docilely acquiesced, repeating the lines he had given her to learn, mouthing words after him, and laboring over her kinked-up letters. Sometimes she walked the three miles to the church, when she felt afraid, to be near him. Now that she could read a little, she would have liked to go inside with the others, but that would have been unthinkable—in her condition. So she waited outside and listened to the cardinal and the mockingbird and knitted or sewed or, if those duties dragged, went off down to the creek to catch fish and hurried home alone with them to surprise Mentor at supper. They talked of her lessons and the lessons at school, and she began to read the paper to him; but she thought more about how thankful she was that William Skaggs hadn't died quite late enough for "his spirit to ha'nt her child." She was always upset by Johnson's visits. He talked so loud and emphatically and so endlessly about slave-sinning. He always had newspapers and books in his saddlebags, and he and Mentor often had a talkfest that lasted until nearly morning. The time she stole out and ran home, crying, to spend the night, they did not even know she had gone.

When Johnson told of a vast new movement toward righteousness, antislavery papers springing up everywhere, Sarah listened and learned. She knew of it when Preacher Hogan and Preacher Warder returned from a three-thousand-mile trip to Philadelphia, making six hundred converts on the way, and of Dr. James Blythe, president of Transylvania College, who was dismissed because he kept a nude statue in his home. His plea that the statue was a copy of fine Greek art only made his crime more heinous; he should be worshiping God, not heathendom's naked statues! In a vague, unhappy way Sarah wondered why people could not let each other alone and just enjoy the woods and the fine weather.

In November, Mentor went to Louisville and brought Sarah a pair of store shoes and a mantle. He told her she was prettier in her new finery than anybody he had seen in Louisville. Sarah liked to read the papers now, little snatches, here and there. She read of some woman warning other women to be on guard against a man named Daugherty who had wooed and wed her only to tell her that he had another wife and that all he wanted was her horse to ride back upon to his far handsomer wife elsewhere. To Sarah's childishly frightened queries Mentor said that things like that happened only in towns. The worst that ever happened on Brush Creek was gander pullings.

Teaching, surveying, making bricks, peddling books, and farming sent the finances of the little cabin soaring; but January took all their savings. Sarah's premature child was born dead, and the little mother lay near death for weeks. But spring came again with its sweet wild crabs, and she grew stronger and more cheerful and walked out to watch Mentor make fence, sow flax, and plant corn and cotton. Soon she had the hoe in her hand and was laughing and chasing squirrels with it when they made sallies after the corn in the hills she had not yet covered.

Mentor had made a reputation as an especially good teacher, and his school grew until his income was sufficient to purchase a silk tile and a cutaway professional coat for himself and a deep-blue silk dress for Sarah. With steady industry he kept the woodpile high, the root cellar well stocked. His steadily growing acreage of cleared land was fenced in Virginia rail-worm style with rails he made at odd times with maul and wedge.[1] After school he cared for his saddle horse, his yoke of oxen, and the pigs and chickens and the cow he now owned. After supper he read. Sarah had no choice but to sit spinning or weaving, waiting the moment when he would look up and smile at her and read out in his clear, ringing voice the special part that had pleased him. Often she could not make head or tail of it. He praised her for her quick skill in reading and writing and ciphering, which he was still teaching her; but these things did not interest her much. Now and then she was perked up by a quilting bee or wedding; but most of her days were dutiful, sinless, and drab.

Mentor was proud of his own fine writing and spent much time late at night setting copies for the children who could not afford books. Sarah helped him make goose-quill pens and boil ink from sumac berries and white-oak bark. She always knew when another learner had arrived at success in writing a "joined hand," for Mentor's joy showed in the springiness of his stride. Together they baked gingerbreads for the Christmas treat and went into town to purchase a long rope as a gift for the children. With one end tied to a tree, a rope could provide all kinds of fun, one child holding the free end and trying to catch any who dodged into its range; with both ends tied to a low branch, it made a swing.

Mentor was different from most schoolmasters, so low voiced, gentle, and patient that the children loved him and begged him to play with them. He always did, not neglecting to see to it that the precious rope was brought in every night and coiled neatly, back of the door. He taught the children reading, writing, and ciphering, tare and tret (how to compute waste, in handling flax and wool), geography, and what, for lack of a better term, might be called "poetry appreciation."

In October, Aunt Lizzie's ninth child was born, and she began to prophesy again for Sarah. This she did at the preaching held at Mentor's cabin in November. Sarah suffered bitterly under the prophecy, too often repeated, almost as much as under the hell-torment doctrines of the preachers. She did each task with the utmost care, lest she sin. But when the preaching was over she carried from it a song which she hummed in her work, the hymn that became her lifelong favorite:

> My God is reconciled, his pardoning voice I hear:
> He owns me for his child: I can no longer fear.

But Sarah was not happy. She began to beg Mentor to sell this unlucky cabin, and persisted until he gave in. They moved to a place near the new Dixie Highway, into a much larger cabin, one in which seven children had been born. The move encouraged Sarah, and she went willingly to Louisville, both to see the sights and to see the town doctor. But when spring came again, the baby died the day it was born. Sarah had known bad luck would be hers. She had broken three needles in making the baby's clothes; once she had put on her Sabbath gown wrong side out; she had inadvertently cut out the baby's clothes on a Saturday.

School went on in the same old way, however, and the lonely days went on too. Sarah wept constantly for Mentor's loss as much as for her own; it was evident to all by now how well he loved little children. He had made and polished until they shone a black-walnut hooded cradle and a trundle bed. He had been as happy as she over the little garments.

If they had only left Kentucky as they had talked of leaving before the baby arrived! Surely, in some other place their luck would change. Aunt Lizzie and Uncle William Greene had gone to the Illinois and wrote that they were "suited." Neighbor Spears had gone and taken Uncle Johnson's son John, as a farmer-apprentice, with him. Johnson and Jeremiah had both been up and considered locating, for it seemed a promising place along the Sangamon. Certainly teachers were scarce there.

But Mentor was well enough content. He was managing to ride into Elizabethtown between terms, to dip into those "abstruce subjects" upon which he had set his heart since the days at Uncle Nat's. According to the catalogue of the Academy, Graham had access to courses in geometry, trigonometry, navigation and astronomy, dialing and advanced algebra, each a six weeks' course at $15. Fluxions, grammar, geography, and belles-lettres came a little higher at $30 each; and extended courses in Greek and Latin could also be taken.

These were days amply recorded in the Severn's Valley Church records kept by Graham's cousin Samuel Abell as church clerk. Grandfather William Graham's wife's folks, the John Popes, attended here, as did the Potters, who soon moved to Sangamon County, Illinois, and the Bushes. The record shows that Sister Hannah Bush had to be labored with for using improper language; but, after "duly acknowledging her fault and shewing much token of repentance, both to the church and the world," she was duly restored to "standing." Hannah was a sister of that Sarah Bush Johnson whom Tom Lincoln, whose first wife had died in Indiana, had now returned to marry. Sarah Johnson was described in the language of the day as a "fine set-up widow-woman" whom Tom was lucky to get.

In October a party of nine—mostly Grahams—went prospecting along the Sangamon. They came back enthusiastic over the new country—not a slave to be seen anywhere, all the land registered, and no boundary squabbles. The Armstrongs had settled there and the Potters, old neighbors. Sarah and Mentor, listening to all this, took the "Illinois fever" and took it hard. That was the place for them.

Leaving his saddle horse for Sarah to ride, Mentor went alone to Monticello to try to persuade his brother Robert to go too. It was no particular hardship for him to walk the sixty-five miles, for he had always loved walking, had resorted to long walks to clear his mind, and had walked all over that part of Kentucky as a boy, hunting work. Over the frozen trace through the winter woods he went, pondering what arguments he should use. His own plan was to keep on as they were for two more years and save enough to tide him over for a year or two in the new country until he got started. But, though he stayed many days and talked earnestly, his persuasive arguments failed. Robert, doing well, was on the point of being transferred to a larger store in Crab Orchard at a higher salary. Slavery and land troubles had not affected him, a salaried merchant, at all. Mentor, however, arriving home just before Christmas, put up his land for sale.

The corn had not yet been husked, and the Grahams "invited in" to a husking bee. The two cousins, both named Felix, captained. Felix Garris Graham's team won because he kicked back the dividing rail in the pile of corn to be husked and thus gave his side less to do. But even the winners got only a tickler of whiskey. Sarah set out rows of her tempting pies and gourds of cider, and the young people ate, drank, danced, and laughed. They went home from a husking bee, sober, for once. Mentor was certain by now that whiskey was not needed except for sickness.

But land was not moving, it seemed; so he went about soliciting pupils in the Friendship Church district, at some distance. He rode horseback daily to this school, except in bad weather, when he boarded round. Sarah had remained with her people; and with the old feeling of security and with fewer duties, she forgot her dreads and became the bewitching beauty she had been when Mentor had married her. She quickly changed her mind about Illinois, pouted, and said she would never go north.

The little log Friendship Church sheltered thirty children. The older boys kept up the fire, and the girls kept the earthen floor swept. At play-spell they baked apples and roasted sweet potatoes before the fire. The winter was unusually cold and long, and Graham formed the habit of helping the smallest children home before he walked to his boarding place. The Raffertys did not need the produce he took in as tuition, so he hauled it to Greensburg and sold it for cash. Little by little his hoard grew; but he realized that, even at this rate, it would take several years to accumulate enough for the trip north and for expenses during the first year or two.

But he was happy, teaching. There, in the quiet woods—if we may judge from his later practice—he talked earnestly, quietly, to those children, patiently telling them again and again what they found hard to understand. And the children loved him. He was fond of telling of this school in later years—how the boys coming in covered with snow after play-spell, their buckskin pants rattling, would crowd about the fire to dry out, the air smelling of both baked apples and drying leather all afternoon. When the children tired, he stopped lessons to read to them from the English poets until they brightened, when he sent them back to their study. As soon as darkness threatened, they sang together and he helped the smallest ones to bundle chins and ears, locked the case of books and pens, and went out into the snowy woods with the children, making them laugh by clapping his hands as if at chickens and calling loudly three times, "Kite for home!"

He punished strictly when students neglected to be polite; and he insisted upon their cap-doffing and curtsying to strangers who passed during play-spell—as he had been taught. Any child who learned to write a joining hand he presented with one sheet of paper. Though he was happy teaching, at home he was a sad-eyed young man. He could not forget the two little mounds up the hill from the deserted cabin—the children who might have been his.

At this time Great-Uncle Edward sold out, at a fine figure, to head for Illinois. Graham again posted his land for sale, in the Greensburg square, but there were no takers. Sarah continued to say stubbornly that she would never go. Since Mentor did not wish to leave her longer dependent upon her parents, and since she did not want to go back to Otter Creek, they compromised. They sold the tulip-poplar cabin in which they had begun housekeeping, and moved to a cabin near the Raffertys'. Sarah's sister Ann, a girl of twelve, came to live with them so that she might attend Mentor's school; also, so that she might be delivered from the clutches of the Greensburg dancing master, who was enamored of her. She liked books, and Graham was prosperous enough to buy her skates and ribbons and a fine Sabbath dress in exchange for her help in the household.

Thus Mentor and Sarah lived for four years, Ann staying with them until she was wed at fifteen. After two years at Friendship, Graham became master of the town school in Greensburg—and now they rarely spoke of going north. "The North" became only a dream when the savings they had been accumulating vanished—like many another Green County man's—in the failure of the Greensburg bank.

Mentor settled down to life on Brush Creek, riding back and forth to teach. His cousin Felix Garris Graham was now married and had set up house not far away. Everybody praised Mentor's teaching, and he decided he had been foolish to think of going north. He bought back the farm, added another room and another bookshelf. Like his Uncle Johnson he was forever buying books. But Johnson was far ahead; his library of two hundred and twenty books was valued at $640, while Graham had scarcely five dozen.

After Graham began teaching in Greensburg, Sarah was often in town. It was a fine sight on court days to see the horse racing and the wrestling, and to hear the medicine hawker calling out cures for rattlesnake bites and gunshot wounds. Country boys and girls offered pawpaws, wild grapes, berries, and nuts, and sometimes the backwoods women brought in patchwork quilts, willow-withe baskets, woven counterpanes, and goose feathers.

Sarah, now twenty and still childless, had submitted to all the leechings, poultices, and pills, all the snake-oil liniment and bitters, that town doctors prescribed and Brush Creek grannies advised. Being childless was her constant grief and shame; and Graham was indeed a sad-eyed young husband.

VIII

THE NEW LOCATION
1823–26

For three years Graham rode back and forth to three three-month terms each year, did his farming between times, and managed to make and lay brick, for large houses were being erected by many slaveowners. He bought fine dresses for Sarah; and, as there were no children and his land was paid for, he was free at last of any twinge of conscience over buying books. And he bought them —books, books, books, and pored over them late at night. Sarah now listened with much interest and real comprehension to what he chose to read aloud, for she had progressed well in her own continued study. She learned "quicker than you can shell a corn-cob."

When news came that Illinois had voted down slavery, the two of them began to talk "locating" again. The big houses of "quality folks" in town were kept by slaves, and all the tobacco plantations round about were tended by them. Some even said that many men were getting rich hand over fist by breeding slaves—and not all of them black, either. Niggers now fetched three times as much as mules on the market, especially yaller Niggers.

Every letter that came from old Green County neighbors who had settled on the Sangamon raised the question of going north again. Things were headed the right direction there, with everybody for Clay and great talk of canals and public schools. They had once talked of going to Bowling Green, Kentucky, but Graham's prospecting trip there sent him home, disgusted: the country south was full of whining, howling Shakers.

In March their child, Almira, was born and lived. At last the little hooded cradle could be brought down from the attic. Graham found his evenings completely taken up with fatherhood. He could

81

scarcely restrain himself from waking the baby just to talk to her, to see her smile, feel her tiny hand curl about his finger. Sarah sang from morning till night, and the North was forgotten in the pure joy of parenthood.

When Lafayette came to Frankfort in May, the proud parents rode horseback the seventy miles, taking the tiny daughter with them that she might see the greatest man of all except Washington. This was a "jewel day" for Sarah, who loved to tell of it for the wonderment of her grandchildren. The crowd on horseback and in Conestoga wagons held back respectfully before the Fayette Hussars in gold lace and feathers, on white horses, who escorted the hero from the Versailles Pike into Lexington. Not being city folks, the Grahams had not gone to the grand ball; but the baby had been awake, and Mentor had held her high as the great man passed them. Later they read that Transylvania College had entertained the general by a program in French, given by the students. It was something to talk about for weeks and weeks.

By this time Campbellism, the New Light faith that believed sinners could be saved, was breaking up Methodist, Presbyterian, and Baptist churches alike. Yet worse was the political tangle in which Kentucky was now involved. The court of appeals judges who had found the Kentucky Bank Law unconstitutional were called before the legislature. When they were judged to be within their own rights, the opposition voted a bill to dissolve the court of appeals; and, when neither the old court nor the new one established under this new law would yield, both courts held sessions and handed down opposite judgments. Settlers poured north out of Kentucky.

When the whole countryside went to the Liberty Fair on the Little Barrens to celebrate the Fourth of July, tradition relates that forty cooks prepared oxen, turkeys, deer, and hams and that there were barrels of whiskey. The assemblage danced all afternoon and at night gathered around the campfire to eat the remnants of the noon feast, topped off with wagonloads of melons and more whiskey—and then danced all night. The Grahams left early in the night and came home to find that Great-Uncle Edward who was going to start for Illinois tomorrow had been found dead at his still, to which he had gone the day before to keg up whiskey for the Liberty Fair.

Once more the young parents talked the Sangamon. Reared as they had been in the midst of comparative law and order, Old Kaintuck now appeared to be declining; but if Illinois land was being set aside for schools, if there were to be salaried teachers with schoolhouses provided, if every child was to have a chance to go to school—that was the place for them. They weighed and re-weighed the pros and cons until finally Graham decided to go prospecting for himself and see how matters stood.

He at once absorbed the enthusiasms of the new country, with its ferries on the streams, its roads just being opened, its unspoiled virginity. Though the fine hunting and fishing were of slight at-traction to him, the Sangamon country seemed to outclass Brush Creek by all odds. Graham and Hawkins Taylor had ridden up to-gether on horseback, and now they were being feted by old Green County neighbors: the Whites, the Spearses, and the Connovers. After ten days Graham prepared to return home, but Taylor stayed. He sent word by Graham for his folks to pull up stakes and come right on up.

The journey home alone was uneventful. Graham had slipped his new botany in his saddlebags and now made good use of it. One of his later habits dates from this journey, the habit of calling by name everything that grew in the woods or on the prairies. To Graham, the tree-lover, the trip was through a veri-table paradise of untouched, primeval beauty: ash, chestnut, and serviceberry; hornbeam, redbud, and box elder; witch hazel, mul-berry, and red haw; wild cherry, crab, and hickory; sycamore, cot-tonwood, and willow; and oaks of a dozen kinds.

His stop at Louisville was enlivened by the feverish tavern dis-cussion of the new charter to build a canal around the Falls. The portage men had drunk themselves into a "conniption fit." What did the law think? Now what was going to become of *them?* They were interrupted by the clamor of a showboat on the river, and they all went out to see it and revel in the magnitude of its calliope music.

In the Sangamon country, Graham had found a man, a preacher to his own way of thinking, John Berry, who talked plain common sense, Presbyterian though he was. Sarah wanted to know what this man might say about their Cousin John, struck dead by lightning. This was news to Graham; and he went with Sarah to the spot where, in August, after the mud had dried enough from the thunderstorm that struck him down, they had buried Cousin John. He had been a dutiful, kind, work-brittle man. Standing there, Graham realized how small a part is a teacher's and said aloud what he afterward said often, that it must be very hard to be a good preacher.

They put their land up for sale, and Mentor went ahead with his fall term as usual. Sarah, singing over the thriving Almira, cared little whether they stayed or went. But Mentor was restless. News that Ninian Edwards had become governor of Illinois spurred him to write again and again to his brother Robert, imploring him to go to Illinois with him. But Robert, having got his promotion to Crab Orchard, would not be persuaded. Graham decided to go without him. He taught through the fall, the winter, and the summer terms before selling out in September.

At last everything was ready to start. On Monday, October the second, 1826, they would leave Brush Creek. Sarah carried the baby about, visiting all the loved spots—the spring, the mill, the ruins of the old weavery, the church, the deep woods. Now that the day was at hand, she shrank from going, and looked at each dear thing, trying to make its image in her mind indelible, in a way that saddened Mentor when he left her thus to go into Greensburg to wind up his last business. He had had to take a note for part of the farm sale, and there was an odd ox to be auctioned. Well after dark he returned, elated over the unexpected payment of the note and the sale of the ox.

At four the next morning they were stirring, shivering in the crisp autumn air. After breakfast Sarah rolled the featherbed and bound it with hemp, stowing it in the wagon in the place that had been reserved for it. Cook pots and johnnycake board, noggins and wooden spoons, she made secure in a firkin suspended beneath the wagon. Much later, when Graham was boarding round in Illinois and her children begged for a story, she liked best to tell of how they left Brush Creek. Mentor held Almira while Sarah climbed up, then he handed her the baby and sprang up beside her. With a "Heyah" to the oxen they moved off slowly and plodded down the winding yellow Brush Creek road in the foggy, chilly air before sunrise. Neither of them looked back. Neither spoke.

A party of others who were going to the Sangamon waited at the old furnace site: Cousin Elizabeth from Severn's Valley and her man, Bennett Abell; Cousin Clara and her man, Peter Elmore; Levi Summers and his family; two Goldsby boys; one of the Rafferty boys, and the Barbees. Most of the group were relatives. Mentor fell in at the head of the caravan, while Bob Rafferty took the job of riding the Grahams' saddle horse and driving the cow that had been hitched behind the wagon. As the line moved off toward the northwest, Sarah shifted her mantle better to protect the baby from the raw wind—and to hide her tears. They were obliged to halt frequently during the first few hours: somebody's cow broke loose; somebody else's feather bed came unbound and tumbled into the river they were fording. Not until midafternoon could Sarah control her tears enough to look about and find a bit of interest in the strange scenes slowly coming into view.

The little caravan snailed along the Nashville-Louisville Pike, a busy highway traveled by such marvelous buckboards, phaetons, gigs, and carryalls as Sarah had never before seen. Some, like themselves, were leaving Old Kaintuck behind, pulling up stakes, going to the Illinois; jaunting hopefully, if slowly, behind oxen, to a land of no slavery and no boundary feuds. But fine ladies and gentlemen drove rapidly past them, stirring up a constant cloud of yellow dust from the highway.

Sarah eyed these grand people wistfully. "I'll build you a fine brick house," Graham offered, noticing her desolation. "Cash from the farm will give us a start. I'll throw up a cabin first and then take all the time it wants to build you the finest house anywhere about.

"Yes, Mentor," Sarah said.

Though she had been in Louisville before, the sights there made her head spin: elegant mansions and carriages, ladies in silks and lace ruffles on their way to church. They stopped at Stoge's Tavern. In delicious excitement the women carried their Sabbath gowns from the wagons to the tavern's ladies' dressing-room, where city women stared as hard at the Brush Creek folk as the latter stared at them. When the women reappeared from their toilets, Mentor whispered to Sarah that she was the handsomest. They walked to the little Separatist Baptist Church, standing on a knoll at the edge of town in the midst of trees that were reddened and purpled by autumn. It was a brick church with a high, tapering steeple. To Sarah, its dingdonging bell was the quintessence of grandeur. Hushed by the unwonted elegance, the party entered, the women thrilling from head to foot to walk the length of the springy, carpeted aisle. Sarah smoothed her blue Sabbath silk proudly and joined heartily in the singing—a jewel day, indeed. However, all of them were disappointed in the preaching, especially Graham. He said the preacher was only middlin' good, neither as logical a prayer as Elkin nor as eloquent a preacher as Whitman.

Next day they were ferried across the Ohio in a jam of little and big arks and flatboats, skiffs, barges, brigs, and steamboats. The ferryman made his slow way with one wagon after another until all were across. Graham's oxen rolled their eyes with fright, trembling at the unreality of moving under other power than their own. Baby Almira cooed at the sparkle of sun on water. "There's no slavery, yon side," Mentor said, happily, as they watched the Indiana shore grow distinct with tree and boat and busy figure looming clear and friendly. "These woods are finer than Brush Creek."

"If only my folks will come . . . . ," Sarah answered.

There was no pike "yon side"; so the wagons lumbered along a dim trace among stumps and heavy undergrowth, swaying dangerously every little while and often halted by downsweeping branches. Sarah watched Mentor, swinging his ax with the rest, lopping off saplings and branches right and left. She saw how straight and wiry he was, not as heavy as the other men. Though his strokes were slighter, his ax rose oftener.

Tuesday it began to rain, a cold east-wind downpour, and the earth became so sodden and miry that the oxen moved forward only with the greatest effort. The men got down and walked, cutting brush to lay underfoot, that the animals might get purchase on the slippery ground. Black ground appeared, looking ominous to Sarah. Kentucky with its dear red soil, its gray tobacco barns splotching the red winter hills, the covered windlass well in her own dooryard, her cabin, her family as she had seen them last— all rose overwhelmingly before her. When Mentor climbed back beside her and took over the reins she had been handling, she said bravely, "Us a-goin' won't stop slavery." She was to become adept in such epigrammatic checkmating, canceling weeks of Graham's carefully piled-up arguments with a few words.

"I don't want to live around it, nor have my children," was all he could answer.

The trace grew more tortuous, and the rain fell day after day until sleep was all but impossible in the dripping wagons. The woods were silent and foreboding, and seemed endless. How unlike the Kentucky woods that had lain close by their cabin . . . . the night before they left Sarah had gone alone to see for the last time how the shellbark hickories made the air in the woods almost as light as if the moon were shining. Now the men talked in lowered tones when they talked at all; they spoke of Indians, and a great dread overtook her and she wept in silence. But when Friday morning dawned clear and the trail began to widen, the trees stood out gorgeously from the mists, brilliant and reassuring. Sarah began to sing to Almira in time with the thub-glub of oxen feet struggling through deep, black mud. It was forty years now since the feet of William Graham's pack horses had plodded through the mud of the Wilderness Road into Kentucky.

The men reckoned they had come about halfway, and they were right. On another Tuesday, two weeks later, with many a creak and rattle the Kentucky wagon train pulled up a long hill and halted on its flat summit, near the spot where the Rutledge Tavern would soon stand. Even Sarah's heart warmed at what she saw. It was a natural "slash," surrounded on three sides by noble timber, the farther, western end opening upon flat prairie. Everywhere the color was as brilliant as Brush Creek, and the Kentucky cardinal was singing. Graham, referring to his penciled map and directions, said, "Just a little farther and we'll hit Rutledge's and Concord Creek, if I have directed you right."

To the last child, the Rutledges came running from their cabin to welcome the travelers. Every one of them offered help, began to untrace the weary oxen, to unload weary children and women, and fetch them in. Graham had met Rutledge on his prospecting trip and had accepted his invitation to stop with the Rutledges till the new settlers could get located. "Aiming to settle hereabouts?" Mr. Rutledge asked.

Graham, the teacher, was spokesman for the party: he knew

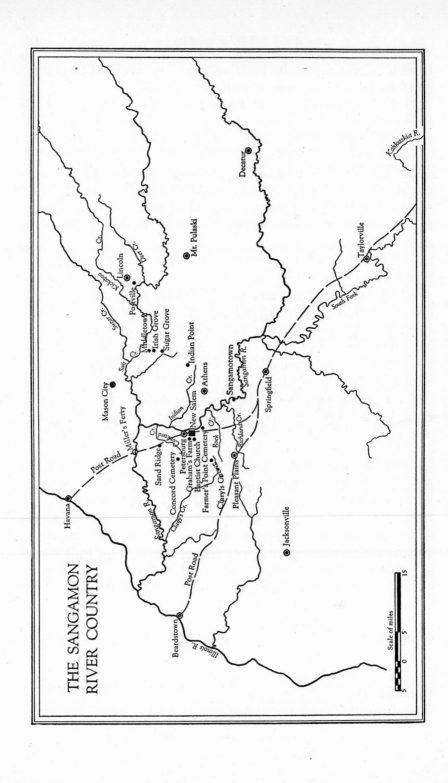

THE SANGAMON
RIVER COUNTRY

Kaskaskia R.

Decatur

Taylorville

Mt. Pulaski

South Fork

Lincoln

Beer Cr.

Postville

Middletown
Irish Grove
Sugar Grove
Indian Point
Sangamotown

Athens

Springfield

Mason City

Miller's Ferry

New Salem

Sand Ridge
Concord Cemetery
Petersburg
Graham's Farm
Baptist Church
Farmer's Point Cemetery
Clary's Grove
Pleasant Plains

Havana

Jacksonville

Post Road

Beardstown

Scale of miles

what to say and the right way to say it. Mr. Rutledge often told of
Graham's answer, which had made them all stare in grave respect:
"These are the Green County, Kentucky, emigrants I told you you
might expect when I was here prospecting on Rock Creek. Yes,
this is our destination."

"Now we'll be having our *a-b—abs*," shrilled one of the little
girls. "He talks like a teacher."

"Do you like your *a-b—abs?*" Graham asked, picking up the
child. "Yes, we shall have our *a-b—abs* just as soon as we can build
a schoolhouse." He took an acorn from his pocket. "Here," he
said, giving it to the little girl, "is a traveler acorn that has come
all the way from Kentucky. It will make a fine cup and saucer for
a doll's dinner."

There were thousands of acorns dropping in the woods about
them, but little Miss Rutledge's eyes shone with the wonder of a
traveler acorn. She took it shyly and, when Graham put her down,
tried it out upon a stone. It sat evenly, for Graham had smoothed
the stem end. "Thank you, sir," she said, smiling.

That afternoon Graham took Sarah and the baby over to inspect the land he had tentatively chosen to file on and other plots
that might be more to her choice. They would take squatter's
rights until the bricks were all made for the fine house, since they
might want to change locations and nothing would be gained by
putting down money. The sun was warm, and the woods rang with
the familiar cardinal and robin—lucky, comforting sounds. Sarah,
seeing her husband's earnest desire to please her, told him the
spot he had picked exactly suited her.

Ten days after the cavalcade had arrived on the bluff above the
Sangamon, Graham's thrown-up cabin was shipshape. It stood
in a wooded niche on the edge of the prairie, near a little creek,
Greene's Rocky Branch, that flowed into the Sangamon. Sarah
sang as she baked her first johnnycake before a fireplace which she
felt was going to be lucky. She was beginning an arduous and
eventful life, with slavery following her, taking its awful toll.
Their going, as she said, would not stop it.

The newcomers had "gathered a church" the first night, thank-
ing God for their safe journey just as Ben Lynn had, long ago.
Next day they raised the church house on Greene's land. Greene

was Graham's uncle who had been north for some time. Two preachers might be had, John Berry and Preacher Clary—but neither was a Baptist. They decided to make out with singing and praying and reading the Bible together rather than engage a non-Baptist minister. For the next twenty years ox-drawn carts and wagons were tied at the hitching rack of this same little church, on Sabbaths and on lecture and lyceum nights.

Graham at once solicited pupils and opened a subscription school in the church, hopeful that the new school law would soon be functioning and that this would be his last subscription school. It was well he did not guess how many years the law would be in coming.

IX

AIRIN' IDEES

1826-27

THE KENTUCKY scene was re-enacted in Illinois. Hard-Shell Baptists who had come up from Green County did not waver an iota in their leanings. Their preacher must wait upon a "call," not a college education. They were unalterably anti-missionary, unalterably anti-temperance-society (the latter on the grounds that belonging to any but a church society divided allegiance to God). But there was a "regular" Baptist church at Clary's Grove, near by—missionary Baptist, a fine 22 × 36-foot meeting-house with glass windows. And there were several congregations of Peter Cartwright's "hallelujah-jerking" Methodists close at hand.

Children of all these faiths gathered in the little log church with its oiled-paper window, on Greene's Rocky Branch, one mid-November morning. There were twenty-seven big, little, and middlin'-sized boys and girls, giggling and whispering about the master's roached, curly red hair and the triple-dented scowl between his eyes. The big boys opined that he was "apter than not to lick mighty damned hard."

Had their parents paid the usual rate for each of them—five cents a day—Graham would have had the fabulous income of $54 a month for a five-day week—from sunup to sundown. But nobody had any money. Butter and eggs and meat Graham earned that term, and a great deal of satisfaction. The free-school law that paid a teacher a salary, which he had so hopefully counted on, was not yet working in Sangamon County. He had to solicit pupils, just as in Kentucky, and keep a tricky account of days absent subtracted from bushels of corn and pounds of butter. Many parents overlooked altogether their promise of pay to the dour Scotsman. But he taught their children with the same care he gave the

others, and had the same hope in them. It was his lifelong fault—
or virtue—that no child who wanted to learn was ever turned away
from Mentor Graham's schoolroom door because his parents
would not, could not, or did not pay his tuition.

As in Kentucky, the children possessed few books and Graham
was driven to penning daily lessons for each one, copying from his
books meaty portions for his advanced learners. Murray's *English
Reader*, Kirkham's *Grammar*, Dabold's *Arithmetic*, and the Kentucky geography whose title-page is too dim to decipher either
publisher or author were his texts. Far into the night, after the
chores and the evening meal were over and he had rocked Almira
to sleep before the fire, this man sat, copying without error in a
precise hand that was to lose but little of its precision even when he
was eighty. From many records we have his carefully penned signature:

Mentor Graham

Graham, a tall, lithe, strong-muscled man of twenty-six, had already taught twenty-seven three-month terms. His granddaughter, Mrs. Mary Graham Bradley, of Greenview, Illinois, a tall,
lithe gentlewoman, once auburn-haired, and a great-grandmother,
is the chief source of information about Graham's early years in
Illinois. She supplies the graphic touch here from her lifelong-
collected store of material about her grandfather. She reported
how, sedulously, paragraph by paragraph, he copied and assigned
these books to each pupil who had "reached the proper perspicuity." For the younger ones, he "originated the larger part of
their lessons out of his own knowledge."

What did Mentor Graham know? A review of his library may
give some hint. He owned an encyclopedic dictionary, a set of
Kentucky and federal laws, Shakespeare, Milton, Burns,
Dante, Hume, Volney, Shelley, Keats, several books on plants and
a botanical analysis, several volumes on medicine, many biographies, a surveyor's manual, many files of Kentucky newspapers
and antislavery publications, several books of commentary on the
Bible—these in addition to a great array of schoolbooks. What he
"originated out of his own knowledge" for those children—the
Greenes, Potters, Rutledges, Armstrongs, Spearses, Camerons,

Sampsons, Abells, Barbees, and perhaps others we have failed to learn of—with each day's lesson adapted to each different mind, all this we can only surmise. A few pages of those hand-done lessons are still treasured by Mrs. Bradley.[1] Tied with a bit of tow-colored linsey-woolsey warp, the careful script is almost like print in regularity. One page begins with the verse:

> Amidst the cheerful bloom of youth,
> With ardent zeal pursue;
> The ways of piety and truth,
> With death and heaven in view.

And, as if doubly to urge the lesson:

> Give God the morning of your days
> And be forever blest.

Then come long-division problems—a few solved, to demonstrate the method: "If 4 men receive $24 for 6 days' work, how many men may be hired for $96?" And, more difficult: "What is the difference between the discount on $227.66 for 2 yrs. 3 mos. and 22 das. and the interest on the same sum for the same time?"

The common conception that log-school learning was very primitive receives complete refutation through scanning the table of contents of Murray's *English Reader*. How many Americans today have read—and discussed, digested, and memorized high spots from—narratives by Dr. Johnson, Blair, Cicero? Arguments of Pliny and Addison? Descriptions by Goldsmith and Fénelon? The pathos of Goldsmith and the Earl of Stratford? The dialogues of Heraclitus, Dionysius, Pythias, Damon, Locke? The orations of Fabricius, Cicero, Adherbal before the Roman Senate, Paul before Festus and Agrippa, Lord Mansfield before the British Parliament? The essays of Addison on contentment; of Quintius Curtius on slavery and freedom?

Add to these some one hundred selections from the great poets and excerpts from English literature upon friendship, fortitude of mind, government of your own thoughts, proper use of your faculties—and you get some idea of what those roughly clad children, going home through knee-deep snow after sunset, had heard within the fireplace-lighted little 16 × 18-foot log church. At the master's command, snow-wetted shoes must stand before the fire until perfectly dry. Feet thrust into them at going-home time went out into the leaden weather as warmed as were the hearts of the children who had, that day, heard great things out of a great and unknown world.

Unadorned by so much as a curlicue to entice the child-mind, Murray's *English Reader* is a tiny volume of very fine paper and very small print. In place of a foreword, the book has one of the preposterous titles of the time; yet how illuminating it is: "The English Reader, or Pieces in Prose and Poetry, Selected From the Best Writers; Designed to Assist Young Readers to Read With Propriety and Effect, and to Improve Their Use of Language and Sentiments and to Inculcate Some of the Most Important Principles of Piety and Virtue, With a few Preliminary Observations on the Most Important Principles of Good Reading,—by Lindley Murray, Adapted to Different Classes of Learners (Burlington, Vermont, Printed and Published by Samuel Mills)."

True to his word, Mr. Murray rolls a college course in dramatics and rhetoric into those "few observations." "The good reading of good writing," he remarks, "infuses a taste for excellence, and produces a habit of thinking and of composing language with judgment and accuracy. . . . . Perusal of the best produces solidity of principle and character which thus becomes able to resist evil when met . . . . too much attention may be paid to amusing youth so that he becomes indifferent to sober dictates and the best in him becomes feeble and transient . . . . read without straining the voice, pronounce with neither hurry or drawling . . . . if the reader attempts to render everything of high importance by a multitude of strong emphasis, little heed is paid to anything he reads; it is like crowding the page of a book with italics. Such reading is strictly imitative, assumes a theatrical manner, and gives offense to the hearer."

This reader was one of the weapons with which Graham sought to quiet the loud Illinois braggadocio that prided itself on having "plenty good enough gray-matter." The majority in Graham's neighborhood were against the proposed free schools and orated long, loudly, and profanely whenever they heard of a new "passel" of land being sold to pay a teacher's salary. In voices as virulent

as their language—which borrowed many of English oratory's
most effective words, pronounced ad lib—they aired their idees.
They were "tooth and toenail agin' all such damn-foolishness."
They snarled against taxing everybody for schools and canals.
"Why, a Michigan canal could wash Gawd's country clean down
to the Gulf," they said, if it didn't flood that paradise with
"damn Yankees." "What if your childer was growd? Don't think
you'd be payin' in to eddicate other folkses' brats? Not by a damn
sight!"

Graham, of course, had the Bible, too, from which every child
read every day: the Bible, and Murray's *Reader* and—surrepti-
tiously—Kirkham's *Grammar;* but he was only one man, after all.
It was a challenging task. Graham, a bit dazed by his summer's
reading of Volney and Paine and their soul-defeat philosophy,
rose to the challenge. In spite of them he would do what he himself
believed was right, for what his pupils learned and believed would
condition tomorrow's nation. With deepened consecration Mentor
Graham bent to the task of making thoughtful, self-expressing
men and women out of the heterogeneous Sams and Susans who
met him every morning—most of them children from homes content with knowing "enough figgerin' to go to town."

When he had signed a sixty-day contract with a dozen or so
fathers of families, the contract had read, "reading, writing, arithmetic, geography, and grammar." But grammar and geography
were stricken off at the parents' demand. The opinion of the
majority had been that these subjects were not needed. Before
them, Graham had drawn a careful line through the two words.
"Nobody needs no grammar," they said. "He kin understand us,
cain't he? Why in tucker cain't he git along? Sugar Creek never
had no grammar. Rock Creek never had none. No skules never,
not ery a one."

Every day without fail, nevertheless, Graham with a clear conscience, taught Kirkham's *Grammar* to every child before him—
though he never referred to the subject by name. "When you are
expecting to accomplish, say 'I shall do'; when you have accomplished it, say, 'I did.' " No, there was no grammar in their skule,
they'd saw to that t'onct. So the fathers rested content with
the almanac to satisfy their intellectual needs. Their women had
the *Missouri Harmony* at singing school—which was "a damn

good place to spark for the young bucks, too." A fellow could roar out with gusto, superior to pitch, as befitted those whose mothers were wildcats and whose fathers were alligators.

Meanwhile in the intent quiet of the little Baptist church, Mentor Graham put the pulpit to one side and walked back and forth, back and forth, bringing goose flesh to his youngsters by reading, with awing gestures, "Horatius at the Bridge." Those children, only a few frontier-generations removed from Old England, the Scotchman won completely, with words. Long years later his students of those times reported that Graham still let no day pass without a mental treat. Towhead and black-pate would become suddenly grown-up, their faces shining as they listened to his flashing speech. Only in his schoolroom was Mentor Graham really himself; outside, his speech rarely rose above the utterly commonplace.

At home they were sure to be quizzed. "Wall, did the schoolmaster collar y' ter-day?" Slight surprise at the answer, "Nope. He never." "Well, belike he got up his dander and thumped y' on the gourd?"—the Illinois word for "head." The answer, "Nope," might bring on that Illinois superlative, "So help me Gawd, you don't say? Jest went the whole hog and give y' a larripin'?"

Home folks could only respond with "Wall, I'll swan!" when no collarin's, gourd-thumpin's, or larripin's were reported. The pupils were more likely to repeat to them the story of "Horatio at the Bridge." They would exclaim with amazed pleasure: "I reckon he be'n't one these here reg'lar schoolmarsters." In spite of their set conviction that "nat'l hoss-sense was better nor larnin'," more braggarts sent their children to school and paid their hard-earned corn and bacon to the stern, unbending young man of whom they were secretly very much in awe.

The battle was more and more to Graham until, at play-spell, rather than play, the children would beg him to read to them. Could a man forego such an opportunity? He read them *Aesop's Fables*. Unbending a wee bit, he declaimed a few of them without the book, taking the part of crane or fox in an exaggerated low chuckle or a high squeak that set the children roaring with laughter. If they piled their ears with twigs for quill pens at play-spell and held little imitations of his performance down by the creek, it was not surprising.

Graham's old Kirkham that he dared to teach lies before me, eloquent with use. The text might well amaze a grammar student of today. We have our own smug definitions of the subject; but with Kirkham's, guided by such an understanding mind as Graham's, what ambitious log-school scholar could not be led to the heart of learning? For Kirkham's *Grammar* included spelling, with the classical derivation of every word; and, of course, parts of speech, their various forms, and diagraming. Then it proceeded to prosody —the forms of poetry, their accents and meters. Next, rhetoric: sentences of various kinds for various uses; eloquent word order; punctuation and its theory; words oftenest misspelled and mispronounced; colloquialisms of various sections of the country and their correct forms. Then came a section headed "Good Writing," which went directly to the heart of the matter in one sentence: "One who understands his subject well, directed by common sense—that is the foundation of all good writing."

Every illustrative sentence held a moral: "None performs his duty too well," "A good man is a great man," or "Mercy is the badge of true nobility." The entire book is interlarded with confidential chats of the author with the learner. For example: "Do not commit and rehearse this book. Read one or two sentences, then look off the book and repeat their contents in *your* words, in your mind. . . . . It is an evidence of a weak mind to be discouraged by the obstacles every learner meets. . . . . There is nothing more effective than grammar to enable you to think. . . . . Learn to unlearn what you have learned amiss."

Mentor Graham's was a blab school: but not a sound was permitted when a learner, having announced his lesson learned, stood before the rest to recite. There was no ruleering for error. The smallest child said his letters from the master's knee, encouraged by nod and pat and smile when on the point of faltering. But woe to the youth who had whittled secretly and recited like a dunce! Graham's switches were hickory, long and strong, and he knew when to use them. The tales that have come down to us are contradictory: a whipping, domineering Graham; a gentle, patient, kindly Graham. He is described by those who disliked him as cantankerous, extremely odd; by his friends as high-strung, with an extreme mental and nervous energy that kept him pressing lessons at a smart clip all day long—lessons in which he never wavered from his one overmastering objective: to teach the child to say what he thought audibly, clearly, and well. Yet even Graham's enemies admit that under his unrelenting eye the student learned accurately, permanently, and with an inspiration to do his level best. It was Graham's theory that it did not matter so much whether the learner liked his labor or not as that he should do it exactly right; for this would make a valuable citizen of him and, incidentally, one whom others would trust—even love. He never relaxed in any way his demands for exactness in letters being written, or figures; and, especially, the way words were said: none of this "mush-in-the-mouth" talking! Under his exacting sternness, however, lay a tender heart and an almost feminine love of children. After the final spelldown he helped the smallest with fastening and mittens, tied small chins and ears securely away from the stinging cold with yarn mufflers. His "Goodnight, one and all," to the families of children as they ran off for home was more tender than stern.

During the day he remembered how short legs tire from dangling from high benches and wrapped the nodding little one in his own greatcoat for a nap before the fire. Or, seeing fatigue overtaking the older ones, he would release them with a sudden, unexpected "Books aside!" and slowly, with as much of a smile as he ever gave them, would tantalizingly draw a book from his pocket, put there for just such an occasion. Then he would administer a stimulant in the form of a story or verse, striding back and forth to give free rein to his gestures and interpretation. Or they sang some rousing song together. Or, best of all, he told them how he had learned the vice-presidents of the United States and all the officers in the Revolutionary War to the "ker-chunkie-wunk-wunk" of the hooves of his Uncle Robert's horse, as they went picking their way through the boggy paths of the Kentucky wilderness. Then with a sudden "Books again!" he would send them back, refreshed, for renewed efforts.

Both the children and their master were constantly subjected to the influence of majestic natural beauty and the grandeur of a noiseless peace, of flaming wood-aisles and the incomparable benediction of winter shut-awayness. Indeed, a more idyllic scene could scarcely be conjured up than that of the young folk arriving from every direction through the thick timber that surrounded the church on Greene's Rocky Branch. The road leading to it ended at the west door, near which the mounts of those who lived farthest away stood patiently all day at the hitching rack.

The capacious fireplace was on the east, with its outside "feeding door," provided so that fire-mending might disturb church meeting as little as possible. In the coldest weather it took Graham and several big boys to ram through this door all the logs that would warm the room through the day—and light it, too—for when it was very cold even a western door might not stand open with a "norther" whipping sleet down. But the log hinged on the outside in the south wall was rarely drawn up.

Three long, low puncheon pews of graduated heights sat, a little off center, to the south, leaving a north aisle. Along the north wall hung the drab wrappers and coats of the children and the master, brightened by the stripe of knitted muffler or the scarlet of mittens, and punctuated with the rounds of lunch baskets. This was the room in which Abraham Lincoln and Ann Rutledge would soon be studying Kirkham's *Grammar*.

Graham wore the weighty look exacted of his profession. He wore his cutaway coat and stovepipe hat; he awed, and later won, both the children and their parents, perhaps as much by the meticulousness of his necktie as of his grammar. Yet his fine speech, not his necktie, is the thing remarked upon by friend and foe alike. His later students repeated to me his conviction that "a commonplace 'whang' bespeaks a commonplace thought, or none." The alert brain, searching for words, the trained tongue, lips, cheeks—through which thought is made apparent—these were the essentials for putting the world ahead. It was almost an obsession with him. If the twenty-year-old, "ketchin' up a bit," would grumble that "larnin' ain't such great shakes; no farmer has a needin' to larn sechlike," Graham would scorch him with: "Lazy minds make a dying nation, young man!" His patriotism grew more intense with the years; love of country and duty to her carried over to every learner.

Sometimes he joined the boys at "bull pen"—not very often but often enough to win their homage, for he could take, as well as throw, a stinging ball.[2] Lads coming home with tales of the schoolmaster's prowess at stinging increased Graham's standing among the unlettered older males, whose standard for measuring men was "grit." Gradually, the schoolmaster was winning out. Many a settler at his wit's end, many a booby, tied his horse to a church-door sapling while he interrupted school to seek an answer to his problem—law, land, letters he could not write, calculatin'. "Why, that feller could tell a man *any* damn thing!"

Half a mile from the church, Graham's forty acres lay near the edge of the timber, west from the Sangamon and not far from open prairie. Beyond the maples and walnuts, mulberries, locusts, oaks, sycamores, hickories, and cottonwoods, he and the Greenes had opened a brickkiln shortly after throwing up their cabins. Most pioneers were obliged to practice more than one trade, and those who were not chose to do so anyway, since so many opportunities to amass wealth lay on every hand. Ninian Edwards owned five stores in Missouri and Illinois, practiced law, farmed, speculated in land a little, ran a sawmill, and practiced medicine during his governorship of Illinois.

From the first there had been a good market for hand-pressed brick. Pressing brick is slow, hard work; but Graham, faithful to his promise to Sarah, gave brickmaking every minute he could manage, piling up the bricks he did not sell for the fine house that he intended to build. The Alkires, on Sugar Creek, made a house all of brick; but it was only a small one patterned after a log cabin. As Graham finished a cartload, they hauled it away by oxcart, a homemade cart whose wheels were slices of a log. The heavy wheels caked and bogged down in the all but impassable "gumbo," where the crane-swamp settlers had pinned down logs and covered them with swamp grass to make a road.

Graham made bricks for the fireplaces and chimneys in Spears's and Connover's new houses, watched as he worked by that prince of loafers, the groggery-keeper, John Clary. Graham's were the first bricks Clary had ever seen. He opined they were only for "stuck-up folkses' houses."

X

NEW SALEM IS BORN

1827-29

*F*OR A TIME, Graham felt so humiliated that he had half a mind to return to Brush Creek: his youngest brother, who idolized him, ran off from home and came to live with the schoolmaster in Illinois. He fitted well into the routine, for he knew brickmaking and did creditable carpentering. He and Mentor worked on the brick for Sarah's fine house and on Spear's and Traylor's new houses, until he—or was it Obedience Traylor?—horrified the little community. She, with her baby in her arms, left her other four young children and decamped with him for parts unknown.

Sarah's pleas to return to Kentucky rose to a constant wail. She couldn't and she wouldn't live here disgraced like that! If Mentor would not go back to Kentucky with her, she'd go without him and take Almira, too. But then came a letter with the news that Jenny Simpson—Sarah's cousin—and her illegitimate son, Carrington, had come back to settle in Green County and had bought the farm cornering on the Raffertys'. Sarah's threats wilted.

So went the humdrum of hard work and little successes, of battered hope and great humiliation, of happy days teaching at the church-house school, and of unhappy, berated hours at home. Mentor Graham strengthened under it. There were more lessons, new ones, out of his own knowledge, at the little school in the woods.

At first Sarah had been delighted with the tumult of wild turkeys, cranes, and geese coming back from feeding on the prairies to roost in the timber at night. As in Kentucky, wild pigeons flew by in flocks that hid the sun. Cardinal and catbird made her feel at home. She had planted rhubarb seeds and had found sarsaparilla and pokeberry in the woods, thus making sure that Dr. Abell, Mentor's cousin, could concoct the right kind of bitters for her and the new baby when it would be born. There was "nothing like these things to drive out pizen," everybody knew. Mentor had built a high "stand-table" at which she could grit corn without having to get to her knees as other women did. She had laid by a roll of weaving. But she had taken to weeping as she sewed and hoed and spun and wove, and to begging to go home for a visit. She made new pillow-coates and baby clothes, and a bright-blue wedding dress for Mentor's sister, Elizabeth, who was going to marry James R. Herndon in Green County. She gathered great nogginsful of wild crab and wild plum, lady-slippers and violets, and let the cooking go. Mentor had to go to St. Louis in August for supplies—sugar, salt, coffee, books—and left Sarah to tend his thriving patch of sweet potatoes. The Abells and Greenes, near neighbors, promised to look out for her. On the verge of another motherhood, Sarah's tongue-lashings kept them at a distance. The books which Mentor brought back were the last straw.

Autumn saw the rafters of their cabin festooned with strings of dried pumpkin and onions, and the vegetable hole beneath the cabin floor was level full of turnips and potatoes, for their garden had produced better than any in Kentucky. But when Sarah walked to the woods, the green and yellow "worm-eaters" (paroquets) made her so homesick she would go back to her sewing and her weeping. At night the hoot owl made her homesick enough to die. All day long the prairie chickens kept up a cackling at the edge of the prairie that made her nervous enough to scream.

At last she lay with her new little daughter, Minerva. Through the open door she saw deer in the frostbitten truck patch, cropping at the few green leaves among the bronzed rounds of pumpkins. "Hit would so pleasure me to go back home, Mentor," she said. Her tears fell in a stream; and Mentor, helpless before them, promised that they would go to Kentucky for a visit before he opened his fall term. From the trip, made when Minerva was only two weeks old, Sarah returned unwillingly, even while admitting that Mentor had done noble by her.

Things took a turn for the better when James Rutledge and John Cameron bought the wooded hill half a mile east and began to build at the bend of the Springfield road. They obtained a per-

mit and laid out a town. Sarah reckoned that such a big house as
Rutledge's meant they were expecting a big town. She was placid
again, for the baby was thriving and she had seen her own people.
Her own brick house had begun to rise. Mentor, careful craftsman
that he was, was building a house that stood seventy-five years
and would still be standing had not fire destroyed it. Her luck had
changed, Sarah knew, now that she could bear a child often, and
now that her brick house was going to be only half a mile from a
town. Along with the electrifying information that town lots were
for sale came steady work, money-work, on Saturdays and after
the winter term.

The twenty-by-forty tavern-to-be of the Rutledges was not
much larger than Sarah's own fine house. Hers, twenty by thirty-
eight, was to have plaster, and windows of glass that had been
bartered from Harry Riggin, and three fireplaces. Sarah forgot to
be sharp-tongued and glowed with pride in Mentor. What other
man, almost singlehanded, in less than two years had planned and
executed the best house in the neighborhood, and that at odd
times between teaching and working on other peoples' houses?
It was tucked in among tall trees, with a wide, cleared dooryard
facing south, and a spacious root cellar, a covered well and a proud
weathervane, and was within walking distance of a new social
center—a house with *five* rooms!

That second autumn everybody helped with the milldam and
the mill. Graham took his oxcart and worked with the rest, gathering the boulders from the little stream that flowed by the church.
A sawmill and a gristmill would make eating and house-building
easier, attract more settlers. The little community was suddenly
buzzing with industry. A thousand cartloads, so legend says, they
hauled and dumped into log-pen piers in the midst of the Sangamon, upon which the mill was to rest. Graham worked late into
the night over figures on the mill with which Cameron had asked
his help. Sarah could always tell the depth of his concentration by
the intensity of his taps—key or coin—rat-tat-tat, sharp, quick.
It was hard on a body trying to sleep in the next room. But Sarah
held her peace: a mill and a town! And Mentor had said: "Now
the school law will be getting around to us!"

The coming of winter slowed the work; and Graham again found
himself in the little Baptist church, facing lads uncomfortable in

breeches and jacket after having "shirt-tailed around" all summer
in knee-length shifts. Many new children arrived—some in moccasins, some barefoot, some in shoepacks, some in store shoes. Between keeping the backlog supplied in that long, hard winter of
1828, attending to his farm, and writing out the necessary lessons,
Graham found little time for money-work. While the children ate
cornpones and grape jam stickily, at noon, he read them *Gulliver's
Travels*, then made them wash their hands and dry them at the fire.
After school he saw the smallest to their own doors: timber wolves
were bolder than usual, because of the long snow.

Butter and eggs, corn and deermeat, skins and sweet potatoes,
Graham earned that winter, and a great deal of satisfaction. For
his advanced learners were losing their Illinois drawl and outland-
ish lingo. They weren't going to be "mudsills" any longer. The
master answered furtive questions about what a college was—the
institution hotly ridiculed by parent and preacher. But that stumbling block had been mastered by Graham. At twenty-eight, constantly prodding his own attentive mind, he had reached some
conclusions. In fighting kings the fact that learning was no part of
king-crime had, he decided, been overlooked. Kinging it and education belonged in two distinct categories, and the world had
cheated itself by not acknowledging that fact. Almost feverishly
he applied himself to the task of trying to make the incoming settlers education-hungry. He would show them that they would
prosper doubly if only they learned to think and to talk. Buoyed
at his task, he let no opportunity for purposeful speech and effort
go unfilled.

Spiritually, he was a lonely man. Time constantly hounded him
on to the next duty, and he had little refreshing companionship at
home. Bowling Green was his one real companion. From the first
they had been warm friends—he and Green, the cultured man, the
thinker, the man with refined manners, the lawyer whose authority
might have some effect upon the rising rowdyism around the mill-
site. They talked together of the new town, free schools, river navigation—stealing their time out on Sunday afternoons or after
chores on Saturday. They exchanged books and ideas about
books.

When, after many months, the mill was finally completed, all
rushed to patronize it. Boys and men waiting for their grist talked

and joked, ran races and had "wraslin' matches" to while away the time, for the meal was only a slow trickle between the hand-hewn stones that had been quarried near. When John Clary opened what he called a "grocery" (some termed it "doggery"), temperance-thinkers like Green and Graham did not have to be told that jokes were now off-color and that the wrestling had turned into eye-gouging fights. A drunken man would draw his gun at the first word suggesting slander of himself in this new place that was made to order for "sittin' an' spittin'." Graham added lectures on drink and profanity to the growing curriculum of his school.

By the end of the year a few town lots had been sold. Sam Hill and John McNeil opened a store. On Christmas day a post office was opened; and Graham mailed, for only twenty-five cents, one of the first letters, back to Kentucky, telling the relatives they had better come on up. But the state borrowed the accumulated school funds for other matters, and the day of salaried teachers was again deferred.

After Hill had returned from his stocking-up trip to St. Louis and had opened his store, a decided enmity had developed between him and Peter Cartwright, Methodist circuit preacher on the Sangamon, who had come north from Kentucky in the early 1820's. Sam would refer to Cartwright as "Uncle Peter" with the same patient forbearance as if Cartwright were a doddering old man, and Cartwright would clap his emphatic lips together in a fighting grin, sit down upon the bench before Hill's store, and tell all comers that Hill, who "hired his fightin' done for him and paid for it with blue dishes," was bound for hell. Bent upon accumulating dollars and cents, Sam let Peter pile up whatever fancy vituperation he chose while he measured out calico and cotton-chain, coffee, forty-cent jeans, tallow and beeswax, muslin, hops, laces, powder and shot, ribbons; and Old Monongahela and tafia from the barrels at the back. Yet by all frontier standards, Hill should have knocked his slanderer edgewise.

Graham and Hill, about the same age, had also disliked each other cordially from the first; and though Graham patronized Hill, he did not keep his ideas about whiskey-selling to himself, for Hill sold liquor to the men who came in before he waited upon the ladies. As a consequence, there was likely to be cussin', and worse, at Hill's store; and that made it no place for the ladies. Green and Graham talked the matter over. Something ought to be done about this. Hill charged three prices for his stuff, besides.

Since Cartwright's booming utterances always stopped the passer-by, he really served as a ballyhooer for Hill's customers and loafers. Graham, who had been the public's letter-writer and banker, now lost the banking half of his free service to Hill, who not only banked the people's money but disposed of their extra produce as well. His store was the focus from which news of prospective weddings and wolf hunts, of births and deaths and river-doings, of church meetings and horse races, went out, until people began to know people fifteen miles away. Hill presided with a fine flourish, never more the first citizen than when handing out the mail, for he was also postmaster. He performed before an admiring little knot of folks—the regular loafers and the women who had come in to exchange a great deal of butter for a few yards of the precious posy-calico. They stood around, eating the holiday treat, store cheese and crackers, while someone read aloud from the newspaper —regardless of whose address was upon it—until the subscriber appeared and claimed it. Every item called forth a burst of spontaneous and overloud discussion. Temperance advocate and groggery-keeper, Yankee and southerner, ignorant and college-bred, argued and discussed all kinds of subjects, concerning most of which they differed widely.

Graham was willing to have his *Kentucky Gazette* and *Washington Globe* help him thus at Hill's in his fight against ignorance, but he did like to get them finally in a state in which he, too, could read them. He exchanged papers with Squire Green, and afterward the two talked over all they had read. Both figured the new steam engine was bound to change things; so Graham read up on it, found out how it worked, and taught that to his learners.

And just as what his learners heard from him soon got abroad, so what teachers at Indian Point and Irish Grove were telling their pupils sifted into New Salem, as the little settlement springing up around the Rutledge and Cameron mill was now called. Now there were missionary Baptists at Clary's Grove, Peter Cartwright's jerking Methodists, Rev. John Berry's Presbyterian preachments —Graham was being asked many off questions by the young folks sitting on the stick-leg puncheon pews of his little church-

house school. He read them the Bible—parts that seemed plain—
but he made no comment. They read those parts back to him.
Yet they understood what the schoolmaster did not put into
words: all these differing grown-up theories were what grownups
thought the Bible meant. His keen blue eyes had a way of flashing
delicate messages, and not a child but would quail under their di-
rectness when his drawled phrase, "Well I reckon?" had not
stopped a prevarication; not one but softened under his tenderness when those eyes filmed a trifle over innocence. Even the lit-
tlest knew for certain that nobody knew for certain just what all
of the Bible meant.

In contrast to their bewhiskered sires, Master Graham was
shaven, his shirt collar was white and lay smoothly, and his wonderful vest was of black velvet, his stock, shining satin. His tall hat
seemed only right; he would have looked odd in a coonskin cap;
yet Graham doffed the uniform of his calling after teaching hours
for rough farm clothing while he did the stable chores and the carpentering and brickwork and other things by which he managed to
make the ends meet that never would have met from the proceeds
of his slowly paying school. His was a lithe, erect figure, swift of
gait; always hurried a little by the self-imposed task of replacing
raw boasting with the power of knowledge. His hands were red,
rough, calloused, from cutting brush to feed his livestock during
the drought; but he always kept his face smooth-shaven and his
bushy hair combed evenly, and sent any besoiled learner out to the
creek to wash his face and smooth his hair. "You can't do your
best when you're dirty," he said. "Dirt and brains can't work together."

If new books found their way among his crowded shelves, Sarah
learned to content herself with a biting "New books won't mend
old shoes," while she herself read the books—and sometimes let
the mush burn. She seems finally to have caught Mentor's thirst to
know and, as a grandmother, was often heard to boast that he had
never been too absorbed in a book to be kind to her, never too concentrated to let the wood box get empty, never careless enough
with his money to chew tobacco or spend a half-dime for Old Monongahela.

She began to understand that he could no more help trying to
find answers to hard questions than she could help wanting to be

among her people. She stayed back when, restless from his books, he got up without a word and went off alone into the moonlit woods. If he did not return until after she had gone to bed, she roused from sleep to listen to his carefully worded dissertation on New Lights, or whatever it was that he had struggled with. She made Almira corncob dolls, but Mentor bought the child books and took her little four-year-old fist in his and guided it to write her name—on expensive paper, with his new steel pen.

Sarah kept her new house with an orderliness and cleanliness that demanded incessant toil. She, with her cutlery, fancy dishes, and leather-seated Windsor chairs, was envied by many. On the mantle shelf in the best room sat a tall clock and candles and snuffers, exactly spaced. Almira had a little chair Graham had made, and he kept the hooded cradle polished like a mirror. With only infrequent tiffs, they grew back into their old love for each other, and she braided wheat straw for his work hats and he sanded wooden slats for her sunbonnets. She had a best and second-best store hat, and they were considered a dressy couple when they set out for church.

Good neighbors, among good neighbors, they had only to mention being "scarce of corn" or "down bad sick" and the meal or whiskey would arrive. They jolted grandly about in their new screechy-wheeled wagon, invited the preacher home for Sunday dinner, and attended singing school. Saturday was baking day and churning day; and Sarah, inviting guests in often, served fresh wheat bread, fresh butter, fried prairie chicken, and wild-plum jam, thus gaining a reputation as a wonderful cook and housewife.

Not long after the mill began to operate, foot and horse races began to be a regular Saturday-afternoon event. Acquaintances bet a one- or two-bit drink with strangers on the farm horses and farm boys. Mentor loved a good race, though he was never known to have entered a bet. "My opinion is that the sorrel will win" was as far as he ever went, standing among the rough men with their loud "Old spavin kin lick the bunch! Go it Bowlegs!" Graham went once to Shawneetown to an advertised race. There metheglin (fermented honey), the mead of ancient England, could be bought by gentlemen with temperance leanings. There he is reported to have shouted: "Go it! Get there!" Since grist could neither be brought to mill nor be ground on Sabbath, except sinfully, these conscience-quieting frontiersman made Saturday their grist day and played like schoolboys while they waited. A lot of talk was heard, too. Somebody who had been west or north was always setting the community to talking about Texas or the Indian Territory.

The Grahams, like the others, did a great deal of dancing. To the wheeze of an old accordion, guitar, or fiddle they danced all night, resting from dancing by watching others dance, and, if they did not live too far away, walking home by the light of dawn. It was something to celebrate when the corn was all shucked. You could forget fatigue before outdoor tables laden with food and drink, and there was no law against sleeping most of the next day. Far from the humdrum of duty, the ordinarily darkened cabin would be candle-lighted, its furnishings hauled out by strong men and women eager to release their pent-up primitive joy in primitive fashion, and soon the puncheons would be rattling beneath their flying feet. They danced three- and four-handed reels and jigs, and cut out partners to make the dance last longer, to the tunes "Money Musk," "Devil's Dream," "Fisher's Hornpipe," and "Yankee Doodle."

Thus time sped, and with it came news that Elizabeth and James R. Herndon were now married and coming to live in New Salem. News, too, that Sarah Bush Lincoln had been back in E-town selling her cabin. While Graham and Bowling Green talked of fluctuating currency and getting pigs to market by water, Tom Lincoln's son, Abe, a lanky young farm hand, was thinking about that too. Graham, reading up on Kentucky and Henry Clay, taught river transportation and stable currency to his oldest learners.

XI

SCHOOLMASTER VERSUS CAMP MEETING

1829–30

CONTENT reigned within the Graham's fine house during the winter of 1829–30. News that Illinois College would open on the fourth of January at Jacksonville quickened Mentor's step to school and set his ax twinkling at the woodpile. He was going, if he could cut wood enough ahead. Christmas was over, with its striped peppermint candy and corncob dolls, its barring the teacher out for a treat of apples, its knots of children with their shrill "Christmas gift!" demanding presents from those they hailed. Sarah had knitted new mittens for Almira and a hood for the baby. She had knitted a muffler for Mentor, extra wide and two yards long, in stripes of somber colors, except the green. He wore it fifty years.

He bundled Almira in it when she rode to school upon his back, clinging tightly to the gentle hand put back to steady her but never touching the head with its shiny plug hat from which she had been sternly warned. Hats like that cost $15. By now Almira had learned to hop, skip, and fetch it for both parents, to sweep the hearth, and to watch the afternoon shadows for time to put the potatoes on to cook. At six she could read and sew and mind food that was cooking, tend the baby, clean the candlesticks, and shoo the cows from the corn patch. Like all children, if she had been good she received biscuit and jam on the Sabbath. Graham never failed to rock her to sleep, even when he was all keyed up and about to start over to Bowling Green's for one of the talkfests in which the two men sat the stars out.

Sitting before the fire after he had rocked her to sleep and Sarah had tucked her in with "cisslin' hot bricks" at her feet, the parents worked late. Graham shelled the best of his tuition corn for seed or cobbled the family footgear. Though Sarah would have liked to go barefoot in summer, as most farm women did, she dutifully wore the neat-soled moccasins Mentor made for her. She wore her store shoes every step of the way to church, too, instead of carrying them until within sight of the building, to save them, as most did. After the shoes, Mentor again turned to his books—copying out lessons, reading a few pages in a new book, "exercising the mind." Something was forever pricking through the batten of humdrum living and demanding Mentor Graham's consideration—the propositions that have baffled men from the beginning.

It is easy to imagine them thus—Mentor at his last, or slowly rocking and reading, stopping the rocking to think through what he read, reading those inevitable bits aloud; Sarah before the little wool spinning wheel, with flying fingers and foot—staying them only when Mentor began to read—twisting the strands between thumb and forefinger, twirling them up from the carded fleece that billowed, rosy-pink in the firelight, from the willow basket beside her. But it was more likely to be the big flax wheel and nettle fiber for rough tow cloth. Wool was scarcer than hens' teeth.

Graham returned from his trip to Jacksonville with renewed vigor and vision, newly consecrated to a self-imposed task. A college within sixty miles! This winter, when he was so far ahead of the wolf, he had his chance. His attic and root cellar were filled: firkins of butter and honey and maple sugar; apples and pumpkins, turnips and sweet potatoes; and, near the never cooling chimney, strings of dried fruit. Fruit trees, set out eight years ago, were bearing now. And there was yellow and purple variegated popcorn. The old Kentucky carders waited the wolf hunt to release them to usefulness again. It had been a good year. Wild turkeys and geese helped themselves, unmolested, at the chinks of log corncribs. His chance to do something about liquor was here: from now on, learners from his select school would be headed toward Illinois College and there wouldn't be a "fip and a bit" bettor on dog-fights among them.

Riding back through the snowy woods, he must have absorbed some of their power. Why else were those snow-weighted trees picked out, remembered, among all the wilderness of trees with which Mentor Graham communed his lifelong? Perhaps it was the uninterrupted solitude of the ride, without other mental demands. Whatever the reason, that solitary ride through trackless snow Graham retold over and over. Whatever the impulse, when he shook the snow from his coat and opened the back door late on the night of his return, he told Sarah of a great new sense of power. She reckoned he had been "called." Perhaps he was—but not to the pulpit.

Preacher Berry was the right man, Graham knew, to bring about the spending of less for Monongahela and tafia and more for books and education. He attended every preaching Berry gave out in town or country cabin. Certain ones referred to Berry as a "milksop," a "whangdoodle preacher," for his intrepid speech had labeled them "tipsy-topers." Graham went to hear Cartwright, who did not mention drink but sent hard-working Jemimah Gum into barking hysterics because of her sins. There was going to be a hard struggle for temperance, Graham saw, for the town and surrounding country were building up fast with new settlers who kept the mill booming by their demand for sawed lumber and kept Clary busy at the whiskey barrel.

Graham dragged logs into his schoolroom to provide seats for the new children, most of them poorly clad and barefoot except when it snowed. They had the seats closest to the fire, with permission to warm hands and toes closer up any time they felt cold. With so many new minds to comprehend and minister to, the hours flew by in the little meeting-house. The master's eye was more accusing than ever when one of his prided advanced learners slipped back into an "I done" or a "you cain't never." If the big boys (in their late teens) tipsied and chawed terbacker, they did not do it at school.

This was the winter that a peddler came banging into the church, expecting it to be empty. He burst in with a loud rattle of tin and a whistling of the wind, then drew up short with a snort of surprise. The master's "Books aside!" wasn't needed. The fellow was half-frozen and hungry. At Graham's suggestion, down came the lunch baskets and each child gave the peddler a small part of his lunch. "It was providential," Graham often related, "that some of the children portioned out mere crumbs, for there were sixty children." But the man ate all they offered to him and then lay down in front of the fire and went to sleep. Nevertheless, the command to "Books again!" was obeyed; lessons went on in regular fashion; and nobody laughed at the man's snoring. At closing time the peddler woke, opened his pack, and presented the school with a wire broiler. After that they brought raw bacon and ham and broiled it over the fire, and toasted their corn pones, too, if the day was very cold. Above the fire hung the iron pot which Graham had provided. Snow was melted in it, and the children drank from a common dipper-gourd.

Preparations began for a trip to Kentucky to attend the wedding of Robert Graham, Johnson Graham's son, whose father was to do the marrying, as he had been restored to the Brush Creek pulpit. But Almira came down with the measles and Sarah had a spell of ague, so they did not get to go, although they sent gifts. Graham's were a hardwood medicine chest from his workbench—in the log toolhouse and weaving-house, just behind the brick house—and a history of Kentucky. Sarah's was five yards of cherry-red linsey-woolsey which she had spun and dyed and woven. There was enough yarn left to weave a piece large enough to make Almira a Sabbath dress.

Months later the gifts were acknowledged. The letter opened by saying that the New Lights, with their belief in salvation for sinners, had split the Green River Baptist Association wide open. The "dress pattern," Robert said, had made the bride the handsomest dress in Green County; and his mother (Cassandra) wanted to know: "However did Sally [Sarah] dye that cloth?"

Graham rode to the wolf hunts that winter among the bushbeaters who caged the black beasts in an ever narrowing circle; but he had no gun. Almost everybody lost cattle and pigs, since they ranged free. New Salem was not yet as advanced as Greensburg had been, before Graham's birth, in its dictum that geese, pigs, goats, and cattle running loose in the village were "unseemly." Nobody in New Salem objected to the animals. Pigs wallowed and grunted in the mud in summer, and in the snow in winter under the two big trees near Hill's store; and chickens, geese, and ducks scattered with a great commotion before the country wagons coming into town.

Nobody branded their pigs, so there was much squabbling over the ownership of shoats. And there were always some who didn't bear respect for ownership. Squire Green was put to it to settle disputes. Finally he hit upon a solution, and with biblical wisdom decreed: "Pick out what you think belongs to you, and keep it, if nobody else claims it. Kill all the rest and divide the meat among the claimants." That made Green famous and won him the faith of all. He got a lot of good meat in pay and thanks to boot, and obliged the pig-stealers to "come of [overcome] their habit." Squire Green was a pippin—no less.

Graham, seeing this, talked oftener and more earnestly to Green with an eye to doing something about the excessive liquor-drinking that went on. Both men were now certain that New Salem had a future, for the new cabins going up were no makeshift, pigpen-cornered affairs. Their logs were squarely, smoothly hewn, the chinking was good white mortar; and some were even ceiled and walled up inside with finished hickory or walnut planking. Some had wooden gutters and unroofed, wooden-floored "settin' places" before the door. When spring came, the air was filled with the creak of log-chain and the gee-haw of ox-drivers and the boom-boom of the mill. In their ten- or twenty-acre clearings men and women were out with hoes, planting corn, and mudsills were breaking open the prairie, out beyond the timber, with five yoke of oxen to the plow—plowing by moonlight when the gadflies left off. Graham's spirits soared: he managed to get the three men— Green, Rutledge, and Berry—together by inviting them in, knowing full well what the talk would run to. April saw him penning a petition for another road into New Salem to pass Morgan's, Rogers', the Bethel meeting-house, Higgins', Good's—twenty miles. The old Springfield road was noisy with settlers, a few headed toward a definite stop but most of them looking for a location, splashing through Purkapile's Ford and on up and through the ford near the dam on the Sangamon, pulling up in the one street of the village, to "howdy" the villagers and learn where they were. Wild-crab and plum fragrance raced the blood in young and old veins, cowbells jingled through the timber, and Sarah sang all day long. She said what a smart thing it had been to come north. Once a week Harvey Ross cantered in, or plop-blobbed through the mud, with the mail from Springfield: the newspaper.[1]

Those who were building New Salem on that level-topped bluff a hundred feet above the Sangamon dreamed of a great city that would be there, some day; they could not have guessed that, instead, their little log village would decay, to rise, resurrected after a century, a shrine for all the world. Only a brief pageant was to be theirs, of oxcart and bar-share plow, spinning-wheel and gritter, well sweep and quilting bee, sulphur purgative and slippery-elm poultice—and young people listening to a redheaded and preposterously earnest and insistent schoolmaster down behind the town, a stone's throw from the graveyard. Already there were big and little mounds there, marked with boulders carried from the brook, which were festooned at play-spell with May apples and wild phlox and violets from the woods by happily chattering, pig-tailed little girls. The town was a prideful place, with its rock chimneys, bricked hearths, and glass windows. Little New Salem on the Sangamon had steamboat dreams.

But in the hot, dry swelter of August when dog fennel was beginning to bloom, it was religious zeal that boiled up and over, not steamboat talk; and Graham went down to Peter Cartwright's camp meeting to see and hear for himself. He came home discouraged. From twenty miles around people had gathered, and he found the women sweating and panting over fires, cooking kegs, and tubfuls of food and setting the children to ward the dogs off, while the men threw up a rostrum.

Cartwright mounted in due time and lined the hymn:

> Think of what the Savior bore
> In the gloomy garden,
> Sweating blood at every pore
> To procure thy pardon.
>
> See him stretched upon the wood,
> Bleeding, grieving, crying,
> Suffering all the wrath of God,
> Groaning, gasping, dying.

An earsplitting exhortation followed—the puncheon pulpit wavered and all but fell beneath the resounding whacks of the Bible-beater as he pounded home his points, defaming the meek, callous-handed assembly before him and accusing it of guilt unspeakable. For hours he went on, flailing those honest men and women who worked from dawn till dusk and spun and tinkered and cobbled far into the night. There was secret sin amongst them; and they were going to be dragged down to hell, where the vilest sinners of all time would stand aside while they were thrust over the brim into the bottomless pit to fall forever through flaming oil, ten thousand thousand hells, blazing eternally—unless they acknowledged their sin. Cartwright's voice was a young thunder, his words fairly leapt from his snapping thick lips that clapped to after a climax with a spasm of complete and awful certainty. He who had made thousands fall in Kentucky was sure of his power. His mane of dark hair flopped with the vehemence of his utterance as he bellowed, pleaded, ridiculed, stamped, threatened—and then calmed off and asked the brothers and sisters to come up for the right hand of fellowship. It might take a good deal of straight whiskey to keep up such steam, Graham decided. But the crowning insult to intelligence came in the final hymn:

> But if you still refuse us
> We bid you all farewell:
> We're on the road to heaven,
> You're on the road to hell.

The effect of the camp meeting on the young bucks from Sand Ridge, Sugar Grove, Athens, Clary's Grove, Rock Creek, and New Salem was such that they undertook to break it up. Graham saw some of his own learners in the gang that rushed Cartwright to pull him down and punch him. But Cartwright freed himself by finding sensitive spots under jaws, and the boys slunk off.

At the first camp meeting on Rock Creek they had sawed the pulpit in two and set it together neatly; and when Cartwright got to beating it, it fell in halves and tumbled down. Cartwright kicked the halves off the rostrum and went on exhorting and beating the air to the accompaniment of Sam Berry's "A-men brother!" and Jim Pantier's "Not so, brother." But the situation had been too sidesplitting for even camp-meeting folk, and Cartwright was obliged to jump from the platform, calling for supporters, to chase the cowbelled boys. After half an hour they caught a few and gave them what they had earned—hot, heavy, and unmercifully—on the seats of their thin tow britches. But the ornery boys came back and broke up the night session with fire-rings set in the near woods, and when accosted by another posse replied innocently: "We wuz jist a-catchin' snakes fer the old Devil's hell-pot." They promised to make tracks for home and disappeared into the woods, but "howsomever had snuck back" later. Their ghost-shrieks so rattled the congregation that some of its members shrieked too. And when a Negro ghost came fiend-dancing out of nowhere, the congregation broke into a pandemonium Cartwright could neither yell down nor fist down. Graham knew what folks said was true: "They would walk through the briars of hell to attend such meetings."

Graham went home from the meeting in a brown study, his mind permanently and unalterably made up against this sort of thing. Brush Creek had been right. He could not know that this very camp meeting was to bear unrighteous fruit, that Lincoln was to suffer slander through this same Cartwright's lips.

A new ally, Dr. John Allen, now arrived in New Salem. He was a thin, middle-aged cripple who had come west to cure his consumption. He wore a cutaway and a silk tile and carried his capsules in a leather case. The refinement of his clipped white beard matched his quiet speech and the refinement of the furniture he brought for his office. Another man to fight for intelligence and decency, Graham knew at first glance. He welcomed Allen with enthusiasm, invited him out, and bought the gate-leg table that would not fit into the doctor's little office.[2] Now there were five to debate and argue, to get their heads together: Rutledge, with his library of twenty-five books; Berry the elder, the able, temperance-favoring preacher; Green, the lawyer; Allen, the doctor and a Dartmouth graduate; and Graham, the Scotch schoolmaster who did his own thinking.

Graham often had all these men out to supper. While they talked temperance, Sarah spread her Sabbath cloth and bustled proudly, serving them her tastiest wild-plum jam and prairie-chicken noodle-soup, and sometimes even fresh fish. Others besides Spears's Nigger Jim seined and gigged fish at the milldam. Like Mentor, Sarah was no "halfway" doer. She scrubbed everything with lye suds and polished her pots and pans with brick dust until they glowed. Her house was tidy, her babies clean, her hands never idle—and her temper a bit short, in consequence. Mentor's late-staying guests were hard on her, trying to sleep in the next room. In their enthusiasm the men often talked until nearly sunrise. When they left, Sarah never failed to say she hoped the likes of them would never darken her door again.

Dr. Allen promoted a Sabbath school which studied the Bible with special emphasis on spiritous liquors. A good many came out of curiosity, just to see this "damned silk-tile Yankee who'd ought to be dogged to death, by rights." He had a pleasant, quiet voice; his logic was bewilderingly simple, and he never contended that his temperance tenet represented God's one and only appointed salvation. These things, along with his kindnesses to the villagers in their distresses, resulted in an office crowded with Sabbath-school attenders. People who had hated him for being a Yankee were first awed and then came to love the crippled little Dr. Allen.

"Stuck-up, silk-tile Graham" likewise grew in favor; but people were slow in losing their awe of him. He knew "too damned much"! Why, that man would write you out a letter faster than you could tell him what to say. He could draw up a will, a mortgage, a contract, a deed, a note, with similar speed and ease. And he was "quicker'n a streak of lightenin' at figgerin'."

When, one day, Dr. Allen offered a temperance pledge, he got many signers. Of course Bowling Green, James Rutledge, and Preacher Berry signed. And Graham signed.

XII

LIKKER AND THE DEBATING SOCIETY

1830-32

*I*N THE AUTUMN of 1830 Johnson Graham and his wife Cassandra came to New Salem for a visit, along with Uncles Edward, Samuel, and Joseph and their wives. Among them they had twenty children. Singing school, spelling school, dancing (although it was now thought godly only if there was no fiddling and the dancers sang their own music), and dinners with the Abells, Greenes, and townsfolk kept the visitors well entertained. Though all of the women worked, it was a difficult time for Sarah until two of the families, deciding to locate, filed on land and threw up cabins. The visit of the other two families lasted until nearly Christmas.

While Cassandra, the professional spinner, spun and wove and stitched for Sarah, the other women kept busy with meals. The men boomed at each other in an enthusiastic survey of everything from horse collars to heaven, in a good old Kentucky get-together; and home-going was postponed to the last possible minute. They brought word that Rachel, Graham's sister, had married a slaveowner and gone to live in Tennessee—she was Mrs. Isaiah Goldsby, now. The visitors, as was customary, brought presents for everybody, and when they went home took a "dress pattern" of deep-green woolen and a book of family medicine for the bride; the Goldsbys would be going to Tennessee sometime during the year and would present the gifts.

The villagers who had helped with the mill more than a year before this had signed for either money or work. Money-signers now had first turn when they brought grist. As Graham was a work-signer, he contrived the scheme of taking tuition-corn to the mill as he received it, so that it could be ground between money-grists. Every few days he brought the meal away; and, as there was much more of it than he would need, he exchanged some of it for shoes and a chest of drawers and paid in some to Dr. Allen, in advance of the arrival of another baby. More than rhetoric was back of what his learners heard in his new maxim: "Do not say you can't until you have exhausted every resource." It was to be a needed maxim in that eventful winter. He also provided an even more piercing one: "Excuses are not truths, but lies." This year the Warfields, Watkinses, Bales, Ritters, Onstots, Greens, Camerons, Rutledges, and two new families of Grahams subscribed to his school, and the little church was packed. Graham folded his great-coat for one child, a cripple, to sit on, and carried him home every evening.

Winter fell early that year of 1830. The cranes flew south early, and wild geese honked by before November. It snowed early and the snow stayed on. Children, rich with their short, wide planks from the mill, slid on them at play-spell or made snowmen. Between Thanksgiving and Christmas storms increased until it snowed almost continually. The snowbanks kept most of the children at home, where there was beginning to be a great to-do uncovering corn shocks to get at the ears, to feed both people and animals. The bad weather had been early and too intense for many huskings. A few of the nearest children struggled in until the last few days before Christmas; Graham managed to keep them warm and see them home. He also kept his own family warm and fed; the idea about the corn had been a good one.

The day before Christmas their first son arrived, a black-haired, blue-eyed, thin little fellow. Sarah, struggling in the keen cold that has come down in Illinois history as "the winter of the deep snow," tended him as best she could, but he did not survive. With her own hands she lined the little coffin Mentor made; and kind neighbors tunneled a path, half a mile through the snow, to the graveyard, just beyond the church. Sarah was too ill to go and could only look through the window as Graham and Preacher Berry and Bennett Abell disappeared down the path with their little burden. Preacher Berry prayed above the open grave they had dug with such difficulty, and the clodded mound was smoothed flat and white before the men found their way back through blinding, sharp sleet.

Day after day the snow fell unrelentingly, making prisoners of every household, piling up against the once brave brick house, now gone dreary and desolated. Graham shielded Sarah from the cold and cooked and fed the fire and tried to make the little girls happy. Though he gave Sarah the largest portion of every precious apple and soaked her corn bread in melted butter, she did not mend. He rocked the children to sleep, but he could not sing to them. Bennett Abell brought frozen deermeat whenever he and his wife Elizabeth came to do what might be done for Sarah, while the snow piled higher and higher and Sarah lay staring, dry-eyed, a hard cough racking her. Dr. Allen wallowed out, but the best he could promise was that she might recover if the weather would only get better.

Late in February the crises of the deep snow and Sarah's illness passed; and while Abell's oldest daughter sat by Sarah, Graham found his way out and up over the heavily frozen snow-crust into an elevated world, with people living below in burrows. Townfolk had had to sit the winter out too, but they had had the solace of health and talk. No child but his had died.

The Rutledge house, now turned into a tavern, was crowded with stranded travelers, among whom there was plenty of loud argument over the temperance question. Dr. Allen had seized the chance to bring it up, with no luck at all. What! Divorce a man from his morning and evening bitters, his "ticklers," his "starters" and "eye openers," in a winter like *this?* Clary had stayed at his farm, and Hill had run out of whiskey. Graham found his store loud with ifs, ands, and buts—and perfectly sober men.

Under heavy rain the snow began to melt in March, and bets were rife upon how high the Sangamon would "boom." Talk of New Salem as a steamboat city was revived and waxed more enthusiastic than the bets. While New Salemites began to hustle to bury dead animals and get at their corn, A. Lincoln, with a stepbrother and a cousin, was setting out on a now-famous flatboat trip to New Orleans—a trip that would thread the pattern, vivid and clear, of that fabric begun by Weaver William when he set out for the new, unknown world. Lincoln, meditative, thoughtful, hungry for knowledge, was to find fulfilment in this ambitious little log village on the Sangamon, at the hands of a descendant of Weaver William. In their secret leanings and ponderings the two men even now saw eye to eye: on hunting, temperance, religion, slavery. Vachel Lindsay, the Illinois poet, sensing this truth, commemorated it in a poem on Graham. The closing line, "And Lincoln found the schoolhouse in the spring," is true except that the find came in the autumn.

Graham solicited for a spring term, having to accept promises of tuition after harvest with "potluck" hunting until then. When a little meat and butter and whiskey came in, he traded the whiskey for sugar and coffee and a bright new calico for Sarah—a new dress might help some. So school went on again, and Graham braced himself to give strict attention to business within eyeshot of the spot where his first wee manchild lay buried. He traded carpentering for fish that could be roasted in the iron pot without butter, if need be; and as soon as the meadows greened, he gathered lamb's-quarters, wild mustard, and sour dock on the way home from school. Sarah was up again, scolding Almira for laying the cutlery at a slant beside the plates, dusting the furniture daily, scalding and scrubbing the horrifying pots, jars, and crocks of Mentor's domestic labors. When she buttered Mentor's neck with goose grease for a sore throat, he "durst not take it off."

A temperance society, the White Templars, had now become a reality. Graham had been one of the first to take the oath and sign the pledge. The result was a fearful new blow. One evening he came in early to find Sarah going woodenly about her work, pale and weak. At first he hesitated to tell her; then he blurted it out in spite of himself: *the Baptist church had dropped him for signing the pledge*, and it might mean he could no longer teach in the meeting-house. Again Sarah was prostrated, and again the hectored husband struggled with pots and crying babies and chores and schoolwork.

Even intoxicated children were not uncommon at New Salem bees and harvest merrymakings; along with a loomhouse, almost every farmer had a stillhouse close to and to the rear of his dwelling. But, stubborn as Lang Willie of the Border, Graham did not revoke his pledge. He attended the secret meetings of the White Templars and set himself resolutely to bear his humiliation. These same Baptists had dropped his father for drinking. As a matter of fact, at the session which dropped Graham for temperance, another man was dropped for tipsying. At this, another member held up a full whiskey bottle and asked, "Just how much of the critter should a feller drink for good standing?"

After this, Graham was sometimes hooted down when he talked temperance and Henry Clay. Some folks wondered if that kind of man should be allowed to teach their children. Abe Lincoln, not far away now since his people had moved to Illinois, was also riling folks with his jackass talk on the same subjects. While Graham endured grief for his child, ridicule, and humiliation, Abe Lincoln, on the verge of striking out for himself, was dreaming of a place with no disgusting topers, a place where a fellow could find out all he wanted to know.

Late in April of this year one of the raftsmen on the Sangamon got his flatboat caught on the milldam, a great excitement for the villagers. It seemed as if the thing was bound to stay stuck, no matter what was done. The fellow who had been unlucky enough to jam his cargo-laden craft was wading around in the cold water, giving instruction to his helpers who were trying to dislodge the boat. Graham, hearing about it and going into town to look the situation over, saw that the young man was Abe Lincoln, the boy who used to "live clost" in Green County. Legend describes the Lincoln boy's brown checkered shirt, buckskin pants, and jeans jacket, though it fails to supply like details of the boy's kin, Johnson and Hanks, who were with him. All of them were just river hands then. Not an eye that fell upon them guessed what one of them would come to be.

Legend says that Graham showed Lincoln where he could borrow the auger of Onstot, the cooper, Graham's cousin, so that the water could finally be let out of the boat, after which it was reloaded and went on its journey downstream. Graham's hand, however, penned words to the contrary. The story has been told a thousand times and a thousand ways, but certain it is that Lincoln hung his flatboat on the Rutledge-Cameron milldam. The heart of the matter undoubtedly is that Lincoln, who, as he himself said, was then only a "piece of floating driftwood," remembered gratefully the little village that had helped him out of his difficulty, and so returned to it when his cargo had been duly delivered.

Rowdyism had now become a real threat to the New Salem community. The village had no whipping post, no jail. Bowling Green, the justice, lived on a farm out of town. It had gotten so that "Git, or I'll set the dogs on y' " no longer availed. Who couldn't "knock a dog out with knucks"? One heard the half-dead squawk of a gander, suspended head down from a low branch, as the young ruffians, riding along at a gallop, jerked but did not quite sever the bird's head. There were loud, cursing altercations; tipsy "wraslins"; and betting by a half-drunken gang on Saturday afternoon races. And only five citizens to combat this trend. Five "fine gentlemen who did not cuss, tipsy, smoke, or chaw terbacker ": Berry, the preacher; Graham, the teacher; Rutledge, the tavern-keeper; Bowling Green, the justice; and Dr. Allen, the temperance worker.

Dr. Allen converted his pay-corn into whiskey and shipped it to St. Louis, where it brought cash; and meanwhile he doggedly pros-ecuted his Sabbath school and talked temperance at bedside, at his office, and at the newly organized Debating Society. But still the farm boys—yes, and their sires—outstayed the firefly, outhollered the katydid, and got lost in the woods, sitting backward upon their steeds, near Sunday sunup.

These Saturday celebrators hailed young Lincoln when he came moseying into town one hot July afternoon, back from his trip to New Orleans. He drifted about the town for days, waiting upon the arrival of goods for the store which his boss, Denton Offutt, intend-ed to open here. Wrestling, pitching horseshoes with the mill gang, shooting marbles with the village small fry, he varied his program by lounging on the wooded banks of the Sangamon, backwoods style. Here he elicited much yah-yahing and prodigious leg-slap-ping with his backwoods yarns, which he told rather better than most. A slat of a river hand who was boarding at Cameron's, he fitted familiarly into the mill gang: he talked its language.

Election day rolled around, and he moseyed into Hill's store for a change of entertainment and looked around. Here we can turn over what happened to the telling of Mentor Graham himself, who that day was clerk of the election. He recounted the story of Lin-coln's first public office to Herndon, in 1865, who intended to write Lincoln's biography:

In the month of August, 1831 we were deficient a clerk for the polls. Mr. Lin-coln was about the sheets, looking at them, and was asked if he could write. He said, "Yes, a little." [Others say he said "I can make a few hentracks."]

"Will you act as clerk of the election today?"

"I will try to do my best, if you so request." [Others say Lincoln answered, "I can try it."]

He was then sworn in and acted as clerk of the August election. There were 49 candidates, it being a general state election. He performed his duties with much fairness, honesty and dependability. I clerked with him the same day and at the same polls. This was the first public act of his life. [See Appendix, p. 250, Graham's letter to Herndon.]

Graham, studying the stripling, noting his clear handwriting, and feeling him out on Henry Clay and slavery and temperance, recognized the young man's mental hunger and decided to try to satisfy it. "Drop in to see me, Lincoln, whenever you feel like it. Drop in to school down at the church when you're not busy," he told him. They were historic words.

He invited Lincoln out to meet Billy Greene, his cousin, and asked them to supper. Sarah, waiting in the doorway for their response, called Almira to lay two more plates. That evening Mentor Graham and the Lincoln boy had a long talk over the drop-leaf table after the supper dishes had been cleared off by Almira.

Graham told of this first talk so often it has been fairly well preserved. The theme was New Salem itself. Graham had taken such a great liking to his guest that he determined to keep an eye on him, if possible; and he talked up New Salem and her future warmly and long. Lincoln said that he thought he had right smart chance of a shake with Offutt and that he aimed to stay on and storekeep, and Graham sighed with relief. He drew the youth out, learned what education he had had, and, that first night, elicited from him a statement of his ambition to be a public man.

Sarah joined in the talk, after they had finished about Henry Clay and slavery; for then the subject ran to old times in Kentucky, how they had been neighbors; and all the preachings on Green River and Brush Creek and the Nolynn. Sarah warmed to this gangling fellow from home, and Lincoln certainly must have felt welcome. Graham's attitude toward his invited guest seems to have been preserved very much as he must have expressed it: When Lincoln came into our house that first time, he walked straight to my book shelves and straight into my heart.

There were now four liquor-dealers in New Salem, and many a blackleg gambler, keeping a sharp lookout for trouble in the shape of Squire Bowling Green meanwhile, took in any boasting loudmouth with his skill and made what he called a "tolerable deal of a winning." Many a rural gallinipper hove in, a "dominacker" rooster under his arm to put up to fight for drinks. Offutt's new store, which young Lincoln helped to raise, was near enough to Clary's grocery for the boy to get a good idea of the brawls, checkers for drinks, eye-gougings, and fist fights that went on there. Sometimes the whiskey barrel was lugged outside, with the bets growing larger and larger when some itinerant hoss-racer brought his raw-boned nags to race and tied them around the brow of the hill until he got

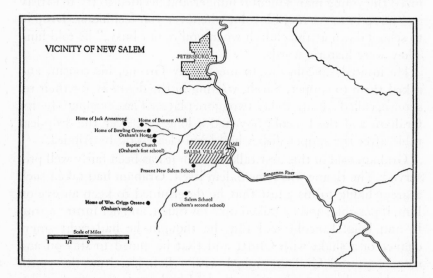

things started. Sometimes it was the groggery-keeper who, being accused of "scruppling measure," went up the holler a piece to settle the matter in a wrestling bout with his dissatisfied customer.

Meanwhile, down the street a Debating Society had been born, its roster including James Rutledge, Sr., and his son, James; Rev. John Berry and his son, William; Squire Bowling Green and Harvey Ross, the mail-carrier; Mentor Graham and his two cousins, William G. and L. M. Greene. When Graham invited Lincoln in, he came, paid rapt attention, and asked to join. Each week they met for debate, sometimes in the tavern, sometimes at the church house. Still the grocery-keepers drew the largest "crouge" (crowd).

Cartwright, with his expansive smile and collar and his thunderous maledictions, didn't happen into town so frequently; and Graham often went to "set a spell," as Sarah said, at Hill's, where his *Liberator*, subscribed for out of Boston, went the rounds among those who could read. The Hard-Shell Baptists saw to it that there were abundant cabin preachings as well as services at the church; they fought bravely against this rising tide of societies—two, now: temperance and debating. But their efforts could not keep the debaters' subjects from being known to everybody in town, and the little village buzzed with lively discussion, not about the church but about the societies' themes: slavery, temperance, water transportation. Against this alien thought, sermons lengthened. Worshipers bringing their long-handled warming pans to meeting, passing them round to each member of the family in turn, sat through half-day dissertations. Yet the congregations finally got to talking steamboats, too, after meeting, or even that New Salem needed a whipping post—though they remained faithful to prodding the children during Sunday dinner to produce the text of the sermon verbatim

Mentor's sister Elizabeth and her husband, Herndon, arrived about this time and stayed with the Grahams until their own cabin was completed. They didn't like Illinois—it was "too onhealthy. A feller had all he could do to stay alive, what with so much snow and all." But they stayed, nevertheless, and visited for several weeks before they moved into their own home. Before the fire the men busied themselves making shoes and harness, sharpening tools, whittling ax-helves, spinning interminable yarns over "dominicker" games, while the women "scraped something together to fill stummicks." The children begged for cracklin's and ate them while they lallygagged around under the table, until at last the welcome call came, "You can come now, all, to a poor make-out."

XIII

GRAHAM'S MOST ADVANCED LEARNER

1832–33

*L*IKE OTHER "hands," Lincoln boarded. The length of time he is said to have boarded with this one and that totals twice the length of the life of New Salem. Certainly he was at John Cameron's, at Herndon's, and at Greene's. He could not have been very long with any of them, nor at the Rutledge Tavern,[1] for that was sold—late in 1832—to Alley, from whom Onstot rented it. He did a lot of visiting and lending a hand, which in those days could mean a week or two. And you stayed overnight as a matter of course if you had talked or worked until it began to storm. "Might as well. Take potluck for breakfast, Lincoln." And potluck would likely be corndodgers and honey and buttermilk.

Here is Graham's statement regarding the time Lincoln lived with him:

In the month of February, 1833, Mr. Lincoln came to live with me and continued with me about six months. It was here that he commenced the study of grammar with me. I was then teaching school. I taught him the rules of surveying. I do not think that Mr. Lincoln was anything of a mathemetician—especially so of geometry and trigonometry—before he came to my house and I think I may say that he was my scholar and I was his teacher.

Mr. Lincoln spoke to me one day and said, "I have a notion of studying grammar." I replied to him thus, "If you expect to be before the public in any capacity, I think it is the best thing you can do." He said to me, "If I had a grammar, I would commence now."

There was none in the village [besides Graham's own which was in constant use at the school], and I said to him, "I know of a grammar at Vance's, about six miles," which I thought he could get.

He was then at breakfast—ate—got up and went on foot to Vance's to get the book. He soon came back with it and said he had it. He then turned his inordinate and almost undivided attention to the subject of grammar. The book was Kirkham's grammar, an old volume which I suppose—so I have heard—is in the Rutledge family today.

During the spring, summer and fall he read law, studied and practiced surveying, and the grammar, and would recite to me in the evening. I have taught in my life four to six thousand pupils as a schoolmaster and no one has ever surpassed him in rapidly, quickly and well acquiring the rudiments and rules of English grammar. This, I repeat, was in the spring, summer and fall of 1833.

He was writing deeds, contracts and other papers for the people. His playful hours were pitching quoits, swimming, shooting, telling stories—anecdotes—and not infrequently, truth to say "sitting up to the fair girls of Illinois."

Before 1833, between intervals of work, Lincoln attended, altogether, about six weeks (according to Graham's written record) of Graham's day school at the Baptist church, where he recited with other advanced learners, young men and women, among whom were Graham's lovely young sister Nancy Ellen and the charming Ann Rutledge. Graham wrote of Miss Rutledge: "Her eyes were blue and very expressive and her hair was auburn—not flaxen— her face rather round—beautiful in outline . . . . she loved everybody and was beloved of everybody. . . . ."

When work kept Lincoln from school,[2] he managed to meet Graham at some fence corner convenient to both of them; and there, in the dusk, hurriedly the schoolmaster heard and corrected the recitation of his begrimed pupil. Graham, after testing the boy out to discover where his lacks were, was trying to make a clean, straight line of Lincoln's "spotty education. . . . . He knew many things well, but not their interrelation," Graham said of him at this time.

After Lincoln had been to school for a short time, he told the schoolmaster: "I believe I can go it alone. I can read and write and cipher a bit." Graham responded, kindly, "Yes, so you can, and better than most; but that is only the introduction to knowledge, only the keys." After that the pupil did not refer again to going it alone. He took Graham's homily to heart: "Best success is not for them who are good enough, or even better than most, but for them who are best."

Among the older learners' exercises at school was speaking— the students' own words or the words of some great mind. Mentor, deaf in one ear, would pretend he couldn't hear, didn't understand —"What's that? What's that you're saying? Didn't get it. Now; again; the *sense* of it!" Advanced learners were likely to understand what they were talking about. He didn't let up until they did. He could spend more time with school than in the past, for he felt less harried now since the school lands were being sold and real money was being paid to Illinois teachers—not much money, but *money*. According to Mary Graham Bradley, "He could afford to stay until dark helping full-grown men and women who were working on rudiments." New Salem was booming, the little room was crowded with children, and Graham's pay was in proportion.

In town there was the excitement of new settlers arriving and the rattle and roar of the mill, eating logs like stick candy. Hundreds of people attended the camp meetings and traded in town. Then—grandeur! The *Cincinnati Gazette* announced that the long-dreamed-of steamboat was to arrive at last. A cabin steamboat was scheduled to make a run as far as Springfield on the Sangamon. The *Sangamon Journal* archly advised prospective settlers to make the trip by boat and avoid the mud.

As the great occasion approached, the countryside went wild. Bogue's "Talisman"! You a-goin' to the Springfield celebration? And, say, how d' y' stand on Lincoln?" That fellow-townsman had capped the climax by announcing for the legislature—steamboat legislature, y' understand. Babble rose to uproar. If you couldn't get to Springfield by ox or horse, who couldn't walk only seventeen miles? The banks of the Sangamon boomed with speeches—hundreds of words to the bursting sentence. Squirrels skittered from flapping flags that had invaded their treetops, and knots of excited spectators sent up salvos of musket fire at every bend. Small fry took out in fighting the enthusiasm caught from their elders: "Y' cain't whup me, I betcha!"[3] Officious axmen armed with long-handled axes mashed down briar and underbrush and cut off any sapling that leaned too far over the sacred river, while gangs of chainmen yanked out the midstream "sawyers"—clearing a path for the steamboat that was coming. At noon the workers "took on wood" in the form of barbecued beef and pork, and whiskey, to keep up their own steam.

Springfield? Bless your heart! New Salem! *Stopped* there, the "Talisman" did, and took on lumber from the mill. And what's more, there was that slat of a river hand who'd got his raft caught on the dam, sittin' up there in the pilot-house, takin' her on into Springfield and gettin' *fifty dollars* for it! If New Salem pioneering had earned nothing else, it paid for itself a thousand times over in the glory of that moment when, with clamor of whistle, the "Talisman" rounded the bend and hove into sight above the dam.

How incomparably she eased over it with the sparkle of turning wheel and bore away over the snow-swollen Sangamon! She, subject of daily bulletins out of Cincinnati announcing her progress— she, the dream come true—swam through the March fairyland at the breath-taking speed of four miles an hour. Barefoot urchins climbed trees to watch her pass, then slid down and "run like hell" to repeat the thrill. So did their elders, for that matter.

Springfield throbbed as with an earthquake: salutes of cannon, speeches, fireworks, whiskey—everybody "hollerin' theirselves hoarse." One yarn has come down of a farm boy, delegated to stay home to keep up the fire and milk the cows, who thought to make up for thus being cheated by adults by telling the other children (who were too little to go) his funniest story. It was how Schoolmaster Graham had been talkin' and walkin' when of a sudden the puncheon come unketched at one end, swung up, and landed the teacher down under the floor as slick as molasses. And how the big scholars had had to squeeze and tussle a gittin' him back through up agin' by twistin' him through by his fancy vest. But the story got no applause, or even smiles. So the lad conceived the idea of their taking turns watching the fire and running the half-mile to the river and back, watchin' fer her and blowin' the cow horn if she was comin.' Thus, against orders, they all got to see her.

And she came back. But not with her former ease. She wheezed and she wallowed, she backed and blew her whistle and butted ahead again; but she stuck on the dam. No auger could solve that debacle. "Why in thunder dam a navigable river?" "*Permission* from the legislature." "To hell with the legislature! Tear the dam down!" "*Touch it if you dare!*"

Somebody suggests a solution—is it gentle Dr. Allen, limping up, or the candidate for legislature in the pilot-house, or silk-tile Graham with his faith in right words, or Bowling Green with his vested authority, or James Rutledge, with his sense of practical expediency? At any rate, both sides agree to remove enough of the dam to let her by and to rebuild the dam immediately. At last she is free and heads out.

As she hove out of sight around the bend, the dream vanished with her. Steamboats could come to New Salem only when the Sangamon was booming with snow-water, a few days in the spring. But chimneys were "smokestacks," ever after—a sort of memorial to what might have been.

Debating society, speaking at school, midnight grammar drill at
Graham's table, along with an inexorable redheaded friend to
starch the syntax and help round the period—by these means was
evolved the platform of the candidate for the legislature. It is not
the great enigma that it has been said to be, neither wonderful nor
inexplicable. Graham had weaned Lincoln somewhat from his Indiana lingo. He had set lessons in such a way that the young man
had had to "add tire to tire, and at it again," and the college-edu-
cated McNeil had given a few pointers. Lincoln and Graham had
worked the wording of the announcement over and over and with
McNeil had argued out every phrase until poor Sarah had packed
up the children and gone over to the Abells'. Graham said of the
platform's content: "He [Lincoln] read attentively the *Louisville
Journal*, the *Missouri Republican* and other papers. His text-book
was the *Journal*. He was a regular subscriber to it."

Just what the debating society debated may be pretty accurately imagined. An early meeting had argued the subject, "Fire or
Water?—Which is the best mode of eternal punishment?" The debaters, Graham and Lincoln, had occasioned a great deal of laughter, Lincoln spinning astounding arguments for fire which he had
chosen to defend because, as he said, he might as well begin to be
prepared for it. He won the debate. Their serious subjects doubtless followed pretty closely—or led—those discussed by Rock
Creek debaters under the leadership of Thomas Nance (who had
been a scholar at Nat Owens' Brush Creek Academy along with
Graham). Both of them very likely got their notions of debate
subjects and debating from tutor McElroy. The record of Rock
Creek Lyceum shows they debated such things as "Are pioneers
entitled to a pension?" "Should United States forgive France's in-
demnity or compel her to pay by force of arms?" "If Negroes
should be freed, should they be educated here or colonized elsewhere?"[4]

The backwoods debating society was tackling vital questions
these days. The cantankerous schoolmaster, Mentor Graham; the
affable jokesmith, Abe Lincoln; the damned Yankee, Dr. Allen;
the teetotaler, John Berry, were no longer pooh-poohed when they
talked of Henry Clay, running for the legislature, sober days and
nights, and responsibility to God. The temperance society reported
only a fourth as much liquor sold this year as in the preceding one.

If Lincoln burned out many a candle, there was good reason for it. Many sawyers and leaning saplings were to choke that stream down which he would be asked to pilot humanity's great ship of the spirit.

Meanwhile, handbills proclaiming the Black Hawk War interrupted both awkward and graceful young folks dancing to

> I won't have none of your weevily wheat,
> I won't have none of your barley:
> I must have the best of wheat
> To make a cake for Charley,—
> > *Then*
> Come ye hither and trip together
> For it's true I love you dearly,
> Heart and hand we true shall stand
> All in the morning early,—
> > *For it's*
> Left hand round your weevily wheat,
> And it's both hands round your weevily wheat,
> Come down this way with your weevily wheat,—
> IT'S swing O swing your weevily wheat!

Farm youths hustled into town. Lincoln and Billy Greene, who had been running Offutt's store, were free to go for the very good reason that the store failed—whether because its owner was lax, because his clerks put too much "on tick," or because they chatted too much instead of tending to business. Mentor's sister Rachel (who had married a Goldsby and moved to Tennessee) arrived—a widow with a little girl—at the Grahams'; so Lincoln decided it was a good time to be moseying on out of New Salem. He would go to war with Billy. People pointed out Rachel as the woman who had "read the Bible clear through seventeen times."

By mid-July he and the boys were all back—much ado about nothing. They had left, singing "Arouse, ye bold Kentucky boys, foremost in the fight"; but the Black Hawk War was only the weakened Indians' last stand for food. Captain Lincoln, again living with the Grahams and now out stumping for his hoped-for election against Peter Cartwright, spoke when and where he could get the chance. If his awkward pose smacked of the comic when he told his listeners what he believed at the pig and cattle auction at Pappsville, it was because the novice *was* a bit unsure. But his ship was launched, and back in the brick house was its living compass that would help point a clearer course if this one proved miscalculated—a compass never too weary to swing to the North Star. And Lincoln had faith in his guide. He followed as earnestly where Graham led in lessons of statesmanship as he had followed the schoolmaster's "set copy" in penmanship during those weeks at the church-house school. The chirography of their signatures was so similar that they might have been written by the same person.

But Cartwright boomed his way to victory. There were ways— when you were "lining" a hymn such as "Methodist, Methodist, Methodist, /Methodist till I die," or "Whip the Devil round the stump, /And hit him a crack at every jump," you could bring in a fervently groaned comment on infidels who joked about eternal hell-fire punishment. It is easy to see how a man as near as Lincoln was to Cartwright's camp meetings, but who did not attend them, would be forked over the brimstone pit in Cartwright's campaigning sermons.

Certain it is that Lincoln and Graham spent many a close hour examining the religion of the times. It was neither logical nor worthy of God, they agreed. Graham refused to forsake his boyhood conception of a forever good, forever merciful God. How easily—having traveled the doubt-road himself—could he show another in doubt, as Lincoln was, why he came to the conclusions he reached. Yet idle gossip was to perpetuate the "Fire or water?" debate, almost to Lincoln's undoing. In years to come what Lincoln said about camp meetings lived to invest him with the character of an infidel, until his old friend, then seventy-four, rose up to vindicate him.

Lincoln, now a storekeeper along with Preacher Berry's son, went ahead with his meditative study of law and letters, bank discount, poetry, and the Bible. Graham continued to be his guide.[5] Among his new acquaintances was John F. Stuart, a lawyer he had met while away at war. When Lincoln had returned to the brick house with talk of reading law in earnest, the schoolmaster had hunted out his old *Kentucky Laws* and his new Illinois volume and put them into the hands of his friend. Law was something, Graham told Lincoln, of which he himself knew the merest rudiments; a subject in which an advanced learner would have to go it alone, unless Squire Green could tutor him. Though Abe Lincoln hurried to read the challenging pages, he rarely did it alone. Green helped him through harder spots, together with Stuart, the new friend.

Lincoln attacked the study of law with great zest. Graham lent him a form-book, since knowing how to make out legal papers was a first step, and turned over his patrons to Lincoln. Graham had always made out papers as an act of neighborliness, free of charge. Lincoln did the same.

Graham sent his scholar to the Rogerses, a family with four sons who had attended Cooperstown College in New York, both to borrow college textbooks and to obtain mental stimulation. The books borrowed and the great talk with the young men over, Lincoln often walked back to New Salem, reading aloud what he had borrowed. The schoolmaster said of him at this time: "He was so studious he somewhat injured his health and constitution. In New Salem he devoted most of his time to the Scriptures, and books on science and to the aquisition of knowledge of men and things." These were the days when Lincoln walked always with a book in his hand, reading; or meditating, a finger between the pages. Graham doubtless told Lincoln what he told his later students: "Read aloud when you are alone. Put the book away. Write out your own statement of what you have read. Did you get all of it? Look and see." He was so intent on *complete understanding* that his usually steady voice would quiver with earnestness. Not a loud voice, never sarcastic or ridiculing, but one tense with the necessity of obliging the young mind to test itself for full comprehension. Out of the schoolroom, he was retiring, extremely and conventionally polite, shy to a fault. But in teaching he was completely self-forgetful.

As another election occurred, there was another dollar apiece for clerking for a lean, rather well-spoken young man and his ever urging, scowling friend—a rather distinguished-looking friend, even if a little shabby as to long tails, fancy vest, and stovepipe hat and very rough and calloused as to hands—a friend whose sharp blue eyes, from under bristling red eyebrows, searched the world for answers to the unanswerable.

Among the names of new voters this year was that of Graham's father, Jeremiah, who with his wife and their last unmarried child, Nancy Ellen, had come north to make his home with his eldest son and dicker in land. There is record of his buying at least one hun-

dred and twenty acres a few years later, in 1836. Their coming
was a godsend to Sarah, for Mary still was, and remained to the
end of her days, "turrible work-brittle." Graham added two
rooms to the brick house, which was beginning to serve as a gathering center for the clan and from this time on was the scene of almost constant visits by relatives from as far away as Tennessee
and California. Sarah, envied woman, placed upon her mantle in
the best room a pair of lipped vases of fluted glass, the gift of
Robert from Crab Orchard, sent on by Jeremiah and Mary. Again
Lincoln said he'd better be moseying on. But no, he could stay.
Plenty of room. They'd never used the attic.

Graham opened his fall term, hailing the children in from play
with the identical cowbell he had used on Brush Creek. History,
referring to the schoolmaster during this year, invariably calls
him "the old schoolmaster." He was but thirty-two, only nine
years Lincoln's senior. His thick mop of upstanding hair did not
begin to whiten until after the Civil War, three decades later.
Now, proud of his advanced learners, most of whom he tutored at
his home, he came down on them harder than ever. Among other
tasks, they were mounting dooryard stumps and delivering their
own speeches. Graham, severe, unbending, mimicked their idio-
syncrasies. He flung out his arms erratically at the least emphatic
words. He jammed a self-conscious hand into a pocket, he rammed
an aimless one through his hair. He held on for dear life to an
imaginary lectern. It was funny enough to double a learner with
laughter, but nobody smiled. His speakers were first warmed up
by repeating some such line as "Ruthless waste makes woeful
want." If one of them had said "*Ruth* less waste makes *woe* ful
want," Graham pierced his incomprehension with some such utterance as "There's a *t* at the end of the word 'want,' young man!
Stress that long *o* in 'woeful'! Get the *sense!* Get the SENSE!"

Mornings, after he had distinctly enunciated and articulated
the rules of the school in a final and warning voice, his advanced
learners read excerpts from the Bible. Every one of them could
make and mend quill pens and write a regular hand. All were "fair
to first-rate at putting their own ideas into words." Professionally,
Graham was never happier. School lands sold regularly, and he
buoyed himself with the satisfaction of money in his pocket; but
more, with the hope that soon, now, every child in Illinois would

surely have a chance. "Two percent of the net proceeds of the sale of the sixteenth section in each township"—how often he had re-read the school-land law!

Because of his storekeeping, Lincoln, when no longer able to make it out to school, slipped in sometimes for the last spelldown on Friday afternoon, or a dip after school into that delectable subject of grammar—along with Ann Rutledge. She was being privately tutored in grammar this year after school, brushing up preparatory to entering Jacksonville Female College another year.

But Berry and Lincoln, storekeepers, were going to have to follow Offutt and sell out, it seemed, for Hill's competition was too strong. Hill's partner, McNamar, had sold out to him and had acquired the Cameron and the Rutledge farms near town. McNamar was the man, everybody knew, who was pledged to marry Ann Rutledge as soon as he returned from a trip east to bring his parents out. Gossip was ceaseless: McNamar was not his real name; no wonder he never voted, even with the polls right under his nose in Hill's store. And everyone knew who received letters at the post-office: "He's quit writing to Ann—the blackguard!" When her fellow-student in grammar said, "I'll try to find him for you, Ann," the girl answered: "If he doesn't care enough to write to me, I'm sure I don't care enough to try to find him." For a logically minded young man like Abe Lincoln there was only one course—already long-denied—to take. He took it.

Now that her father had lost the tavern and the family were ignominiously renting from this very McNamar (or was it Mc-Neil?), Ann was "working out" for Mrs. Short, saving her earnings for Jacksonville. Ardently Abe Lincoln beaued her about and thus gave the gossips a new topic. They say that there was a second very fancy vest in New Salem in those days, and that it was "dotted with little bunches of flowers." Graham, confided in about this affair of the heart as about affairs of the pocketbook, mind, and soul, was as pleased as Puck. "An *ideal* match!"—shuffling his cuffs with nervous joy—"*Both* of you like books!" Legend says the young couple were betrothed on July 4, 1833, after the village celebration of Independence. In 1865 Graham wrote: "Lincoln and she were engaged. Lincoln told me so. She intimated to me the same."

Graham himself had suffered from town talk earlier in the year when his sister, Mrs. James R. Herndon, had been accidentally shot and killed by her husband while he was cleaning his gun. He had been humilitated by the gossip, which suggested that Herndon had "done it a-purpose; he wasn't cleaning no gun." Lincoln, who had been working for Herndon at the time, now found employment with the father of his friend Billy Greene, on the farm next to Graham's. Billy was Mentor's first cousin.

In fact, had you subtracted all of Graham's kin from New Salem —the Abells, Elmores, Onstots, Potters, Goldsbys, Herndons, Raffertys, and Greenes—you would have halved the town. The community of New Salem, before the mill was built, was nothing more or less than a Graham plantation. Nathaniel Owens owned land adjoining Bowling Green's and eighty acres near Mentor's farm. Johnson Graham filed on an acreage adjoining the townsite. Sarah's brother John had filed on a forty cornering theirs but had returned to Kentucky. Now he was back, living on his land, and Sarah was conniving to get others of her family to come north too.

XIV

MIDNIGHT SESSIONS

1833–34

*N*OW THAT clearing was nearly finished, farmers like Graham had more time. His land, unlike most, had needed little axwork, since it lay largely on the prairie; but he had spent many months building the brick house and fitting it with cabinet-true woodwork of black walnut. The town now rang with heated discussion and argument, where once it had been noisy with drunken brawls. Under the temperance pressure Clary had pulled up stakes and gone to Texas. Lukens and Warburton, also bested by the temperance society, in a besotted bet settled on the name Petersburg and founded a new town to suit themselves.

Petersburg was two and a half miles away, and there you could drink yourself to death if you wanted to and nobody could interfere. There would be no pussy, officious Bowling Green to haul you to Springfield to jail, after trying you in a kangaroo court for riding out on Sunday. If it took two days to go to the mill, whose business was it? Certainly you would not need to go to church. Sunday could be a gala day for netting quail, trapping prairie chicken, hunting foxes, drinking, racing, gambling, wrestling, laying and collecting bets on personal skills—and just plain fighting.

While the village men talked, the women worked harder than ever, though the men helped them get the needed quilt out of the quilting frame or helped tie the much-needed comfort. Graham lent a hand in a pinch, and Lincoln is said to have drawn a new design for a quilt block. But to the women's eternal spinning and weaving were now added rag-carpet weaving and stitching of more and fancier dresses. The old daily routine of three square meals, of pots and crocks and kettles of heavy milk, the Sabbath feast, the butter churning, the "puttin' up" for winter—all this must be accomplished, along with bearing a baby each year, and spanking and petting and trying to keep clean a houseful of growing children. Many of Sarah's wants and wishes were disregarded in the process; her tongue sharpened, but she held the pace.

Graham's students, Billy Greene and Abe Lincoln, who'd "had an awful hankerin', one for t'other," from the first, clerked the November election. They were constantly together and let scarcely a day pass without presenting themselves at Graham's house to ask a volley of questions and to borrow books. Generously Graham lent them his hard-won, dearest treasures, suggesting in what succession they read the books. They got what they could from them, marked the tough spots with "tail ends of carpet warp." String by string, Graham attacked these pages with them, asking the young men to read them aloud. He stopped them at every word they stumbled over until they "fairly comprehended" what was meant and could pronounce the word "properly and with certainty." After that he read it to them, his nervous smile flickering if their faces lighted with comprehension. Who has ever found a better method? And, if Dr. Allen sat listening, what young mind would not do its best? A mutually cordial companionship sprang up between the young man with hazel eyes, dim with spiritual longing, and the slightly older man with sharply electric eyes, incandescent with a sense of power descended during a snowy January ride through the timber up from Jacksonville—a man who thrilled to questions with the full seriousness of responsibility for true answers which great teachers of all times and places have felt.

There were always the two of them, then, with Billy Greene making a third sometimes, and Dr. Allen, a fourth if he happened to have a call out that way. Mentor sat at Abe's right to favor his good ear. After books came talk, talk, talk. During the day Abe had stayed with the tantalizing page until he had mastered it. He sat, elbows on the gate-leg table, his lean legs disposed of somehow beneath it, his mop of black hair close to Mentor's red one, his eyes fixed on Mentor's face. The smaller man, burning from top to toe with the intensity of the quest, puckered his shaggy brows in the effort of thought, every muscle of his face taut with the necessity of giving complete expression to that answer.

Sarah lay in the next room, fatigued from pots and kettles and crying children and never resting hands and feet. Long ago she had deafened herself to this everlasting talk, talk, talk. She was used to it now—but souring under it. Sarah was having another child, and she had become a nagger. Now that Abe had come to live with them—"Might as well, here all the time anyway"—there was more talk than ever. Still Sarah was fond of the sad-eyed young man who took the baby from her when the food was about to burn; who kept the woodpile higher than it had ever been before and never let the wood box get empty; who told the children stories to hush their crying; who took the heavy tub or bucket from her and carried it for her, and never had to be told to empty the wash water.

Only when there was nothing more that Sarah could think up that ought to be done would Abe sit down and "eat books up whole." His help was welcome to a woman with a baby about to be born; but such a woman also needed sleep. Yet, night after night the two men sat in the next room, talking, kinfast by the love of learning, unconscious of the flight of time. Though their voices were low enough most of the time, the excited flare-up would rouse Sarah from sleep. "If you two goin' to sit up all night, seems like a body oughtn't have to remind you to mend the fire!" .... Hasty and apologetic scraping of feet being unwound; the door opened, shut, as Lincoln went out. And pretty soon the door opened, shut, as he came back with wood..... The log thrown on..... Someone poking the fire. "Now, don't go poking ashes all over the floor!" And Sarah, dozing off to the snap and crackle of the fire, would soon be wakened again by another volley of voices. .... "You two *ever* goin' to bed?" Until finally, from sheer exhaustion, she got up and snuffed out their candle.

Graham's own insatiable thirst to learn, his agony of "sparing" for his beloved books, his need to choose warily to get the most for the small sum he could spend, had produced a remarkably complete library by the year 1833. Originals and translations of Greek and Latin classics he had, at which Abe took an intermittent pull. Histories of America, Europe, the Orient, and the ancients the young man devoured. Poetry and biography he read by spells. He sat upon the low and narrow splint-bottom chair in complete discomfort, never realizing how cramped he was until, after hours of total concentration, he groaned as he unwound his numbed body and tried to stand erect. When Graham came in, or while the two were doing the chores, he asked questions on what he had read. Graham always tried to cast further weight of evidence, from what Lincoln reported reading, to prove his thesis that *convincingly worded thought conditions the progress of the human race.* Little by little he daily urged this idea upon Lincoln as well as upon the other advanced students. Men who could master these two things —constructive thought and convincing expression of it—could be public men, men with the opportunity—no, the *responsibility*— of altering evil and forwarding life. Public men should be able to speak from a depth of conviction, just as surely as eloquently.

Sarah's nerves might well be fraying to the point of collapse in the next room, forgotten by learner and master. Ten, twenty, forty times over—the *same* sentence! Trying it out for inflection, forty ways. There, there, *that. That* gives the best sense and the sense best! Then *that* way ten, twenty, forty times. It was enough to sharpen the tongue of a maternity-worn woman. Now the maddening regularity of a voice conjugating, "If I should be, if you should be, if he should be. . . . ." Somebody poking the fire—"Don't stir it from the *top!*" If Sarah's frenzy woke the children, it was she who scolded them back to sleep again and got up to diaper the baby, give the windlass a turn or two to tighten the bed's rope slats, plump up the bedtick of prairie hay and the featherbed of wild-goose down.

Next morning she sent a stinging "Threadbare clothes, but buyin' books, *books*, BOOKS!" after Mentor's retreating footsteps as he hurried off to school. His fine coat was frayed, his brave silk tile mangy. Sarah, who starched and scoured and laid the knife just so beside the plate, couldn't abide the likes. Nevertheless, Graham, stubborn as Lang Willie, put his foot down: no board money from Abe. Yes, he could use the *new* books. The inescapable teacher in Mentor Graham, having sounded a never-before-reached depth in a student, kept tenaciously to his duty. A fellow who could ask such questions—what were an old hat and a frayed coat and Sarah's bitter comments, compared to that? He had, at last, found a spiritual partner, a young man whom he would help to rise, get on. For this he must have him under his jealous eye, making sure that he did not waste time learning amiss what he would have to unlearn. He was taking the kinks out of Lincoln's back-

SARAH GRAHAM

woods drawl and backhanded wording of ideas, setting him to read Plato in translation. Secretly he knew that Sarah would never be really cross with Abe: he could take Abe's share, and willingly.

Sarah, her black hair all but unmanageable in its luxuriance, was tall, lithe, twenty-eight, the mother of seven children, four living, three dead. Duties had lightened somewhat after Jeremiah and Mary's arrival, for then Sarah was released from some of her exacting household drudgery to go to apple-butter makings and quiltings, where she was always doubly welcome for her nimble fingers and her nimble wit. Here that wit blossomed without bitterness, and she kept folks laughing with her keenly observant comment, though at home she steadfastly frowned upon any such "di-do-ing" by any of her household—including its head. Joking at the Graham home was insipid, and a most infrequent pastime at that. Sarah Graham, so they tell, could cut out the most intricate quilt pattern after looking once at a model, could knock together the tastiest kind of a meal out of next to nothing and in no time; her children were neat as a pin and she herself "considerably dressy." She contented herself with pouring her vituperations upon her husband, whose natural nervousness did not grow less under them.

In those dramatic short pauses when Graham and Lincoln rested from cribbing corn, salting down pork, or sawing wood, they talked, eye on eye. When Graham's parents arrived and had to be considered, the two friends walked oftener to the woods; the old folks must needs be given their rightful honor of being heard. If one of them took the floor before Abe and Mentor had "finished gabbin'," the men would strike off through the back yard for the timber, where they talked as loud and long as they chose.

Old *Kirkham's* was proving a hard nut for Lincoln to crack, and it grew harder as he and Ann advanced through its pages. Ann's father had ordered a book for her from St. Louis, but it was slow in coming. Anyway, for lovers, one book is better than two. Graham directed them to the gigantic task of parsing every word in Paine's *Age of Reason*. Paine was the man who had "upset" Graham the year they came north, when the teacher was just slightly older than Lincoln now was. But Graham had bested it and thus had his own sly way of dryly poking fun at Paine's logic between the parsings. A good teacher toughens his learner's mind by waking up his logic.

Graham never forgot to supply the advice—gently, kindly—about the niceties of bodily posture while speaking, of the disposal of hands and feet with ease and propriety—accomplishments his most advanced learner lacked. Paine often drew forth a written speech from Lincoln, which had to be delivered, criticized, rewritten, and criticized again. The parsing of Paine's language having been completed as a lesson, they next parsed Paine's logic as a pastime. Many years after New Salem had vanished, a repairman found an iron wedge beneath the floor of the room where Lincoln slept while at the Grahams'; it was amateurishly engraved "A.L." With that, doubtless, Lincoln split wood for the three Graham fireplaces. In exchange, Graham's sharp spirit-wedge, driving deep into the philosophy of human existence, liberated, through Lincoln, a power that warmed a world.

Lincoln might bring in as many as half-a-dozen books at a time from as many lenders. Graham poked into any that were unfamiliar to him, or the two of them took the mental impact together, stopping for comment: "He's levelheaded" here, or "He's off his base" there, as they took turns reading aloud.

It is a wonder that Lincoln, with a mind as retentive as his, forgot to include all this when, years later, he was importuned for the facts of his life. Actually, the man went to college and earned a high degree in the unflinching course of study provided by his guide and teacher—one who had been "called" in the woods one January night to lift life as high as his nervous, freckled hands could lift.

The two men grew closer through their mental wrestlings. Graham helped word a petition for the village women who thus succeeded in ousting Hill as postmaster and replacing him with Lincoln.[1] Woman's rights was one of the friends' favorite themes of talk; no reason why a woman shouldn't have her share.

Sober Lincoln and tipsy Berry hadn't "gee-hawed" any too well together in their store. Their business had not even picked up when the store of Radford, another merchant, had been raided by drunken rowdies so that he had to sell out to Billy Greene, who, in turn, sold the good stock to Lincoln and Berry. Berry nagged con-

MENTOR GRAHAM'S MOST ADVANCED LEARNER

Courtesy STEFAN LORANT: *Lincoln, His Life in Photographs*

tinually: "Got to sell liquor, Lincoln, *Got* to!" Finally—who knows how?—a license for a tavern was drawn up for the two; and, among other things in the way of horse lodging and care, permission was given to sell peach and apple brandy, Holland and domestic gin, wine, rum, and whiskey. The partnership dissolved immediately, and Lincoln had much time on his hands.

More often these days, he found his way to school, where there now were a good many Dillworth's *Spellers*. Like Kirkham's *Grammar*, this title was a complete misnomer. In addition to its nine thousand spelling words, it presented fables, prayers for special occasions, preachments on industry, truth, piety, thrift, and many lesser virtues—all to be spelled through. With the utmost disdain Graham required each scholar to mark out the exasperating errors of Mr. Dillworth, for that author remarked blandly that "point," though pronounced like "pint," had a different meaning. "Are" is pronounced like "air," the book asserted in another place. Well, it would not be so long until Illinois schools would have new textbooks to use in big new schoolhouses that would not be overcrowded; and the teacher would not have to hear the least ones first and send them home, in order that the ones who stayed all day could sit down to write.

Legend has it that, upon one occasion at least, Lincoln pointed out a grammatical error in the speech of the schoolmaster. If that is true, it must have pleased Graham. A real teacher's proudest day is the day when his brightest pupil steps ahead of him.

By now the squawk of the gander before some twisting fist yanked its head off, the betting and brawling, the rooster-crowing down at the cockpit, the devil-take-the-hindmost pranks, were gone. A quarry was yielding fine stone for chimneys within a few feet of Clary's old stand. Someone dug into a vein of coal. Jacob Bale was the bustling miller now, with more grist than he could grind. Hill was building a carding machine. The village street rang with the clamor of blacksmith and cooper, cobbler and sawyer; and the odor of tanning leather came strong when the wind was in the east. In candle-lighted cabins the spinning wheel droned and the rag-carpet loom thumped far into the night, while at tavern or church earnest men still debated liquor and woman's rights, slavery and river transportation. Barrels, buckets, firkins, spinning wheels, hats, shoes, coal, stone, lime, flour, meal, carded wool, fish, and garden truck were the products of the industry of the little town of New Salem, which numbered less than a hundred souls.

Another new road was opened, running into Petersburg, the likker town that Lukens and Warburton—both now dead from drink—had founded. Graham wrote the petition for it, and everybody signed it and so sealed their own doom. For down that very road would Petersburg, later the county seat, suck little New Salem, houses and all. And—one distant day—the people of Petersburg, understanding and reverent, would carry it all back again, log for log, window for window.

XV

GOD'S HIGHER PURPOSE

1834-35

*L*ATE IN 1834, believing the time ripe, Graham purchased the forty acres he held by squatter's rights and added three forties to it. He now had seven children; and the demands for food, clothing, and books were heavy. He put out corn, oats, and an orchard on the new land, working early and late. His hands were always harsh from ax helve and plow handle, brick trowel and wood saw.

For once in his life, work had him so up a stump that he could not snatch a moment for study or reading; but he looked forward to the coming of winter, when he could read the back numbers of *Genesis of Universal Emancipation*, which he had had to file away without reading, and to look into the new free-thought aspect of religion. When he went into the village he might listen for a moment to knots of arguers, but work drove him on. As for Cartwright, still prophesying a fiery end for Hill, from Hill's stoop, Graham wouldn't have been caught stopping to listen. He preferred to walk through the timber in company with the sheep and cattle grazing there. Even with the hogs, wallowing and rooting for acorns.

If the coat grew ever rustier and the hat ever a bit more shabby, books still had to be bought. As little as Sarah realized it, he could actually warm his numbed feet by glancing through a new book or reading its Preface, even when his stockings were soaked from snow water that had seeped through leaky shoes. If, day after day, Sarah had to fry side meat in the skillet, and then the corndodgers, and finally use the grease to season the hominy, he was really well filled with her "Shakespeare feast." When she had to grind dried pumpkin to make flour for pumpkin bread because the cornmeal was out, Graham went through her mill, figuratively, with the pumpkin; but his enjoyment of the next chapter after the pump-kin-bread supper did not flag. Lincoln was no longer staying with them. He was working and staying where he worked; but he came by for lessons, eager to dip into the new book, too, before supper, or into the latest paper, after the supper of side meat and corn bread and molasses. And Sarah herself was often the first to finish the new book.

The old evening grind went on as usual. But now the most ad-vanced learner was writing out his own ideas on all sorts of subjects, Graham's recipe for making him more conscious of words and their choice. Hard, rough, calloused hands set a like kind to work upon the finest things in the universe. Plainly, this young man's ideas were above the average; but in spite of all those bouts with grammar he still slipped into his old twang when consumed with the effort of finding and pronouncing the right words to fit those ideas. So Graham assigned him to write them out and memorize them. The schoolmaster, walking to the woods with Lincoln in order to escape Sarah's blighting tongue, was overjoyed: his most advanced learner had become his dearest friend. He always said that he got more than he gave. Lincoln, laughing, had said they might "trade even." Lincoln did trade the news from papers Graham could no longer afford—the *Louisville Journal, Cincinnati Gazette, St. Louis Republic, Sangamon Journal,* and *Washington Globe*—for Graham's interpretation of that news and for tips as to gentle-manly social language and bearing. It is not strange that their lessons during their walks sometimes became intimate confidences. They never tired of ribbing the "Scare 'em through the pearly gates" religion to which Sarah held tenaciously, twitting them for their chats in the wood "with the Devil." They were unalterably "ferninst" it. Graham had seen to it that Lincoln had his bout with logic in textbook form and that he learned to talk in terms of "natural philosophy" (astronomy). With these two fields of knowledge they "knocked the blocks out from under" hallelujah-ing and camp-meeting service to God. All of the village knew this, though few guessed that both men longed for devoutly and be-lieved in a kind God.

On Saturdays and Thursdays postmastering took just enough time to wrap and weigh and make out waybills for the outgoing letters and to distribute the few that came in. In an honest town mail lay safely on the counter for hours while the postmaster finished a rail fence or a plowing job. Lincoln was surveying a little now, walking around town and out in the country to take letters to people, studying every minute he could, chinning with everybody he met. It was a good way to endear himself to the little community he called home. Graham now had no need to argue about going it alone with this "most diligent straightforward young man in the pursuit of knowledge." Walking and talking together, the two prosecuted rock-bottom assignments that could have applied on a doctorate. If Mentor Graham demanded a little less noise from the children when he sat puzzling, striving to wring the hopeful answer to human existence; if he reprimanded them harshly and scowled and relapsed into a brown study—afterward he was sure to rock the smallest ones longer than usual and deal out caresses and praise to the older ones. Ordinarily he let them have their noisy play, unchecked: he could walk. He could walk fast and nervously into the woods, hide his eyes in his hands, and struggle there alone.

In February of the new year, signers for the new road to Jacksonville included John and James Goldsby, from Green County, and two of Sarah's brothers, John and Richard. Graham, rejoicing, drew up the petition and signed it first with a flourish. Another step forward for those learners at the log church whose appetites for knowledge he kept whetted. The petition, with forty-three signers, was granted, and Lincoln got the job of surveying the road. But first he had to be put through a little more drill in figures.

A self-effacing man, Mentor Graham, whose delight in life lay not in making himself, but in trying to make his country, great; a man easily overlooked among the self-perpetuators who have always delayed the world; a man to be dismissed with a sentence by biographers of a national savior. Yet Robert Browne, writing of these years, began the restoration of this humble man to his rightful-place when he wrote: "Mr. Graham must have been a diligent student, a patient teacher and a kindly disposed man. Mr. Lincoln always respected him, saying of him: 'he had more information, better methods and knew better how to tell what he knew than any teacher I had met or studied with up to that time. He taught me about all I had to begin with in grammar. He told me where I could get a copy of Kirkham's *Grammar*, which I got very soon by walking out into the country for it six miles. I like the old book yet; but it was a puzzler at the start with its four, five and six-headed rules, about as complicated to beginners as the Longer Catechism and Thirty Articles were for young ministers.' " And Barton, sensing something deeper, added: "Graham helped Lincoln with literary composition and knew more of Abraham Lincoln's mind during this period than any other."

It was in this spring that Peter Cartwright was chairman of a meeting at Heredith's Mill declaring for James D. Henry, long-time sheriff of Sangamon County, for governor. At the same time, Squire Green, with A. Lincoln as his secretary, chairmaned a similar meeting which made the same declaration at New Salem. The new issue was railroading; and all New Salem attended the Springfield meeting in March, proposing a railroad in that part of the state. With a thousand people crowding in before the speaker's platform, things were on the move!

Dr. Allen wed a bride from Lexington whose silks and kids and laces became historic. Their new three-room cabin had a wide door between the living-room and the bedroom to accommodate the growing Sabbath school. Everybody was asked in to meet the bride, and nobody went home drunk or even tipsy. This household never cooked upon the Sabbath, and even the sick must wait a less holy day for attention, though some say that the doctor gave in enough to sit in church with his saddlebags at hand and went if a call came, giving his fee to the church.

If Graham soundly thrashed some of the grown young men who wandered into school this year just to devil the teacher, he had good cause. He is said, by descendants of the young men who were thrashed this year, to have been ever ready with the whip. But the others have tales of his patience. No child need fear a blow as long as he was trying, even if he did not succeed. He carried the tired little ones up the hill into town or helped them by the hand. Little children are slow to confide their hands to brutes. Most of the echoes coming back from these days are of Graham's indefatigable pursuit of lessons all day long and half the night, of his farming by starlight. Even with the impudent he was patient up to a certain point; then the hickory was laid on just as thoroughly as the master did everything else. Once was enough.

Talk in New Salem about steamboats, railroads, had quieted;

now it was: "Why not move the capital closer, bring it to Springfield?" Sangamon County's candidate for governor, James D. Henry, had died; but still little New Salem might get legislation to make it a big town if the capital were at Springfield—and Lincoln now, wasn't he about the right man to send up for that? Excitement ran almost as high as in the days of the "Talisman." With the capital at Springfield, there would be many travelers coming through New Salem. Even if the stage now did not start at all when the roads were too muddy, and in good weather rarely hit the schedule advertised—the fare then would be less, the passengers more numerous, and the schedule kept. Thus, among the candidates who announced in April in the *Sangamon Journal* was A. Lincoln, for the legislature.

Steamboats were given up. A second one had tried to make it up the Sangamon and had got stuck at Petersburg past ever moving again, and had been torn up to build houses. Railroads were problematical. But moving the capital could be done, just by voting. If the manner of expression, the somewhat stilted style of Mentor Graham, appeared in the New Salem candidate's speeches that summer, certainly the schoolmaster felt only a generous and just pride. He would lend his words—even his thoughts—just as willingly as he had lent books to this beloved, companionable, capable young man. Whether or not his own part was recognized or known did not matter, was not of importance. His object was to forward the world, not to glorify the self; to recognize and nurse ability, enforce strict training upon it: that was his, a teacher's, duty, and all the satisfaction, recognition, and eulogy he wanted, or expected.

Lincoln was now writing up legal papers, tussling with law between odd jobs, walking down the fragrant spring ways, reading aloud. The new postmaster was stopping to talk with fishermen at the dam, playing marbles with the village shavers in New Salem's one quiet little street, clerking for a dollar at election, buying a few books but borrowing most of what he read, visiting men and women in lonely cabins, feeling them out about railroads, canals, moving the capital. He was formulating, first aloud and later in writing, the ideas that came to him through these experiences.

In midsummer the countryside went circus crazy as the news

spread that a circus was coming to Springfield. Young and old gathered wild berries feverishly, sold them at a few cents a gallon, saving up for the circus. Men forewent likker and chawin' terbacker in the same urgent cause. Lincoln attended, but not the Grahams—it cost too much. But they heard about it afterward. Lincoln told the story from start to finish while he played marbles with the Graham boys.

In 1835 Graham's children were Almira, Minerva, Elizabeth, Nancy, William, and Mary. Septimus, Benjamin, Bennett, Sandy, and Harry Lincoln were born later. Graham's sister, Nancy, in her early teens, was one of the family, as was James, a small boy whose parents were dead, a relative whom the Grahams had undertaken to raise. Mentor worked harder than ever.

The Female Seminary opened at Jacksonville, but Ann did not get to go, although her brother David went to Illinois College. Ann and Abe were hoarding what little money-wages for work they managed to obtain. Abe did a lot of walking in the woods with Ann, a lot of walking in the woods with Graham. With summer and electioneering came the usual camp meetings, a real opportunity— for a man who had made thousands fall in Kentucky—to make an example again of a certain gaunt young man who still had not been attracted by brimstone sessions. While the camp meeting waxed fervent, the calm Baptists gathered on the banks of the Sangamon below the dam to immerse their converts. Graham, of course, could look on only from a distance, and Lincoln always chose to stand and look on with him while Sarah and Mary, with great ceremony, prodded the children on down the slope to seats with the elect, near the water's edge, and "never let on" that they saw Mentor. As bank-top spectators of immersions, it is quite likely that they laughed at the antics of the village rogues, baptizing logs and dogs a little farther downstream.

There were crowds at these baptizings, for new settlers still came on, every man of them scheming to buy or trade for more land, every woman patiently waiting for the promised better house she probably would never have. Bacon and eggs and sweet potatoes over and over, and a chance to smooth the shiny blue and pink calico at Hill's, a chance to see town bonnets and dripping converts—this was their only relaxation and release. Competition over the contents of their baskets was keen when at noon the women went to the wagons to bring the family's food. Picnicking, these lonely, mentally starved women got to talk a little with others, perhaps learn a new wrinkle in quilts, baby-tending, healing sores, and "sarviceberry" sauce. A pretty considerable Sabbath it must have been.

No hint of politics ever crept in at Baptist summer sermons and immersions. But Peter Cartwright, riding in a one-hundred-mile circuit across Illinois, up to Rock River and down to Galesburg, took off his big white beaver hat, banged the tuning fork against a hickory, and led off solemnly with

> On Jordan's stormy banks I stand
> And cast a wistful eye
> To Canaan's fair and happy land
> Where my possessions lie.

After the hymn he told his congregations finally and weightily that infidels had no place in the lawmaking bodies of a land, and nobody saw anything "out of whack" with preaching politics like that.

Lincoln held his peace about the foot-washing, Hard-Shell Baptists, for his good friend Billy Greene was one of them and Billy's mother was towel-woman. He knew Graham's position at home, and the two men exchanged comments privately. Graham, however, having been dropped from the church and never making any effort to be reinstated, spoke out flatly and publicly. Dropping folks from church, along with foot-washing and such unimportant things, had nothing to do with real religion, he said at every opportunity. As a child he had heard his Uncle Nat pronounce sentence on men and women for traveling on the Sabbath. Now that notion had been replaced by "the better the day the better the deed" conception. Religion—Graham said it at every chance, and he was not above making chances—went much deeper than such things.

New Salem had now passed her hard-time stage. The children's lunch baskets held white bread and plum jam, twisters (dough-nuts), apples, and hard-boiled duck eggs. Their clothing was woolen, and they wore rawhide shoes. With undiminished enthusiasm Graham continued to teach three terms a year. Painstakingly he adapted to each child the lessons he required of him; for Mentor Graham did not believe that all men are created equal in mental capacity. His aim was to feed each according to ability.

The hardest problems, the most demanding mental gymnastics, he portioned out to Lincoln, knowing that that young man had the capacity to master it. Sarah, listening to their eternal arguments, now began to top them off with her summary when they had "run down." If their theme had been women's rights, she would "run them both up a stump" with "Couldn't make any *more* mistakes than men do." If it was railroads: "Iron rails won't get stuck on the dam; but they could wash out with freshets, and an augur hole wouldn't make a train float on by."

Ann and Lincoln were studying grammar again, after their day's work was done. The two of them and the teacher sat at the gate-leg table or before the open fire, grammar their infatuating subject, until Graham dismissed them with "Well, I guess it's about time to sing the Doxology and go home"—early enough so that they could walk home without scandal. Even if a man who had gone to work and was going to marry couldn't go to college, there was no reason why the girl he was going to marry shouldn't go. Ann continued to prepare and hope for the Academy.

Many New Salem folk had jumpers (sleighs) that might be borrowed by an ingratiating young man or rented in exchange for a day's work. There was more than one long road down which young couples might jingle under the sharp stars of winter. If Ann and Abe went sleighing after their work and study were done, no record of it exists. But this once, forgetting musty courthouse records that will be dust some day, may we fancy they did? Graham owned a sleigh.

Some months back Lincoln had come in asking: "Graham, can you teach surveying?" Having dug into the rudiments of surveying alone, as a boy, and having gotten his credentials later in the difficult college of experience in Kentucky, Graham could. And he could introduce Lincoln to the county surveyor, recommending him as a man who could be depended upon to do a thing right. Yes, Graham could teach surveying, or tare and tret, or Plato and Paine, or logic and astronomy.

"Can you master it in time to take the job?" had been Graham's answer. Yes, Lincoln could. Those mental gymnastics he had been put through since he first sat at this table had developed his capacity. Yet surveying was hard for Lincoln, the philosopher. He ground away at it, stubbornly, tenaciously, doggedly;

and he grew pale and thinner. "Do eat something more, Abe. Have some more," said Sarah, all concern. But, chewing as he left the table, Lincoln was already deaf and dumb, again tackling a paragraph that had not given way under his attack. Mentor knew that determined agony. He had been through it, with the bewitching face of Sarah Rafferty his challenge. He had had little help, having gotten his first inklings as a lad of thirteen carrying chain, watching surveyors. Listening to his father, he had learned more, and finally had mastered the mathematics of it from a book bought with hoarded money. He had had to brush up on Gibson a few days before he began to teach it to Lincoln. Thus, while Peter Cartwright was overly busy, in camp meeting and out, exhorting the faithful to exclude infidels from the legislature, his competitor was sweating out the summer over surveying problems. And, after surveying, rehearsing speeches and re-writing them, listening to Graham criticize.

If Lincoln was heard to talk freethinking and Paine's *Age of Reason*, that was all Cartwright listened for. The candidate for the legislature had good reason to know what he was talking about— hadn't he parsed both its language and its logic? Since Dr. Allen had come, people spoke up more. It was not unusual to hear it said aloud that the Hard-Shell Baptists' doctrine of God's creating the Baptists for heaven and the balance of men for hell made a demon and not a god of God. Allen held that repentance could save anybody, that preachers like Cartwright were off on the wrong foot. He held that a preacher ought to know at least the physical structure of the universe. Graham came to his Sabbath school, and he and Dr. Allen and Lincoln talked astronomy when they got together. Meanwhile the debating society's "Fire or water?" debate continued to be retold so often that Cartwright made out a case that should have been effective.

But it was not. Freethinking or no freethinking, people who had come to know upright, earnest, friendly, simple Lincoln elected him; and New Salem, not by steamboat or rail but by her awkwardest, most popular young man, moved into her place in the sun. At the barbecue on Sugar Creek two days before the election the candidates had been feted. A. Lincoln, of New Salem, made a speech accompanied by clownish gesture but full of common sense and a mental and moral honesty that shone through and through it.

Old records show that Graham did not have his reliable election clerk to assist at that election, on August 4, 1834—"The proudest day of my life—but one," as he said often afterward, when his favorite student had been chosen to lead the nation. He opened his fall term, happy and elated. His theory of teaching was right. He would work harder, keep an eye out for other young fellows of capacity. Billy Greene, who had been "reading up" with Graham, had gone to Illinois College, the president of which was Edward Beecher (brother of Harriet Beecher Stowe). Billy had brought home with him a very capable young man, Richard Yates, nearly through his course. Graham glowed when the three—Greene, Lincoln, and Yates—were his guests, saying little, but basking in the delight of hearing Lincoln hold his own in their discussions. Ann still had not gotten to go to Jacksonville, but she was keeping on with her study under Graham. The young legislator was out surveying most of the time now, unaware that a much younger man than he, Stephen A. Douglas, had come west and was teaching a country school near Jacksonville.

Lincoln was now working on English composition, spending a lover's hours with Ann, studying to be a lawyer, looking forward with some little nervousness to being a legislator. He had no money: election clerk in October, one dollar; a few jobs of surveying at three dollars a day; a few dimes as commission from his *Sangamon Journal* agency—and a note he couldn't meet on his failure as a storekeeper. He lost his surveying instruments to the highest bidder—but he got them back. Would Mr. Short have bid them in and given them back to Lincoln if Ann Rutledge had not been working in his household? Sarah, forgetting her old tempers now that Abe was really going to the legislature, urged him to rest a little: "You're likely to get sick, Abe. There's lots of cholera around."

At last the great day. In clothes bought with borrowed money (there was one calf less in the Graham herd) Lincoln mounted the Yellow Bank stage, a "little shaky in his boots," with the whole town up at six o'clock of a chill November morning to see him off. "Do right by us, Abe."

While the earnest young man got his first taste of lawmaking, Peter Cartwright opened an academy in his home, at a fee of five dollars a scholar, one dollar a week board in advance. But the academy went only as far as the three R's, and it soon stopped operating and Peter returned to farming. Graham, too, in a new hat and with the old coat spruced up by a new binding, mounted the stage one morning and went down to Springfield—the delegate, by ac-clamation, of Sangamon County to an education convention whose subject for discussion was common schools at state expense and their curriculum. The convention sent its findings to the legis-lature and to Joseph Duncan, the new governor, who was favorable to their plans.

Early January brought the death of William Berry, Lincoln's one-time business partner, the man who had said: "You've got to sell liquor, Lincoln." Dr. Allen, Dr. Jayne, Dr. Henry, and Dr. Abell couldn't do a thing for the young man, who had drunk him-self into the grave. His sixty-two-dollar estate was just one hun-dred dollars less than he owed. Thus Preacher Berry's son died; and Preacher Berry, a founder of the temperance White Templars, and Graham, a teetotaler evicted from church for that virtue, buried him in a coffin Graham made. Preacher Berry had been able to convince Lincoln of the evils of liquor but had not been able to do as much for his own son. A month before William's death New Salem's legislator, who had dissolved the Berry-Lin-coln partnership over liquor-selling, had presented a bill to relieve insolvent debtors. He was doing right by New Salem.

Back in New Salem by mid-February, Lincoln resumed his old associations. He and Ann were radiant. In a year or two. . . . . Ann was sewing for New Salem women who had less time and tal-ent for the needle than she, although there were the younger chil-dren to help with at home and, in between times, studying. Again the winter fire found the three of them sitting about the gate-leg table, reviewing the knotty grammar, composing speeches, read-ing up on chemistry, natural philosophy, a little Latin—that might put a bright girl ahead in Jacksonville, that might come in handy to a young lawmaker. Sometimes after Lincoln had seen Ann home he came back to Graham's to talk until Sarah drove them to bed. And, at breakfast next morning, Sarah pressed the new buck-wheat delicacy that was supplanting corndodgers with "Do have another stack of flapjacks, Mr. Lincoln. . . . . Sick, Mr. Lincoln?"

"A little fever and ague, I reckon, Mrs. Graham. No, not sick."

In the chill, wet spring, railroad talk died down, somehow. Like other farmers, Graham got into his fields late, his corn was slow, and school took most of his time. Ann was often at the Rogerses'. Arminda Rogers could help her with grammar, and she could sew for Arminda. Helping was the backbone of America in these years: putting in and harvesting crops; throwing up a cabin, quilting, learning; it was a stable and happy society. There had been four doctors to wait upon the insolvent, dying William Berry. Everybody they knew helped Ann and Abe. Mrs. Hill and Ann, in green riding habits just alike, the talk of the town, rode horseback together, but Ann usually walked out to where she was going to help. Her calfskin shoes were sturdy, and she tied her glossy auburn curls beneath a cheap straw bonnet and doubtless dreamed as much of being Mrs. A. Lincoln as of graduating from Jacksonville.

As summer heat increased, a plague of chills and fever set Graham to making coffins. Lincoln helped him, the deaths came so often. Ann's family fell ill. Lincoln helped there, too,[1] doing the chores, sitting up with patients who were "low," until he himself succumbed to the disease and had to be put to bed. Sarah and Mrs. Abell nursed him until he could stand shakily on his feet.

Then one day James McGready Rutledge came galloping in from Sandridge farm: "Ann's calling for you, Abe! Hurry!"

A week earlier a tornado had leveled crops and snapped trees in the woods and scattered fence rails like straws. Sarah had gone about shaking her head. It meant death—more death. "A bad year," everybody said. . . . . Hurry, Abe Lincoln! Hurry to meet and master—if you can—the hardest lesson of life.

Ann? Buried under the ground, out in the whipping rain. . . . . There is nothing to live for now.

Kind Dr. Allen leads him away from the grave, takes him in to Bowling Green's motherly wife, not to see anyone or be seen; not to talk or be talked to. Nature, young blood, might heal the wound—but the scar would be there always.

Autumn again, and a dejected surveyor trudged the sodden roads and fields and woods, dragging back to his friend, empty-eyed. "Do eat, Abe." A head bowed above the table feels the pressure of the hand of the older teacher-brother. Could a teacher of grammar and surveying, of tare and tret, of Latin and logic, of astronomy and a kind God, help with the answer?

"Nothing to live for now, Graham. I feel like taking my own life. . . . ."

"God is bringing about a higher purpose, Lincoln. Surely he is, Lincoln."

A pitiful reaching up and out of awkward hands; the quivering lips, the weeping eyes. "May be you're right, Graham."

In 1865 Graham wrote: "Lincoln told me that he felt like committing suicide often. . . . . He said that my remarks had done him good."

How could Lincoln study at the gate-leg table or go to school at the little church-house? That September Graham clerked the election without him. Patrons complained that the postmaster was careless with the mail. A bad, bad, year. Flocks and herds died that autumn of poisoned weeds; wild turkeys came robbing the slim oats stacks; the winds blew high and endlessly; and no help came to a stooping young man, pounding down stakes, marking land boundaries in the bitter falling leaves of what had once been paradise.

Student was ahead of master now, having faced the hardest problem. Winter found them reading *Pilgrim's Progress* but not analyzing its grammar. They read history and biography; but never again opened the old books that wept aloud with anguish. "Eyes to the future, Lincoln. Other men have lost their dearly beloveds."

"May be you're right, Graham."

Bright-eyed children, scampering through the woods back of New Salem gathering nuts, tried to win over the wan-faced sufferer: "Tell us a story, Mr. Lincoln. I kin beat you at marbles!" At Graham's the children hovered about his chair with their love for him shining in their eyes, begging his return to them. Mrs. Abell and Mrs. Greene asked him in to supper: "If the boy would just eat!"

In December, A. Lincoln, a melancholy look upon his face and a sadness in his heart that remained there always, went back to the legislature.

XVI

MATCHMAKING

1835-40

*T*ALK IN New Salem still flared up over the way to heaven—
"Water or dry land?" Still Methodists taunted Baptists: "The
balance for hell and the Baptists for heaven?" Still Mrs. Johnson
managed to be taken with the jerks at camp meetings; and in town
the same questions continued to hold attention: "Who deserves
salvation?" "Should slaves be freed?"

But change was creeping over little New Salem. Those who had
made her what she was began to take wing, to settle elsewhere.
Many were going on west; others to the coming town of Petersburg.
Petersburg lots were as feverish a topic in New Salem as her own
town lots had been. Lincoln, announced in Springfield as of good
moral character (the first step in becoming a lawyer), was putting
his money in Springfield lots and a certain little stretch of land
along the Sangamon that would always be dear to him. Old Jeremiah, having experienced this very kind of fading-away at Brush
Creek, invested in a section of land on the theory that it would be
valuable, being so near the live town of Petersburg. Graham's
youngest brother, Jackson, came north and bought half a section
with the same object—realizing on it, after a while. Graham, expecting thinned ranks at the schoolhouse, bought nineteen acres
from the Greenes who moved on west to Tallula.

Still New Salem folks chinned and argued to the trampling of
oxen at the carding machine and the rumble of the mill that still
pulsed the air. Sarah told of seeing the storehouse at the carding
machine piled high with a hodgepodge of wool and grease and
finished cards. Women had more time now that they did not have
to card—time to read and talk. The steamboat "Utility," which
had got as far as Petersburg but was too large to proceed, supplied

—in the form of its engine—the power plant for a steam-roller flour mill, and the countryside changed over to light bread.

Family affairs took a hectic route. William Greene went to court with his neighbor, John Purkapile, over trespass, with Abell, Lincoln, and Bowling Green as his witnesses. Travis Elmore, a cousin, went insane, and Graham was driven to petitioning the county for his safekeeping. Many moved away, leaving their children's tuition for school and for private tutoring unpaid; hard times faced the Grahams. Jeremiah managed to be subpoenaed often as a witness and added his fees to the family fund. Nancy Ellen, Graham's sister, a girl in her teens, sickened and lay at the point of death. There is a legend that Lincoln, riding through New Salem, met Graham on the way to the mill with such a pitifully small grist that he urged a bill upon the schoolmaster. Though Nancy Ellen was young, she had studied grammar with Ann and Abe at the church; and after she was married and a teacher herself, pioneering in Shasta County, California, she told both of the grammar lessons and of the money Lincoln gave Graham to buy the family food when they were down to cornmeal and nothing else and to buy the medicine that brought about her recovery.

Lincoln himself was not having any too easy a time, for in the years 1836–39 he sent money regularly to his father. When he was commissioned to survey a section of land three miles from New Salem for school authorities, hope flickered again. But when the post office, New Salem's first crown, was removed to Petersburg and the postmaster advertised a final day for claiming letters, everybody knew that New Salem would soon be deserted. Now the polls were at Petersburg, and Graham rode horseback in to earn his election-clerk dollar or to serve on some roads committee. Lincoln was not clerking elections any more; Mentor's co-worker now was that Thomas Nance, Rock Creek schoolmaster, who had been his schoolmate at Nat Owens' Brush Creek Academy. Together they read Lincoln's platform, posted in the polling place: *Equal sufferage for women:* "All should share the privileges of government who assist in bearing its burdens." And there was a clause favoring the speedier sale of public school lands.

Court and the political campaign were as usual; but this time Stephen A. Douglas prosecuted a man for forgery and lost the case on the testimony of Jeremiah Graham and James Goldsby.

Graham sat in at court as ever, but the debating society no longer met. He fell back for the mental stimulus he needed on listening to lawyer and witness, especially if Lincoln was the lawyer. Usually between sessions they had a chat, which always ended by Graham's asking Lincoln out to supper. Lincoln usually accepted. If Lincoln was going to speak, Graham went to the political rallies; and he went down to Springfield to hear Edwards and Lincoln argue for the Whigs. Political rallies were so numerous that speakers rode from one to another, heading out immediately after speaking for the next rally. After they left, the assemblage would argue a bit on their own. Fights and fisticuffs were common, and rallies were almost as lawless as camp meetings once had been.

Mrs. Abell now made a stir by returning from a visit to Kentucky and bringing her sister with her. Mary Owens was buxom, black-eyed, and witty; and even if her silk dresses, leghorn hat, and kid shoes and gloves did contrast sharply with her relatives' slat sunbonnets and homespun everydays, they all dressed in their best for the great visiting back and forth and the parties for Mary to which townsfolk were invited. The Abells' house was an eighteen-by-twenty frame, built of walnut, with three fireplaces and a full upstairs, and had from the first been a center of New Salem social life.

Brush Creek doings and Kentucky slavery and church news were brought up to date; and talk went to the old days when Mary, a toddler, had been too young to study lessons in the academy. She knew she was being inspected as a possible wife by Legislator Lincoln, and she knew quite as well that she intended to inspect him as a possible husband—and inspect carefully. Mrs. Abell, according to the custom, had told Lincoln of Mary, suggesting her to him as a wife: "Mary's well educated, loves books, and can keep house. Ann would wish you to, Mr. Lincoln." Very matter of fact, Lincoln had said: "It might be a good match."

Now that Mary had arrived, Lincoln shuttled back and forth from Springfield, on horseback or walking, sometimes by stage. He took Mary out, and they got along famously. Everybody nodded approval; everybody was eager for Lincoln to marry; and the couple was feted and asked out and beamed upon by mothers of families. A good match; Lincoln would forget Ann, be himself again. And he did grow less morose, entertaining the Grahams with sidesplitting imitations of stump speakers at political rallies; and with one famous tale of how, when he was campaigning, the guests had slept two to the bed and four beds to the room in a tavern where a polecat had come in between the logs. For the suitor's cause, he reported his law examination at Springfield for a license to practice. For Graham's delight, the Whig election returns. The two men found opportunity for a little time alone in which to read Webster's "Reply to Hayne"—no better speech ever made, Graham thought.

Party to a match that was being made, Lincoln was earning money—and spending most of it riding the Springfield stage to New Salem, a crowded stage with nine passengers crushed in seats built to accommodate six, fighting gnats and mosquitoes, shifting their weight to the driver's "Now to the right, gentlemen . . . . ; now, left . . . ." as the coach struck the boggy places and careened madly and all but went over. If it got too bad, the passengers walked around the quagmire.

Mary spent a great deal of time at the Grahams'; and if Lincoln called at the Abells', and found her out, he went, properly enough, past the Grahams' and dropped in to supper. Boyishly nonchalant, making his call seem pure family friendship, he always fell in with his old character, helping with the chores, rocking the baby to sleep, carrying out the ashes, chopping wood, acting the monkey for the children. Sarah beamed and bustled, with Mary in a very domestic ruffled apron as her kitchen assistant, and the little girls putting flowers on the table and "carrying" during a meal that consisted of both women's choicest cookery: bean soup, roast duck, gooseberry pie, and hot biscuit with honey, and enough jams, butters, and preserves to stock an ordinary modern cupboard for a month.

"Do have some blackberry custard. Have some more, Abe. Maybe I should call you Mr. Lincoln? Mary made it." And Mr. Lincoln would have some more and would praise Mary, and everybody would laugh. After supper the little girls carried out the dishes and poked at Mr. Lincoln to make him tell them funny stories; until Mary came in, flushed from her dishwashing (which she never did at home), bright and sparkling and pretty as a picture, when the children would be shooed to bed, "instanter."

Again there were three at the table; but Mary, unlike Ann,

spoke as often and as emphatically as the men—a matured, brainy woman of twenty-eight, with a cultured, brilliant speech any man might envy. The men heard her through respectfully since both believed in woman suffrage, whether she was setting forth her ideas of government, transportation, wood-sawing, or schoolteaching. As the Illinois dialect had it, "They didn't fault her, but they did have a bad time." After a little while Graham would find some reason to leave the two alone: "Excuse me, I have papers to finish."

If Lincoln arrived and Mary was at Abells', Sarah—conniving openly for this hoped-for match—would say, "Make ace, now children, tell Mary Abe's come. Belike she'll be eating supper with us." Then Sarah would tackle Abe: "I asked Mary to supper to-night, Abe. Can't you stay, too? Might as well. Stay all night." And Abe usually stayed both to supper and all night.

Then Mentor's little son, Septimus, fell ill and lingered many weeks before he died. Lincoln and Graham took their turns with Mary and Sarah and Almira, watching by the child's bedside at night. Lincoln often dropped in on his law tours long enough to ask about the little fellow or to talk to him, telling him about a funny bird's whistle he'd heard, how the bullfrogs croaked and swelled up; and he seemed well satisfied if the child smiled weakly or hung onto a finger when he rose to go. He was there the night Septimus died.

At the funeral Lincoln wept openly as with gentle hands he helped lower the little coffin into its grave beside the baby who had died in the winter of the long snow. After the burial he returned home with the family, did all the chores, and talked to the children. When he left, late at night, he could muster no farewell words or any syllable of comfort when Graham followed him out and stood, watching him saddle up. Lincoln started to mount, threw down the reins, folded both arms about his friend in a brief embrace, swung up quickly to the saddle, and rode off without a word. Mary had been helping in the house, she had been at the funeral; but Lincoln did not seem to know it.

From that time on a coldness crept into Abe's relationship with Mary. Graham's granddaughter tells of their estrangement as she heard it from her grandfather and the Abells. "The day before Lincoln was to go back to the legislature," she says, "he sent word to Mary by one of the Abell children, whom he met at the post office, that he would call that evening. She had planned to go to Grahams' to supper and, thinking that Abe would come on over as usual, went early in the evening. But when Abe arrived at Abells' and found Mary gone, he concluded that she wanted to avoid him. Sarah put a plate on the table for Lincoln, but he did not come.

"After the children had left the table, Sarah said: 'Now, Mary, you must not get out of patience with Abe. He is going to amount to something some day.'

"Mary began to stack the dishes. 'I think you are right about his future,' she answered, 'but our whole outlook on life is so different, and our training, as for instance what he has done tonight, that I think it would be a mistake to become serious about him.'

"Mentor spoke up: 'But you could help him, Mary—and you will never meet anybody again to compare with him.'

" 'Well, maybe I do think too much about the little niceties of behavior, but his lack of knowledge of etiquette might be due to some lack which he does not realize, or even try to overcome.'

"Sarah said, 'Oh, Mary, he is one of the gentlest men I ever knew. Think how he helped and comforted us when little Septimus died—laid him away. . . . .'

"But Mary let down the leaf of the table with a deep sigh. 'Yes, Sally, I know. I know he is good all the way through but—' and she called goodbye to the children and went out to walk to Abells' alone. Ordinarily Sally and Almira would have walked with Mary to Abells', then back home."

Without seeing Mary, Lincoln went to the legislature at Vandalia that voted to remove the capital to Springfield. Letters came and went between the oddly estranged and very frank young persons, parties to a match that wasn't making.

A cold and deeply troubled suitor returned to New Salem in March. He had been back several times to court his unyielding Mary. He had been admitted to the bar, had been asked to address audiences, had worked for the removal of the capital and against slavery, had been offered a law partnership, and had won his first case. He had proved himself worthy; but Miss Owens remained aloof, obdurately indecisive, her black eyes calmly impersonal. With nothing to keep him longer in the little village that had been his home, A. Lincoln moved to Springfield to answer the call that led through a tangling maze of years. His despondency at this time is little to be wondered at. He had lost his first love through death. His second had flouted him. He still owed debts from his storekeeping days. He had failed oftener than he had succeeded.

Against Mentor and Sarah's advice, Mary went home. August had seen a coldly polite letter from her suitor: ". . . . willing to bind you faster, if I can be convinced it will, in any considerable degree, add to your happiness." That had settled it, finally. Mary terminated her long visit. The Grahams settled back to the old routine, planting their little patches of wheat, oats, and corn out on the edges of the still wild prairies. Sarah and the other women still counted on fried quail and wild honey and the jams and jellies from wild crabs and berries, pecans from the woods, and wild turkeys and geese for roasting. But now work was not so pressing. Supper over before candlelighting time, folks gardened a little and knitted and sewed. But they visited more. Visiting was, of course, largely arguing about everything from atheism to Zion.

Sarah was the only woman present when Graham made the speech at the Society for the Promotion of Education, in Springfield, which brought him an appointment to the committee to select textbooks.[1] Her pride in him mounted when he set himself the task of reading and appraising every textbook obtainable. The Torrys, a local family, had sniggered in court when he had articulated his answers in faultless grammar when witnessing for his cousin, Felix Greene. They could understand every word he said, even at the back of the courtroom, where they were loafing around the door. "Are" pronounced like "air"? Just wait!

The society had begun in a small way in Sill and Town's private schoolroom in Springfield. It now met twice a month and had its standing committees, and was considering a series of uniform texts, discussing the "propriety of a uniform mode of instruction" and what subjects should be taught in primary schools. With quickened step Graham walked to his new school made of sawed lumber, with its benches and desks and its Franklin stove that burned coal supplied by the public. A new start. A new tin bucket and a new tin dipper; no more melting snow and drinking from a gourd. Only one young lady refused to abide by his rule: "Come to school clean."

He wondered how he would outwit her. Shaming her had only made her laugh rudely, only made her shrug her shoulders. Day after day she wore the same dress, "slick as grease with dirt down the front." At last he said: "If you come to school so dirty tomorrow, I shall have to punish you." He was little prepared for her reaction. Of course she wore the same dress, but it was now ornamented with a large, newly sharpened butcher knife. Graham had his worries until the school board arrived and suspended her. Salem School, after that, would have ranked in cleanliness as a model school of today. Lessons progressed more speedily from books and with good light from half-a-dozen big windows. There was more time for helping slow pupils when no wood had to be be sawed. The children were eager and interested.

But a big cloud began to darken the horizon. Illinois mass meetings were finding abolition "unnecessary and un-Christian." Even though the Whigs were gaining, they were not gaining fast enough to meet the coming issue. When Lincoln stopped in, both men were too concerned about the threatened national disaster to talk of the lost Mary Owens or the lost New Salem. Lovejoy had been killed at near-by Alton while defending the printing press that was to defend abolition. The mob had destroyed the press, even burned the warehouse where it was stored waiting removal for use. Lincoln hoped, now that the capital was at Springfield, that there would be no more drunken candidates dancing down a banquet table as they had at Vandalia, and thought the black eye that W. C. Bryant, the eastern newspaper reporter, had given Springfield wouldn't make much difference. Bryant had described the town as "a conglomeration of hog wallows and log cabins with a few squatting frame stores around an unpaved square that is dominated by a red brick courthouse."

Sarah, discussing all this with her husband, was still tremulous with superstition, constantly on the lookout for signs. When the temperature suddenly dropped to twenty below in December and froze animals to death in the woods and livestock in feed pens—a thousand hogs frozen into a lump on the way to market—she said the catastrophe meant war. Mentor lost most of his livestock and Sarah her flocks of chickens and ducks. Burying the dead animals, Mentor suggested to her that she was a poor prophet, that she had missed the sign of which this was the catastrophe.

If the country was going to escape disruption, Lincoln said, slavery would have to go. If the country could be persuaded against slavery, Graham offered, a system of free schools was the one method of persuasion. But free schools were not getting very far: Illinois was no longer unified either on the question of slavery or on the question of free schools. Graham hopefully and exactingly labored with his pupils, vastly proud that he was preparing five of them to enter college. He drew up a petition for the sale of school lands in the new Menard County, obtained twenty-five signers, and sent it in.

One by one, the men who had contributed to Graham's mental vigor and spiritual growth left New Salem: the Reverend Berry, Dr. Allen, James Rutledge, and A. Lincoln. If the intervals were overlong between the times when Lincoln dropped by, Mentor would saddle up and trot into Springfield, climb the stairs to Lincoln's office over Hoffman's, on the chance of seeing him or chatting with him, hearing him advise a client or plead a case. They went together, jogging and talking, down to Porter's Grove west of Springfield to see Daniel Webster arrive with an artillery escort, and to hear him speak.

New Salem might make it yet. Pork was up to six dollars a hundred, and the wheat that year was five feet high. A few new settlers drifted in. Bale, who had bought Hill's carding machine, was doing more business than Hill had ever done. The *Cincinnati Gazette* told of German immigrants on the Ohio wharves with their "Guten morgen" and their well-pleased palms rubbed together as an accompaniment to "Ja, ja, mein Herr!" elated and loud on their way to settle the rich Illinois prairies. But around New Salem hill old settlers, wanting to move on, were cracking the well-worn joke: "I'll give you two-thirds of my land if you'll take the rest off my hands."

For now, as old Sangamon County was cut up to make three new counties—Dane, Logan, and Menard—with Petersburg the county seat of Menard, New Salem became "Old Salem"—a memory. It had vanished, man by man, child by child, house by house. Bale, the last man to go, took the marvelous carding machine to Petersburg with him, down that very road that once friendly little New Salem had signed for as "needed and convenient." The railroad had come—but to Jacksonville, not New

Salem; a college, too, had come—but to Peoria. Nothing was left alive, but the mill which was still operated; and the Graham boys, taking grist to it, played in and climbed over the decaying cabins while they waited for the whistle of the miller, telling them their grain was ground. There were many such deserted villages on the frontier; nobody mourned as the cabins were hauled away or fell to ruin and the grass came back to heal the scars of root cellar and well and coax away the street that had been rutted by noisy wooden wagon wheels, until it became a pasture for deer and a nesting place for meadowlark, quail, and prairie chicken, as of old.

Graham was completely absorbed in his new office.[2] He made frequent trips to St. Louis to explore catalogues and bookstores and meet with the committee on textbooks. Sarah, her round of toil thus increased, was tending yet another little redheaded son— Samuel. She sometimes went with some of the children and Mentor to plays at Springfield, Graham having been won by Lincoln[3] to the opinion that plays were educational; but he went alone to lectures at Jacksonville and to see the new railroad there and watch the train come in.

Searching for textbooks, Graham came across the "Penny Dreadfuls, Horror Stories for the Enjoyment of the Young." Fifty years later he could not relate that find without trembling with rage. "As the mind is fed so it fruits," was his maxim, his idea of educating the young. He could see only one outcome for this "moral rubbish," this "degenerating commerce": crime. Graham, who by this time, through the press of Lincoln's duties, had all but lost the one understanding friend of his life, flamed under the challenge of cheap, morbid print for children's consumption—"an easy way to make money and debase a nation." He threw all his might into fighting this sort of reading, girding on an armor that he wore the rest of his life, to fight a battle for constructive books for schools—a battle that he died still fighting.

Out riding circuit or stumping for his partner, Stuart, Lincoln stopped by and kept his friend posted on affairs at the capital. The Graham farm was handily near Petersburg, the county seat; and Lincoln could stop both going to and coming from court, always certain of that heart-warming welcome: "Do stay to supper, Mr. Lincoln; stay all night, might as well." Graham couldn't be dragged from court when it was in session. He sat at the rear of the room, his silk tile resting on his knees, while he listened and appraised logic, justice, and language, shuffling his hat with nervous joy when Lincoln, with a short, logical speech in which no words were wasted, "skunked" his adversary. It "starched" Graham, as he said. He went away fortified. This speaker had not been fed on Penny Dreadfuls.

Graham never threw his hat in the air in applauding, as most men did in those days. He repressed his emotion into a vigorous nod of the head and a wave of the hat. He walked off very fast under the impact of genuine approval. But he almost ran to school for weeks after the election that returned Lincoln to the legislature and Lincoln's partner to Congress, a Senator, as everybody said, by the grace of Lincoln's piercing wit and logic. With new consecration, hoping that another youth with capacity might then be under his thumb, Graham put his college-preparatory class through a grueling course in logic and composition.

Jeremiah went down to Springfield and by his evidence swung a "not guilty" verdict for William Hodges, a Springfield schoolmaster, indicted for selling liquor. Talk had it that the man was "sure guilty as hell," and Graham felt the prick of humiliation when Jeremiah was feted by the talkers. Whiskey, ten years ago, had been legal tender; now a man could be indicted for selling it—that was some comfort.

Household affairs were going smoothly, with every child performing his duties; so to humor Sarah's wish as well as his own inclination, Graham took his wife on a steamboat trip, leaving Jeremiah and Mary to manage the farm and house. The two landed at Louisville and went by stage to Greensburg, arriving in time to witness the death of Johnson Graham, who had been ill for some months. It was a sad home-coming. The day after the funeral, the news arrived from Georgia that Graham's youngest brother, Jackson, had married and gone south to live. When the Civil War came, he was a wealthy Georgia planter, the owner of two hundred slaves.

In St. Louis, waiting for their boat, the "Henry Clay," Graham had looked at books and had bought Sarah a bombazine dress with gold-lace ruchings. Their stern-wheeler had raced the "John Duncan," while ladies in false curls and little girls in lace-ruffle pantalettes strolled the deck, men played whist, and Negro deck hands "patted juba" and "popped corks" between wharves. At night, while the upper deck was gay with fiddling and dancing, lighted up with baskets of burning resin, the Negroes danced below to their own singing:

> Heah dat steamboat coughin' down de ribber
> I'se gwine back to ma Sal an' ham an' aigs.....

Leavings from the whites' tables, scraped into a "grub pile" on the lower deck, were attacked by black hands, clawing in to snatch what they could from other digging hands. The Negroes fought and scrabbled, eating between bouts, stuffing with both fists or the back of a hand not employed in defense. From above, the whites watched these "rat rousters" heave cargoes on and off at the landings, singing as they sweated and tugged:

> Push dat load, coon, jest a little quickah,
> Grab dat calf by de eah an de tail—
> Toss dem flour barls jes' a little fastah
> If y' bus' a single one of um, yo' sho' lan' in jail.....!

The Grahams gladly returned to Illinois, where there was no slavery. Yet the rivers that ran through Illinois were filled with steamboats with their rat rousters and grub piles. Many farmers, seeing how simple it might be to grow wealthy by slave labor, talked slavery and hooted down the very idea of prohibiting it.

As a salaried public school teacher, Graham was at last getting ahead financially. He came back to his beloved teaching, his farm routine, his committee work, and took up where he had left off, now adding a little campaign of his own to his program. He ran for county clerk. When election day came, he voted with a flourish for the Whig candidate for presidential elector, Abe Lincoln; but it took several days for him to rebound from his own defeat, skunked, 9 to 265! He saddled up and rode into Springfield, sat in the back of the unfinished senate room, visited Lincoln, came back "helped up."

He and the entire family attended the Harrison parade—not unlike a camp meeting in strong emotion and noise, with its tented thousands of country folk, its paraded canoes, frigates, and steamboats on wheels, its white horses and silk-sashed riders. A giant oil painting of William Henry Harrison, Whig candidate for the president of the United States, headed a long procession that was brought up with hundreds of carriages and thousands of people on foot, yelling and cheering and waving flags.

All summer long, Whig and Democrat speakers mounted the rostrum that was thrown up in one corner of the Petersburg square, shouting out denouncements and threats whose virulence and lengthiness smacked of Cartwright's camp-meeting sermons. Ninian Edwards gave fourteen acres of his private grounds in Springfield for the use of political speakers. Politics had won the center of the stage. Religion took a back seat, though in deserted Salem—"Old Salem," now—an exhorting Hard-Shell Baptist, Abram Bale, had settled on the bluff and was immersing converts by the dozen in the mill pond. Folks began to call the Old Salem site "The Heights of Abram." Deer browsed there, unmolested.[5]

XVII

LOSSES

1840–42

*A*FTER Sam Hill moved his store to Petersburg, it continued to be a gathering place for the New Salem cronies. At first Graham walked or rode in to talk and listen there and at other Petersburg loafing places, as Sarah called them. But the old interest, the old intensity of themes, was gone; talk was all small talk. Besides the pressure of farming, trips to Springfield and larger schools to teach cut down on Graham's free time. But he was always on hand during court and came in to trade on Saturday. His chief associations came to be in Springfield, where he attended debates and educational meetings, and at Jacksonville, which had similar attractions.

In high hope he attended the Education Society regularly, elated that it had begun to publish a journal, called *Common School*. But there were only four issues, for lack of funds; just as there were as yet no full-salaried teachers for the same reason. Still, as long as the *Union Agriculturist* and the *Prairie Farmer* continued to use their power in behalf of education, Graham worked hopefully, still piecing out a living with cabinetwork, brick making and laying, and farming. His and Sarah's must have been a successful sort of thrift, for the 1840 tax assessment showed them prosperous, with a Petersburg lot and a great array of horses, wagons, cattle, clocks, a buggy—and books. Mentor had enlarged his bookshelves yet again and filled them, and he had not forgotten the new carpets Sarah wanted. He also found time, somehow, to make new beds and chests of drawers and chairs.

Sarah was proud and happy, content to be pointed out as a "stiff dresser." She had two best dresses and a second-best, besides the bombazine, and three everydays. She had relented not one whit in her exacting housekeeping, nor in demands that the children perform every assigned duty. Almira and Minerva, now young ladies, must have smoothly woven woolens and linens and many hand-hemmed ruffles. Grandame Mary helped with all this and with like clothing for her own daughter, Nancy Ellen, who was growing up, too, and needed many things her mother had only heard of. Times were different; young folks had "a heap sight more than they needed." Elizabeth and Mary and Nancy, Graham's daughters, and Nancy Ellen were being unmercifully trained in the arts of housewifery, with two inspectors, in mother and grandmother, to make certain nothing was slighted. The four sons—Samuel, Bennett, Benjamin, and William—poor lads, were kept busy almost every minute lest Satan find the proverbial mischief. Graham superintended the younger children's lessons and saw to it that each one spoke with distinctness and chose his words before he began speaking. Both parents insisted upon kindness and deference for Grandsire Jeremiah and Grandame Mary. The old folks smoked their pipes in the chimney corner and puttered around garden and kitchen, happy and proud parents of a son who was "looked up to." In April, 1841, another son, Sempter, was born to Sarah and Mentor.

A fine family of children, enough to make any man beam with pride as they gathered promptly about the table. Each face was scrubbed until it shone, each head of water-slicked hair bowed during the grace which Graham pronounced. Mentor now had nine living children (five had died—three in Illinois, two in Kentucky). He did not accompany them when, trigged out in their Sunday best, they rode off to church with Sarah and Mary, leaving at home the two men, who had been dropped from church, the one for drinking, the other for not drinking. Jeremiah preferred to chin with Mentor, with the house to themselves and no one listening disapprovingly to their religious discussions; and sometimes the two walked into Petersburg and slipped into a rear pew of the Presbyterian church.

As in Graham's childhood, he and his father attended court together—"wasted precious time doing nothing," as Sarah put it. By arriving early, Graham could usually manage a chat with Lincoln, who now tied his horse before the brick house only rarely. It was a memorable delight to the entire family when Lincoln did come tromping in, stampeded by the children, to toss his hat under the best-room settee and sit down to a sumptuous meal. His face was the focus of a double row of intent, approving faces as he told them of the wonders of Springfield. How admiring they all were when Lincoln, hearing the baby fret, would get up to take it from its hooded cradle and dandle it until it crowed. But off to bed at a punctual eight o'clock the children must flock. "Good-night Mr. Lincoln," "Good-night Mr. Lincoln," .... each in turn.

Elbows supported chins about the table as the talk turned to abolition, while the older girls cleared away the supper things and afterward sat and sewed, or joined in the talk. But the old intimacy was rarely reached. Lincoln's widening horizons, his growing self-assurance, his mention of his new friends—unknown to Graham—made the two men more nearly strangers. They talked—but without the old camaraderie, eye to eye. The greater man—did he realize the yearning of the lesser, his one-time generous, unrelenting teacher?

Lincoln was courting again, a Miss Mary Todd, a sister of the wife of Ninian Edwards. His mien had settled permanently into a melancholy one, a sort of dejection of spirit.[1]

"Graham, death took my mother, and my sister, Sarah, unnecessarily. It took Ann. And now—it is my evil luck—I shall always lose the women I love."

He had expressed almost the same fear when he had been courting Mary Owens. Graham told him now, as then, that he suffered from superstition. He pointed out the younger man's public successes to him and reminded him of his ability to appeal to other men's minds; but Lincoln couldn't be moved. Sarah's comment was: "Well, Mentor, sometimes a person has a feeling, and you can't deny it." Lincoln preferred Sarah's outlook. But this couple, long past their youthful ardors, parents of nine children, did not give any satisfaction to Lincoln, the wifeless man. He went to Kentucky to talk it over with Speed, a newer friend, and Speed's newly and happily wedded wife. Graham was assigned the role of second-best confidant.

Thus shorn of his friend's intimacy, long since deprived of his White Templars, his Debating Society, and the never failing inspiration of talk with Dr. Allen and Preacher Berry, Graham clung to his first and oldest friend, Bowling Green. Even after a day of hard farming, the spark of intellectual curiosity was strong enough to send him afoot, across the fields and through the woods, for the refreshment of a talk with Squire Green. The two men read the latest books together and redipped into certain ancient ones that promised an answer to current questions. But this stimulus, too, was doomed to end.

One February night Green, leaving his wife to milk the cows because of the exigency of a discussion afoot, hurried over to the Abells', climbed their hill, and sank down in a chair, dead. Graham, on the next farm, was roused from his last-minute reading on the subject under discussion by one of the Abell children bringing the news. He fumbled at his coat as he made ready to answer the call for help; he could scarcely keep up with Sarah, walking the scant quarter-mile. The women tried to soothe Mrs. Green, who had been brought in, while the men carried the body to a wagon. Graham held up under the test of laying out his friend; but on the way home Sarah was the strong one.

The weather was too bitterly cold for any pomp of Odd Fellows or White Templars. Only neighbors drove in farm wagons up the hillslope on his farm where the grave of Bowling Green had been hacked out with mattocks. Frozen clods covered the homemade coffin that Graham helped lower. On the way home Graham became ill, succumbing to one of the three "sick spells" of his life. He did not attend the later Masonic ceremony above the grave, nor see Lincoln, too overcome with grief to pronounce the eulogy he had come to make.

No matter how heated their discussion and argument had been, Graham and Green had always parted friends. A lonely lapse now beset the days of Mentor Graham. His face saddened and softened. It seemed only right that the old mill should burn. The old days were over.

He managed to get to his school, but he was the ghost of his former self. He had entered forty pupils in the new register of South Fork school in this year of 1841. The old records show he twice received his pro rata of the school fund, in July and in April. The entire sum for the ten school districts of Menard County was only $452. Graham's share could not have amounted to more than $45. But it was cash, not whiskey or corn.

When spring came and the birth of another child became imminent, Sarah had to go through her ordeal in double suspense; Mentor had gone to Springfield and did not return for several days. The child was born while he was away seeking, it turned out, some consolation, for his grief. He had been to see Lincoln. He must have found some comfort, for he became more like himself, renewed his efforts at home and at school, and celebrated with the rest when his sister Nancy Ellen married an Elmore cousin. She went to live at Weston, Missouri, not far from the farm where lived Mary Owens, now Mrs. Jessie Vineyard.

Illinois law now established, for each county, a school commission under whose direction teaching must be done. Public funds paid only part of the students' tuition, and subscription rates varied with the amount of public funds distributed. Times were not of the best, and many subscription schools still functioned in the old way in sections where school land sale had not been pushed. Many parts of the state that had so long voted for public schools now began to question the wisdom of it. Graham rose earlier to get farm work out of the way that he might be free to strike whatever blow he could for the cause of the public school.

He saw Lincoln only once that spring, but reported him to be in better health and spirits than he had been since the death of Ann Rutledge. The presidential elector was courting Mary Todd, dancing and dressing and making addresses, sitting in the legislature, and contributing articles to the Springfield newspaper. The article that denounced a man named Shields resulted in a duel for Lincoln. Graham walked to Petersburg five times during the three days when the public waited to learn the outcome of that duel. He ran home when the word came that John Hardin of Jacksonville, riding breakneck to Bloody Island, had "cussed the two fools apart."

Ambling into Springfield on his farm horse, Graham sat in on the meetings of the Washingtonians, a temperance society, and on the doings of the society for deporting Negroes. He listened to the debates at the Young Men's Lyceum. But he had no part in all this, as Lincoln had, and as he himself had once had in New Salem. He enjoyed only the fringes. Lincoln's was now a wider world than one of an old gate-leg table and the puncheon pews of a log church used as a schoolhouse. Like a parent who mourns the loss of a son gone out from home to inherit his world, Graham mourned his loss of Lincoln. But he did not complain, as hopefully, constantly, he kept an eye out for capacity learners—though none with *that* capacity had thus far appeared.

Thrown back entirely upon himself, he talked of Dickens with Sarah and the girls. Dickens had been in the section, inspecting the Illinois prairies and the people, and reported them as a "Dang it!" population, rushing childishly out to see the packet boats and steamboats come in. "People probably don't do it where he came from," Sarah said, "because they don't have any to come in." But she agreed with his criticism of packet boats playing a tune at every landing, both day and night. "Folks need their sleep," she said. "Seems like any fool would know that."

Dickens ridiculed the snailing canalboats from which passengers jumped to shoot squirrels or have a drink or two and, by running, jumped on again with little fear of being left behind. He caricatured the berths on these boats as swinging bookshelves; and he didn't forget the clouds of mosquitoes, the red calico curtains of the ladies' dressing-room, and the "Come Haste to the Wedding" kind of music played aboard. "Well, he didn't have to come and nobody ask him what he thought. If we went over where he came from things would probably look meaner than pusley to us," Sarah said. "He can't string-halter us, even if we are only fair to middlin'."

Dickens, master of human observation, for once saw only the shape of things and not the spirit of this "dang-it" population. For out of it even then was developing the man whom the learned halls of England would one day eulogize with bronze bust and a certain Gettysburg speech placed above her own greatest. But to Graham, piecing out his drab days as best he might, that future design of the weaving did not show. Nothing stayed him in his self-imposed, difficult routine but faith in his fight for the good.

Forgetting his humiliating defeat when he ran for county clerk, Graham ran for constable. Laws being what they were, it was his ambition to make of Petersburg as temperate a place as New Salem had finally become. But the election was no simple affair. Seven other Whigs took the field against eight Democrats, the leading candidate receiving only thirty-four votes. With a return of her old sarcasm, Sarah said that even a tail-end candidate should have gotten at least ten votes, especially if he was a man who had never owned a gun and couldn't hit a haystack at ten steps at noon. Graham's retort was that as long as so many fools had learned to shoot he thought he might also, but it was scarcely enough to match her banter. He quit office-seeking, for good.

But again he reaped resolution from defeat, and once more bent to the single task of sending out successful young men to fight for public virtue. He took the Tonica school, which was at a distance. For the first time, it meant boarding round—a good change for everybody. Sarah had her undisturbed rest and a chance to pursue without restraint her meticulous ideas on housekeeping and child-rearing. As for Mentor Graham, he could read and think—at last —without the prick of Sarah's words or the pressure of farm work. A man of forty-two, nobody's watchful eyes were upon him for the first time in his life. And there was much to think about: Was Dickens right? Could hog cholera be cured? Could the Mississippi be dammed to avoid flooding every year? Could women's suffrage be voted in? Could he afford a Stephen Foster songbook?

Sarah took great pride in laying out the school money and making it reach. She made a real occasion of it when Mentor came home, with company meals and pie on Friday, Saturday, and Sunday. The children came running to meet him, fighting for the chance to help with the saddlebags, stable the pony, and fetch the bootjack—thus being able, without any loss of dignity to their mother, to slip from the disgrace under which most of them suffered most of the time for work inexpertly performed.

For the time, at least, they were a happily jesting family as they laughed together and enjoyed the Friday pie. Knowing full well that the extra piece was meant for him, Mentor ate it with great gusto after having passed it so rapidly around the table that no one else could take it—his way of showing how pleased he was that they were all so glad to have him home. Later in the evening he called each child to him, unkinking any hard spots in lessons that were now learned under another teacher than himself.

Saturday he picked up the round of farm work where he had left off the Monday morning before, and carried through until Monday morning again, when he rose early, built the fires, put on the kettle, fed and saddled his horse, ate his bread and jam and coffee, packed his saddlebags, and cantered off through the cold gray woods before the rest of the family were stirring. It had

been a refreshing time, for the neighbors all came in visiting, knowing he was away the rest of the week. His children had hovered
around, enjoying him, eager to help, eager to talk.

Farmers stopped in surprise that winter when they heard some
youngster declaiming at the top of his voice from the snowy school-
yard of the Tonica school, repeating some memorized piece from
the reader. Henry Coffee was the little boy who wouldn't speak up
in school, couldn't be persuaded to use his lips, almost whispered.
He had obediently marched out into the cold one day, mounted a
stump as directed, and, whether from the elixir of the cold or the
absence of staring eyes, shouted so lustily that his father, a school
director living near, sauntered over to investigate. Though the boy
was well bundled against the cold, when the elder Coffee saw it
was his little boy on the snowy stump he approached the schoolmaster standing in the door and said: "Shut-mouth men like you
are bound to be cruel. You take that boy in from off that stump!"
Graham took the boy in; but he also took the question to the other
directors, who voted to retain him over Coffee's agitated accusa-
tions, and Graham sent Henry back to the stump. And that was that.

Graham's last child, a son, was born in June, 1842. At a time
when no one recognized Lincoln's ability, at a time when Lincoln
seemed to be headed for mediocrity, Graham named the child for
him—Harry Lincoln. The boy was a hazel-eyed, black-haired little
fellow, who developed winsome ways and an aptitude for pantomime. Big Lincoln and Little Lincoln—that is the way Graham
distinguished them, though Sarah always called her son "Harry L." Big Lincoln was mightily pleased with his namesake. But
he said he wondered why anybody would name a child for him,
who had never amounted to anything and never would.

Certainly Sarah had won her place among women. She had now
borne fifteen children, ten of them living. A matter-of-fact person, she was, by now, only a trifle superstitious; a well-read woman,
with ideas often as startling as they were original. Incessant toil
had made her old-looking at thirty-six; yet her hair still curled
and was as black and heavy as ever, her eyes were stilling snapping blue. Childbearing had robbed her of her teeth, but her cheeks
were still rosy. She liked to try out new things—*Phlox drummondii*
seed, Jenny Lind hair-glow, buttermilk pancakes. Almira was
teaching her first school, saving her money, at Sarah's suggestion,
to buy her wedding clothes.

XVIII

EXAMINATIONS FOR THE TEACHER
1842–52

*A*LMIRA WAS going to be married, and the Graham house was due for a cleaning from cellar to garret, in preparation for the event. Such scouring and scrubbing and polishing as followed the siege of quilt-making that had taken most of the winter! Almira had her battery of quilts, each one of her mother's design and workmanship. These finished, the entire family was drafted for the great cleaning that lasted until within a few days of the wedding date—just enough time being left to prepare the wedding feast. There would be no dancing. Almira thought that countrified.

As her mother had done, Almira chose blue for her wedding dress and April as the month. A tall young woman with black auburn-glinted hair and a very white skin, she was highly skilled in household arts, a graduate of her father's school, and, like her father, an omnivorous reader. He had sent her to Jacksonville for two winters, where she studied Latin and reed-organ playing. She was marrying a distant relative (probably a second cousin), Ed Goldsby, high sheriff of Menard County. The phrase "Kentucky cousin" had come over intact to this section of Illinois, which was settled largely by Kentuckians. Distant and near cousins intermarried, generation after generation, until it was hard to say just what relation existed. Almost everybody was some kin to most of the rest.

Like her mother and father before her, Almira had had her share of merrymakings: apple stirrings and parings, corn shuckings, and fulling bees, when the young folk played the old kissing games—the same old ones from Kentucky, of course, along with new ones, mirroring a different period:

If I had as many lives
As Solomon had wives,
I'd be as old as Adam.
Rise to your feet,
Kiss the first girl you meet:
"Your humble servant, Madam."

After the couple left for St. Louis to buy furniture for the new home in Petersburg, Sarah went straight to "clearing up and straightening things round, again," assigning the duties that had been Almira's to Minerva. Almira, who had always been Sarah's right hand, was sadly missed. She, the eldest, had been under the constant responsibility of setting an example for the other children. She had not dared to balk, falter, or fail. As her father, when he began boarding around, had been treated as company from Friday to Sunday night, so Almira now wasn't allowed to touch a bit of work when she came from town to see the folks. Mentor missed her intensely: she had been his haven from Sarah's tongue. She could always manage to show by an extra song or a secret squeeze of the hand that she didn't share her mother's views. Sarah, driven by the hourly necessity of making both ends meet, continued to be "more than peppery." Even when the Graham family was fairly prosperous, to support thirteen people the income had to be stretched fairly thin.

Big Lincoln had finally "taken the jump," also, and married Miss Todd, though with the same sort of melancholy disinclination upon his part and the same sort of uncertainty upon the lady's part as had marked his courtship of Mary Owens. The Grahams were not invited to Lincoln's wedding. They were living at Springfield, but Lincoln never brought his wife to visit the Grahams on the few remaining occasions when he himself called. Stephen Douglas was deeply piqued at losing Mary Todd to Lincoln; and Graham worried over the harm he could do the cause of abolition, in revenge, now that he was in Congress. He talked to Lincoln about this, with little or no satisfaction—a slow smile and a slower head shake.

Like other farmers, Graham had a bad year in 1844. Wheat froze out and corn was slow, and only a thousand not very fat steers were driven to market from the farms of Menard County. Nevertheless, in July, after every member of the Graham family had worked all day and well into candlelight to save the crops,

Sarah and the girls went on a visit to Kentucky. This was an ideal time for Graham to catch up on his reading. He learned that Lincoln had taken a new partner, Herndon, Graham's cousin. He had not seen his once inseparable friend for weeks.

Instead of paying teachers, a new school law now portioned out school funds among patrons of schools in accordance with the number of children attending school and set the tuition rate which the patrons were to pay the teacher.[1] With six children still attending school, the Grahams received their due portion; but it all added up to pinching times, in the end. Other patrons' school money—in the press of hard times—went for shoes and food, and Graham went back to receiving tuition in the guise of turnips, pumpkins, corn—small amounts coming in, much bookkeeping, and many tuitions never paid. Even in 1845 many a cabin had cracks between logs "big enough to sling a cat through," many a child considered raw turnips a treat.

Graham took to peddling books between terms. He walked a territory thirty miles in diameter, leaving the horses at home for the boys to farm with. He managed to make ends meet, and reaped a fortune in satisfaction, for the old lost life of mental intercourse was reopened; free schools, Mormonism, abolition, were the subjects he discussed most often. Many farmers were against all three. If night or bad weather overtook him, he was sure to hear that cordial "Do stay all night, Mr. Graham. Might as well." If Graham stayed all night, he sought out the children, discovered what they were interested in, gave them little books on birds and animals, and told them stories. Nobody forgot him or his intense delight when, with the family gathered round, he turned the pages of the books he had for sale, reading out little bits here and there. He usually made the sale.

In the summer of 1940 Mrs. Lucy Robertson, of Tallula, Illinois, recalled one of Graham's bookselling visits to her home. When he arrived, her parents were away; but though she was a child of scarcely five, according to training she asked him in, took his hat, and asked him to be seated. She was alone in the house; the other children were about the farm, working or playing. She tried, but could not think of anything to say that seemed proper. Graham asked her questions, but she was too shy to answer. Finally he asked her if she could tell time by a clock. She couldn't. "So he

stood me before the Seth Thomas clock—which I still have," she
said, "and explained it over and over to me. When we saw my
parents coming, he said: 'Now you surprise them. Tell them what
time it is when they come in.' It was a memorable day. I remember
going round for days bragging to my older brothers and sisters who
did not know how, 'I can tell what time it is.' "

During August of 1843 Lincoln visited Graham twice while he
was stumping the state for Henry Clay; but Graham realized how
they were growing apart. The two men had a final talkfest one
sultry night, sitting under the dooryard trees. A last long talk, not
of marriage success, or of New Salem, long called "Old Salem"
now; not of Volney and Paine; but of the impending national
disaster being slowly and surely precipitated by slavery. Once
more they communed as of old, both men shabby with the times,
both forgetful of personal problems and finances. Graham never
forgot how Lincoln at last rose to go, recalling the lateness of the
hour, and held out his hand: "Well, good-night, Graham, I'll go
on. I've got to think." Nor how the stooped figure, grotesque on
the head-hanging, jaded nag, was lost in the starry night, down
the road to Springfield.

Graham attended the political rallies, carrying his ash pole
topped with a likeness of Henry Clay and adorned with a homemade flag like the ones all the farmers' wives were making, dyed
with pokeberry juice. These flags the farmers carried were brave
enough in the autumn sun; but on the cold, rainy fifth of November, when Polk and not Clay was elected, they became mottled,
blotchy rags.

Graham had his personal compensations for the defeat of Clay.
McGuffey's readers had become a reality. What teacher could ask
more? School directors were now required to provide a comfortable
schoolroom and all needed equipment; tuition was raised to $2.50
per pupil. With twenty-five pupils enrolled at Farmer's Point
School, Graham loaded his roan pony with children on his way to
school, and pegged away with greater precision than ever at the
engrossing task of feeding the child mind. He registered Perkinses,
Houghtons, Kennedys, Davises, Irwins, Goldsbys, Fraziers, and
Weatherbys. Menard County paid him $54.70 in March. Doubt-
less that sum had to be deducted pro rata from cash his patrons
paid in. At $2.50 a pupil, it should have amounted to $62.50. It is

easy to see why many who had been against free schools now began to talk for them; the new law required a superintendent of
schools for each county.

Meanwhile the slavery issue was ever growing in importance.
A rather unrevealing record in the old files at the Petersburg
courthouse is the only extant document concerning one of the
earliest runaway slave cases in the county. Graham, together with
Coleman Smoot, Samuel Denton, and C. W. Ballard, were subpoenaed as witnesses in an indictment brought by a grand jury,
first, against Marvin Pond and later against David Pond, brothers,
for harboring John Hauley, a runaway slave from Kentucky. The
Pond brothers awaited trial under bond from June until November, 1845, when a verdict of not guilty was returned. Petersburg,
in spite of early abolitionist leanings, was still more South than
North, and the Civil War found the town rabidly proslavery. Like
Thomas Lincoln, who was against slavery but for law and returned runaway slaves to their masters when he was slave patroller in Kentucky, Graham did whatever witnessing he could with
fairness. He was never anything but against slavery, though his
family, like many others, was divided, two of his brothers being
slave-owning "hot rebels."

Who in Menard County did not need money in November,
1845? Petersburg court and Springfield court were busy with cases
of hog-stealing and brand-changing, crimes that became more
common as times grew harder. Many a man stood to take his
thirty-nine stripes for a first, or be branded for a second, offense.
For his client, Mrs. Bowling Green, Lincoln sued Graham for
payment of a note for one hundred dollars. Certain it is that in
November, 1845, Graham did not have and could not borrow one
hundred dollars.

Lincoln dropped by to talk the matter over. He handed Graham
a due bill made to himself for work he had done for Bale in New
Salem for which he had never been paid. The due bill happened to
be the exact amount of tuition Lincoln had owed Graham since
his log-school lessons at the Baptist church in the woods. Lincoln
suggested that Graham use this due bill for ten dollars and add to
it the various sums for one thing and another which Bale owed
Graham. All of these items totaled one hundred dollars. That list
of "one thing and another," still available in its original form at the

Petersburg courthouse, shows an entry dating back to Brush Creek days when Graham had cut brush for Bale for fifty cents a day and had never been paid; tuition for many children, both in Illinois and in Kentucky; butter and eggs, and "smoothed lumber" from Graham's workbench. Jacob Bale, who had been rich enough to buy out everybody as they left New Salem, paid up. And Graham paid Mrs. Green (see Appendix, pp. 255–56).

Peter Cartwright, now that being called to preach was no longer considered the one essential for preaching, received an honorary degree from McKendrie College, which he had helped to found. Now, an aging man, a gentleman with a degree, he entered the congressional race again against the country-schooled Lincoln. The lawyer was now riding as wide a circuit as Cartwright had once ridden as a hell-fire preacher: Tazewell, Coles, Logan, Christian, Menard, and Champaign counties. When Lincoln's habitual melancholy expression vanished and the old ardor of creative thought returned as he stumped Illinois for Clay, the literary allusions he made were readily comprehended. Country-taught listeners knew what he was talking about. Cartwright didn't do so well with his old method, trying to make men fall in politics as he had in religion; after all, an honorary degree couldn't supply the long years of intent and earnest study the lawyer had put in. This time Lincoln received the cheers and the invitation to come back. And he was elected to Congress in 1846.

Lincoln had been speaking in Indiana, also, and took occasion to visit his old boyhood haunts and hear the old "Indianner twang" with an ear long trained to spot improper pronunciation. The sojourn brought to mind old sorrows; and when he came home, he came out to talk them over with Graham, just for the comfort of it. It was like a prayer answered for Graham, for the visit lasted several days: Lincoln stayed at Graham's house during the session of court when he prosecuted Chester Moon, and won the case. Moon had shot and crippled Johnson Elmore, Graham's cousin. The case for an unpaid note against Graham's new neighbor, Hardin Masters, he also won, and another note-collecting suit for old Jeremiah.

In the evenings they did not slip back into the same comradeship as in the old days. After the children had given Lincoln a concert of songs from their new *Clark's Songbook*, which Graham had bought on his last trip to St. Louis, they all talked of Kentucky and family history, the subject inspired by the news that Daniel Boone had just been brought home from his Missouri grave and reburied with much pomp at Frankfort.

Their songs were of the type popular then, songs long since forgotten. Most of them were mere parodies set to well-known tunes, as witness the

SONG OF THE COFFLE-GANG
(*Sung to the tune of the* "National Anthem")

My country 'tis of thee,
Dark land of slavery,
For thee I weep.
Land where the slave has sighed,
Land where he toiled and died
To serve a tyrant's pride,
For thee I weep.

May brought trouble with Mexico and the call for volunteers. Lads who had squirmed and wriggled while they declaimed from stumps back in '36 and '37 now mounted the gangplank of the "Mary Jane" at New Orleans. Many died of yellow fever on shipboard and were buried near the mouth of the Rio Grande in Texas. Others made their grueling way, five hundred long miles, on the march to Tampico. "A strange world," Graham said, "that fosters youth, only to send them out to kill and be killed, and—for what? Still, if giving their lives was going to insure the passage of the Wilmot Proviso, would keep the new territory free of slavery. . . . . ." But the Senate which had made the proclamation of war failed to pass the bill.

Whether Lincoln and Graham together attended the demonstration that was staged in Chicago in 1847 is not clear. Graham was not a delegate and seems to have gone merely out of interest. The assemblage drafted a memorial against President Polk's veto of the Inland River and Harbor Bill. It was a rousing meeting, with all of southern Illinois well represented; but it got nowhere. The improvement of inland rivers had always been one of Lincoln's and Graham's pet themes for dreaming upon; Graham died still hoping for it.

While Lincoln was away at Congress, school matters grew difficult for Graham. He now had to take an examination for a certificate to teach. He was one of the few granted a first-grade paper, but he found himself faced with a new and vexing problem. Menard County received an influx of German, Norwegian, and Portuguese immigrants whose children could not speak English. Indeed, the parents were not sure they wanted to spare children from farm work, just to go to school. Through an interpreter Graham first had to persuade these newcomers, who argued that they had come to a free country and could send or not as they pleased. With the few children who did appear he worked tirelessly. Teaching a language was a new kind of teaching. Again he labored far into the night, copying out lessons for children whose parents didn't please to spend money for books. While Lincoln, returned from Congress, was riding his old circuit again, these freedom-seeking immigrants were swinging, by their very numbers, the rising proslavery tide in Menard County back to a free-state majority.

With the return of Lincoln, going to court again became the necessity that it had somewhat ceased to be in Lincoln's absence. In court week, come what might, Graham attended every session and afterward made one of the party that sat up all night talking. Mrs. Bradley says:

"Grandfather was friendly with almost everyone. But some of his best friends that he liked to visit were the Purkapiles, Goldsbys, Maltbys, Kennedys, Irwins, Sampsons, Currys, and especially Robert McNabb, a great story-teller. He is the man who kept the Rutledge Inn after Onstott. Grandfather rode to Sugar Grove on his pony to visit Leonard Alkire's family; and in Sweetwater he had a good friend in William Engle, storekeeper, politician, and story-teller. Sometimes these friends met in Petersburg during court week; and at night, instead of going to bed, they talked all night and listened to Lincoln's experiences and humorous illustrations. Grandfather would make almost any sacrifice of time, money, and comfort to be of that company."

Others besides Lincoln owned a copy of the *Facetious Pocket Companion* and adapted the jokes with great relish to their own experiences and those of their acquaintants. Most of them had seen the play *Six Nights with the Washingtonians* (the temperance society), which survived, after being a bit remodeled, as *Ten Nights in a Barroom*.

The family and the entire neighborhood were enlivened by

a protracted visit from Nancy, Graham's sister, who had lived in his household before her marriage. She was wealthy now—in California gold. She presented each member of the family with a nugget and made a decided stir in Petersburg with her velvets and laces. She and her brother engaged in hot arguments on religion, politics, and how to teach. A well-read woman, she had herself been a pioneer teacher in Shasta County, California, before her husband struck gold. Her niece remembers her saying of herself, "I'll be nothing but a question mark to my dying hour. The idea, of letting myself be lost in a book, like this, and forgetting my housework!"

Lincoln at this time, saddened anew by the death of his first little son, looked on and listened morosely when the children brought out their nuggets and when Nancy said archly: "All intelligent people are for slavery, aren't they?" He reckoned she'd done well if she could afford to go on clear to Georgia to visit.

When the news got to Kentucky that Nancy was in Illinois, a younger brother, Jackson, came on from Green County to see her. He was high sheriff of Green County, and now that his term was all but up he planned to move to Georgia. He and Nancy would go south together. He brought the news of the death of Graham's grandfather, that William Graham who had brought his children and his Nancy Elizabeth through The Gap in 1790. As things went smoothly in the Graham household and as there were many books Nancy hadn't read and her two little boys and Jackson's two little girls played together without distracting her from her reading, Nancy stayed on, from day to day, from week to week.

One May night they were all seated at the supper table, shortly after a hailstorm that had stripped trees, killed swine and poultry, and covered the ground with hailstones that would not melt for days. The men had mended the roofs and buried the dead animals and were just saying how lucky it was that the corn was not yet up when Ed Goldsby came galloping up, scattering the hailstones right and left. He burst in with "Almira's got a baby girl!"

"Now, don't tell me I'm a grandmother, Ed," Sarah said, beaming. "I can scarcely stole it. Belike I'll get right ready and go back with you. I knew this storm was a sign of something."

Little Lincoln wanted to know of his father: "then are you a grandfather now?" Graham, seeing that the child was perplexed to the point of tears, took him in his arms and explained to him that becoming a grandfather hadn't affected his being little Lincoln's father one bit. He delegated the boy to ride into Petersburg behind his mother, to see the new baby of which he was uncle— though still his father's son—and bring back the horse.

There were plenty of hands to do the work if Sarah stayed a week, even with preparations for Minerva's wedding going on. So Sarah went into Petersburg and helped Almira, and took her joy at being a grandmother. But she came back after a few days, responsible for the next wedding. Minerva was a handsome young woman with spit curls and a watered-silk wedding dress. She was going to marry Samuel Kennedy and was "mortified to death" because her grandmother smoked a pipe in church. She sang "O Susanna" with a good deal of dash, and thus impressed the neighboring farmers who were still dancing hoedowns to—

> Old Dan Tucker was a fine old man,
> He washed his face in the fryin'-pan,
> He combed his hair with a wagon-wheel
> And died with the tooth-ache in his heel—O!

> Get out the way for old Dan Tucker,
> He's too late to get his supper.
> Supper's over and the dishes washt
> And nothing left but a piece of squash.

Nancy matched this dance tune with temperance words—she was "strictly teetotaler":

> Get out the way, you whiskey seller
> You have ruined many a feller . . . .

But Minerva preferred ballads to temperance songs. She always "sang for company": "Bell Mahone," "Lily Dale," and, like her mother and father before her, "Barbara Allen." She had a choice among the men, and she had snubbed more than one country bumpkin who told her how purty she was and rolled his eyes like a dying calf. She had dressed them down aplenty.

As the summer wore on, there was much sickness in the family and much watching by bedsides. By working at night in his fields, Mentor managed to keep his farm work going, sit up with the sick, and get to Bloomington and several other points to hear Lincoln speak. Everywhere that Lincoln stood up, the torchlight flickering over his rough visage, he talked with such inescapable logic that he was cheered to a roar. When Robert Graham came on from Kentucky for a visit, the brothers attended the rallies together. Robert appraised Lincoln as "a deep thinker."

When he arrived, Robert showered the family with gifts, and the house was noisy with childish chatter and grown-up talk. Robert told his brother that he had done well with such a fine house and fine family and praised his farming and teaching until Graham, unused to praise, beamed with joy. Robert had been twice to the Kentucky legislature and said that Kentucky was not as strong for slavery as might be supposed.

When Nancy and her children and Jackson and his family and Robert and his family all left for home at the same time, Graham accompanied them. They had a gala steamboat trip, rode on a locomotive train, stopped in Green County to visit round, and went on to Crab Orchard. On the return trip, alone, Graham stopped in Louisville and bought a book for everybody at home, and a bright pink rattle for Almira's baby.

XIX

L̸ASTING GLORY

1852-61

BOTH ALMIRA and her baby died—a sad, despoiled grandfather stopped his horse in the corn row he was plowing, lost in meditation upon the ways of God. Less vital, less interested, his nervousness aggravated, he had a second "sick spell" that lengthened into July, after the news came of the death of Henry Clay. In August, leaving Sarah with her needle and loom preparing for the wedding of their third daughter, Elizabeth, he went to Kentucky for solace. But he found only a sharpener of his grief in the deserted, windowless, tulip-poplar cabin where Almira had been born.

Other fathers have lost their beautiful, devoted daughters. Eyes ahead. Life is still to be lived. But that formula for easing another's grief did not salve his own. Lincoln, at his suggestion, had delved into Euclid as a means of numbing sorrow, of strengthening the mind to the point of wanting to go on, trying to find something to live for. On returning home Graham took a near-fatal dose of his own medicine. For months, until he was thin and pale, he worked at it stubbornly, and finally Euclid proved to be something more than a mathematician. For Graham came through the self-imposed study with strengthened faith—how he never could have said. That things in the physical world were plumb and true, and according to some plan, gave hope. And there was that new idea of foreordination. Lincoln argued for that.

Gradually Mentor brightened back into something of his former cheerfulness. His favorite sister, Nancy, came for another visit and brought many gifts for each of the Grahams. She had just lost her husband; but her very presence must have dispensed cheer and faith, for she, too, was a deep and constant thinker. Her niece, Leila Elmore Masterson, of Chico, California, in whose home she often visited, says: "She had a pleasant expression and very pretty hands. Her blue eyes were sharp and shining, and her brown hair was curly. She was forever making notes, cutting items out of newspapers and magazines, and made many, many scrapbooks. She carried on a large correspondence with friends and relatives in the East. I remember she could quote the Bible as pointedly as any pastor." It is likely that she had a great part in restoring her brother, for her philosophy at that time was a stronger one than his. Upon the flyleaf of her Bible she wrote: "I believe that sorrow, remembered, sweetens present joy; nor yet shall we be always sad, for God has given peace."

When the new town near by was christened by Lincoln[1] and named for him, Sarah remarked acidly that the circuit-riding lawyer had evidently found his rut and would stay in it. At the request of the new town's proprietors to christen it, Lincoln had carved a watermelon, squeezed juice upon the ground, and said, "We christen thee Lincoln, Illinois," after which the crowd ate the melon and buried the rind. "Probably wiped their mouths on their coat sleeves," Sarah said, when she heard the details. "That Abe Lincoln has no idea of manners." But Graham was mightily pleased, and he set his irritable wife on edge by humming "Yankee Doodle" morning, noon, and night for days afterward.

Graham sought out Lincoln, and they held a long session on the subject of death. Lincoln had lost his father and his little son. Though the two read Wordsworth's "Ode" together, taking long hours to stop and discuss and ponder over and wonder about its meaning, final help did not come to Graham, whose deep sadness lasted for many years and colored the remainder of his life. He became more tender than ever with children.

Still, he roused out of his lethargy somewhat when the old infidel charge was once more brought up against Lincoln. Henry Pollock, a student in his school about this time, quotes Graham as saying: "Now they curse Lincoln and throw all kinds of abuse on him—call him Nigger-lover and infidel; but the time will come when he will be looked upon as the greatest man in the nation." He seemed to get a little respite from his grief when he was defending the friend in whom he had utter faith.

Lincoln drove into the Grahams' yard several times that fall, a poor-looking, deeply melancholy man, his clothing unkempt, his carpetbag near collapse, his faded, greening coattails wrinkled, his deep-set eyes seeming larger and more gloomy behind the glasses he had taken to wearing. Sarah greeted him as ever, but after he had gone invariably remarked that he didn't seem to be amounting to so much, after all. She didn't see why Mary Todd, high-up as her family was, let her husband go looking like that. Why, even the knob was off his umbrella handle. Sarah was deeply impressed by the new *Parlour Magazine* with colored style plates which she was expert in copying. She read of the doings of her own family in the Petersburg paper. Proud to be somebody, by these two standards, she never for a moment let the family forget what they must live up to.

They always sang when Lincoln came. (After its appearance in 1859, "Dixie Land" became his favorite song.) While the children shouted around the organ, Graham and Lincoln made a show of singing. The new member of the Graham family, a nephew of eight, had a high, shrill voice that rang above the rest. His parents had died, and Sarah was bringing him up. Graham had little desire to sing—Almira had always played the organ—though all the Graham girls could sing and play. But Lincoln loved to listen to the children and called for one song after another—patriotic, religious, popular. Sarah frowned on some:

> Good-bye Lize-Jane
> She died on the train,

or

> Grasshopper sittin' on the sweet tater vine
> Long came a black bird and nab him up behin'.

And she made them stop singing

> Molly was a good girl, good girl, good girl,
> Molly was a good girl,—
> And a bad girl, too.

After Grandame Mary's death, Grandsire Jeremiah, who had been spruce and able as a cricket, dimmed and failed, content to be a chimney-corner pipe-smoker. The census of 1855 reports him between eighty and ninety, though he was only in his seventies at the time, according to more accurate records. Remembering Old Kaintuck, he entertained his grandchildren with many a fine tale,

just as Mary had done. To these two story-tellers we are obliged
for many of the details of their son's life—their son of whom they
were inordinately proud. Like Sarah, they basked in the glory of
being somebody, with others referring matters to Mentor. He
had fulfilled their hopes—if only they might have known how
exceedingly well!

The old home paper, recounting the death of William Skaggs on
Brush Creek, at the age of more than one hundred, brought old
times back to Jeremiah; and he told them all about Skaggs Station as he had heard it from his father, when there was nothing
else on the Creek. Finally, as Andrew Lynn had died in the home
of his son Benjamin, as William Graham had died in the home of
his son Johnson, so Jeremiah died in the home of his son Mentor,
flickered out amid kind words. Though he had for long been quite
a burden to care for, he had love and respect and was "Dear
Grandsir" to the last.

When, in 1856, Illinois put Lincoln up as candidate for the vice-
presidential nomination, Sarah refused to believe it, since even
smart men like Richard Yates couldn't rise to such heights.
Richard Yates combed his hair and changed his shirt. How a man
with such baggy trousers, unkempt hair, battered hat, and un-
polished shoes could be chosen for such a high place was beyond
her comprehension. He was just as likely to get there as Offutt—
in whose store he had once failed—Offutt who, as talk had it, was
traveling with a circus of wild horses in Georgia.

She was right this time. And in 1858, after Douglas' election as
Senator, Lincoln again practiced law and Graham paid strict attention to teaching in a schoolhouse that was provided, heated,
and equipped by the public. But there was a new trouble. Big
boys taunted other big boys with "Damned abolitionist!" and
"Nigger-lover!" Graham was kept busy thrashing for the fist
fights that ensued. Albert Rothschilds, of Petersburg, one of these
students, told (in 1940) of the Honeyhart school: "Graham went
right down the line, first with the least, then the next least, and
right on up to the oldest without flub-dubs of any kind. He rang a
dinner bell to call us in and kept us strictly at it, and no funny
business. He boarded round and always carried a bag of whole
wheat flour with him. He couldn't abide white roller-flour. He
taught us to sing

"Voyager upon life's sea
To yourself be true,
And whate'er your fortune be,
Paddle your own canoe.

"He would move his head from side to side, vigorously, to the rhythm of the chorus:

"Paddle your own canoe, boys,
Paddle your own canoe:
And whate'er your fortune be
Paddle your own canoe.

"He lectured us often on freedom and free states and told us that Douglas had been booed when he spoke in Chicago and had been offered thirty pieces of silver in Ohio."

Graham also taught these children to sing "Ho! For Kansas, Free Kansas!" That is, he attempted to, for half of them refused to sing it or sang "Ho! For California!" instead. Finally Kansas won out, for he lectured every day on the evils of slavery. But he was dismissed as a consequence.

He collected on a few notes in court, sold a quarter-section of land he had been holding on speculation, and did not look for another school. His old silk tile got a stiff brushing every time he stepped briskly into Petersburg, which was almost every day. He walked like the wind, they say, his familiar, well-kept scarf of dark stripes muffled about his ears. Honeyhart school had thought him the best teacher they had ever had until some of the Copperheads hadn't been able to answer the arguments for common freedom which their children produced at home, after having been required to learn them, letter-perfect, at school.

Kentucky papers now carried the story of a black congregation that had bought its preacher, paying for him through weekly donations. White men were trafficking in their own blood: not all the slaves knocked down at auction were black. Beautiful octoroon girls and young boys brought the fanciest bids. Deeply roused, Graham was striding into Petersburg for the sole purpose of standing up for Lincoln, the enemy of slavery. This he made it a point to do as he paced from hardware store to courthouse, from Hill's store to the bank. He literally patrolled the village square, intent on stopping any slurring of Lincoln in its tracks.

One Saturday he arrived earlier than usual, for he had heard that certain men were slandering his idol. He rolled up his sleeves, paced the square all day, shouting at intervals: "Come on out, you slave-drivers! Come on out and face my fists!" Though the square on Saturday was usually filled with groups of excited arguers, no one answered his challenge. But, after that, when Graham went from group to group of wranglers, he did not hear anyone "throwing mud on Lincoln." The Petersburg newspaper, however, ridiculed abolition and certain abolitionists.

The decade 1850–60 had seethed from its beginning. First to Kansas, then to California, migration kept people in a flurry of indecision. Armed parties leaving for California gold or to make Kansas a free state were frequently held up in Missouri. The sacking of Lawrence was the signal for Illinois patriot women to hold sewing bees for Kansans and for men to lend money to prospective settlers. Many indentured Irish and German orphans from the East arrived in Menard County to be bound out as house servants and farm hands. Along with all this there was the hog question. Graham advocated keeping sick hogs separated from well. Even in Springfield, hogs ran loose on the main streets, rooting and wallowing when and where they pleased. In the East, Illinois towns were referred to as "hog-towns"; and actually there were more hogs than people in many of them. But Graham got no further than being laughed down. "Hog" factions won over "Anti-hogs" until nearly 1860.

Freed from the responsibility of teaching, Graham attended most of the Lincoln-Douglas debates as local feeling grew more bitter. Someone carved a likeness of Lincoln upon a sycamore growing in sight of the Old Salem mill, near the spot where the Lincoln-Berry store had stood. But secessionists chopped the thing to chips—nobody knew who or when. Nor was Graham the only schoolman to suffer. The *Illinois Register* publicly denounced Illinois college professors: "You should not be tolerated for telling infamous lies about 'bleeding Kansas.' Beware, gentlemen, what you do. You are accountable to your country. The honest citizen will not contribute to your college."

During this time Graham had gone on a note for four hundred dollars with his son, William, who was marrying. The notice was served by Ed Goldsby, a "secesher" and the man who had been Almira's husband. The schoolmaster sold more land. He collected on a few notes, sold a few cattle, and came through out of debt and with a Petersburg lot, taken in trade. He was in the field most of the time, having all but decided to give up teaching and farm for a living. His children were growing up, marrying, or teaching; and he felt he could supply the family's decreasing demands from eighty acres.

He took the family to the Springfield rally in September when seven thousand are said to have gathered to hear Lincoln speak. The speaker, catching sight of Graham in the crowd, called out, "Things are bound to move, Graham," and waved his tall hat exuberantly. To this greeting Graham bowed with his usual perfunctory courtesy and an unusually brilliant smile. But he shouted, "Go it! Get there!" at intervals during the speech. Lincoln was certainly "skunking them."

Local tension increased when a Republican paper—"damned abolition sheet," the Copperheads called it—began publication at Petersburg. Its editor also printed a Baptist church paper. When Graham walked into Petersburg, he was mimicked behind his back by young and old rowdies, who tipped imaginary silk tiles and quirked a hand elegantly in an imaginary flowered satin vest. But they did not dare to speak against Lincoln in front of Graham, and "straightened up like lightning" if he started to turn around. He was tutoring private pupils in Petersburg; and though Petersburg square was not safe, he refused to carry a gun as other abolitionists did.

However, the bad signs that Sarah and others besides Sarah had been talking about—destructive storms and floods; destructive frosts; the aurora borealis shining all night long like a rainbow— seemed destined to do their worst. And January brought the catastrophe. Lincoln, making the "most logical, most penetrating, most constructive speeches of anything on record," as Graham said, was defeated by Douglas, the repealer. Lincoln couldn't even draw a crowd—that was seen to—when, after election day, he tried to lecture at Jacksonville on "Discoveries and Inventions." The Copperheads rode smilingly about the country, and political interest died down. Almost the only safe topics were such commonplaces as that Jemima Gum, now that Tom was dead, was running the four-hundred-and-twenty-acre farm alone, or the exercises at the academy, or that the roads were too icy for safe driving.

Farming was not very successful in 1859. Killing frosts came late in June and early in September, making short forage and food crops. It looked as if it were going to be another winter of skimping and scraping. But the directors of the Concord School sought Graham out and hired him to teach a large school of seventy pupils. Again the schoolmaster trod on air. He was *needed*. Besides, almost every scholar under him had an ambition to enter Sangamon Academy in Petersburg.

For a time Graham considered moving into Petersburg. He owned lots, and two married daughters lived there. He planned to do private tutoring to earn a livelihood. His daughter, Mrs. Elizabeth Bell, who lived at what is now 121 West Jackson Street, was the town's temperance leader; and he was eager to support her. As things were, he was spending a great deal of time going back and forth. But when the Concord school offered a position, he accepted, and life went on as usual. Sarah had wanted to go, but the subject of moving to Petersburg was dropped.

Then came 1860, fast moving, overflowing. Graham's school prospered: seven of his advanced learners were accepted by the academy in Petersburg. Crops were good. Home from a trip to Springfield one day, Graham ran from stable to house, shouting: "Halloo! HALLOO! Abe's been nominated for President! PRESIDENT!"

Sarah, forgetting her numerous disparaging remarks, greeted this unparalleled outburst with "Well, if he gets there, you can thank nobody but yourself for setting him on the right track."

"Maybe so. Maybe so. But *he* will set this country on the right track. I tell you, right from the start, I saw that fellow had capacity—CAPACITY!"

All through that summer of the famous rail-splitter campaign Graham almost ran behind his plow. He repaired the house and stable, pens and sheds. He mended all of the farm tools and implements. He edged in a summer term of school where he taught the children the song all patriots were singing:

> Stand by the Union, stand by the Union,
> Stand by the Union, and be on the right side.
>
> Jump in the wagon, the old Union wagon,
> Jump in the wagon and we'll all take a ride.

He laughed and shouted with the ante-over players and joined in games of town ball. He galloped off, singing, to rallies and galloped home, singing, from them. He bought Sarah the finest dress she had ever had.

Sangamon country was noisy with rallies and mass meetings. The little near-by village of Athens put on a horseback parade of thirty-three women in white—the states—accompanied by mounted and uniformed Wide-Awakes (a political marching society), followed by a line of people in buggies, wagons, on horseback and afoot, carrying rails (which had been split by Lincoln on his father's Coles County farm the year he was twenty) and shouting for Abe Lincoln. History relates that a good one hundred thousand trekked to a mass meeting at Springfield. For days they labored down the muddy roads toward that mecca, where, when the hour struck, they formed a procession eight miles long, one whose members reviewed their own pioneering. Ox-drawn floats exhibited stone churns and spinning wheels, log cabins intact, shoemakers, blacksmiths—and rail-splitters. Again thirty mounted women impersonated the states, followed by a solitary woman rider bearing the banner: "*Kansas*—They won't let me in." There were ten brass bands and four thousand Wide-Awakes. At night the demonstration was reenacted—a torchlighted procession. Later, speeches went on in four places at the same time (shades of Caneridge Camp Meeting!), and knots of people sang and kept up a hullabaloo until after midnight. They say there was a light in every window of every house. Folks were singing

> No servile politician he,
> True gold, without alloy:
> Unanimous our vote shall be
> For Abe of Illinois.

Or the Douglas champions came by with

> We'll raise our glorious banner high;
> Douglas and Johnson, live or die!
> We'll vindicate our glorious cause,
> The Constitution and its laws.

On election day, when Lincoln spied him in the press at Springfield, Graham threw his stovepipe hat into the air so many times he had to buy a new one. This was the proudest day of his life, the day when his believed-in, most advanced learner was chosen to lead the nation.

As inauguration day approached, he weighed the pros and cons of going. Sarah finally decided the matter: "You go, Mentor. I'll make out." And Graham went to the capitol dressed in a new suit and kid gloves, carrying a new carpetbag. And, of course, the hat was all but new.

Perhaps one high hour of life is worth living toward, struggling up to. Perhaps one hour, if it be high enough, is worth long, slow years of declining away from, once it has passed. Such an hour was Graham's. For as he seated himself at the front, that his good ear might catch all that was said, Lincoln sent for him. He sat, quivering—almost palsied—with pride and joy on the platform at the inauguration of A. Lincoln, president of the United States—A. Lincoln, to whom he had given his first public office as assistant clerk in little New Salem's election. It was a lasting glory.

XX

COPPERHEAD CONTROL

1861-64

*W*HEN THE 1860's began, Menard County was a sadly divided place. Petersburg was becoming less and less safe for a Unionist. Even while Petersburg folk heard the Union cannon booming away down in Springfield, many of them were cheering the nomination of Breckinridge by the seceding states.

As, state by state, the Southern Confederacy formed, Graham decided not to teach but to produce supplies for the northern army. Then his sons volunteered; and one of them, Samuel, drafted his father to teach out the term at Curtis school. So Graham went back to the old schedule again, at it every minute—teach, farm, teach.

Little Lincoln, now six feet tall and seldom called by the old nickname, had a sweetheart he was going to marry if he came back. He had volunteered. So had the sixteen-year-old nephew the Grahams had taken into the family at the age of eight after the death of his parents. Sarah was right: their crossing the Ohio River had not kept slavery's war away. She reminded Mentor of this the morning the boys marched out of Petersburg.

The call had come on the fifteenth of April. The Union paper at Petersburg said: "If we have any disunionists amongst us, let them show their colors." That night the home guards met. If Graham was absent-minded sometimes, finishing out Sam's school, who could wonder? The volunteer company had organized and gone; and mothers were sending letters and roast chicken after them, and blankets and quilts, for the weather was unseasonably wet and cold.

Though signs were bad and army worms beset crops that promised poorly, spirits held firm, and on the Fourth of July the countryside rang with "The Star-spangled Banner." Even so, there was unrest. A man was killed by assailants who said they had only meant to thrash him, not break his neck. One Saturday folks from Salt Creek, in town trading, settled their differences by a free-for-all fight in the Petersburg square.

Most citizens, however, kept the peace and managed to skimp out every morsel of food and every inch of cloth possible to give to the Union Concourse that came through regularly to collect supplies for the boys who had marched away. In September, Petersburg Unionists called for a meeting in the square for the purpose of pledging fidelity to the Constitution. But down on Salt Creek "secesh men" gave the secret sign and in the dead of night marshaled the Knights of the Golden Circle to drill.

As 1860 slipped into 1861, Graham, although he belonged to it, ceased attending the Intellectual Improvement Association, which was composed largely of slavery men. It often met at the farm next to Graham's, owned by Hardin Masters, who was a prominent leader. Graham did not want to be caught hoofing it down "Secesh Lane," as the entrance to Master's farm was known locally. He spent his entire strength and time in teaching and in keeping a constant stream of farm produce trickling into the Union wagons. He now had more spot cash than most, for his school was large. But hard and harder times were the general lot, with potatoes at ten cents a bushel, butter six cents a pound, eggs five cents a dozen.

Bells in Petersburg tolled on June 6, 1861, and flags were draped in mourning at the death of Stephen A. Douglas. He had been their candidate. (Today, Petersburg's main street is Douglas Avenue.) The two town papers carried excerpts from the *Atlantic Monthly*, or such blood-boilers as "Paul Revere's Ride," while dealing vituperously with current patriotism—the one, with "secesh currency and disloyalty," the other with "northern shinplasters and brag." Meanwhile loafers pitched horseshoes back behind the saloon, where the talk was more likely to run to the best cures for ague, salt rheum, and teters. The cure most in use was plenty of whiskey.

Fort Sumter had fallen in April, but still no one at home had any personal word from Lincoln. Graham saddled up and trotted into Springfield to find out how things stood with his idol. But there was little to learn. The headlines and the street talk were alike:

what was going on in the conflict, how the battles came out; not what Lincoln was thinking, suffering, hoping, fearing, praying about. As far as available records show, Graham and Lincoln did not communicate while Lincoln was in presidential office. Graham had no political favor to ask; he wished none. His was a much larger satisfaction, already achieved. His job was teaching. He was only inviolably proud of the man he had helped to save the nation. Perhaps his time was as burdened as Lincoln's. He felt the personal responsibility of doing his utmost for the cause. Certainly there was no better way to show faith and uphold a dearest friend. Those who wonder at this do so doubtless because being repaid in a worldly sense is what most people would expect, what the world seems to consider only right. But none need pity Graham nor consider him snubbed: the glory of achievement was his reward. He wanted nothing else.

Late in August of this year the Beekman boys from a near-by farm, passing the Graham house on their way to the mill (which had been rebuilt after burning) missed the schoolmaster. Often he had pounced out at them in jest, bringing the horse up short, squinting clownishly and reeling off some impossible problem with the injunction: "See that you have the right answer before you get back." This time they planned to gallop past and have the joke on Graham. But he was at a picnic. His boy, Sandy, was home on a furlough.

Graham taught the Curtis, sometimes called the "Smoot" school, during 1861 and 1862. An old man now, by some standards, he had taken to wearing a gray woolen shawl. He rode one of his farm horses, and the silk tile assorted oddly with the shawl. Yet his was still a vital figure with a fighting erectness of shoulders as, with the silk tile in place and the shawl flapping in the wind, he stopped by to swing up the smallest child before him and the next smallest behind. His was a small world and a small fight, but a thousand times responsible. These little children might, some day, have to face a harder world than his.

The Curtis school has been preserved in the memories of many students who attended it during the years Graham taught there, men and women with whom we talked eighty years later, in 1941 and 1942. If one thing more than another struck us in talking with these one-time pupils of Graham's, it was their precise and thoughtful language, a joy to hear in contrast to the usual speech of the present day. John Terhune, an erect, well-groomed, and courteous gentleman, welcomed us to his rambling Illinois farmhouse near Sweetwater. It was an orderly, peaceful, homey place; lilies of the valley and violets bloomed among the steppingstones about his piazza. His white head shone against a background of orchard bloom as he came out to meet us. He held out his hand.

"Yes," he said, "I knew Graham. He was my first teacher, I believe, when I was little Johnny Terhune, some eighty or more years ago. Come in. I think I can recall something about Curtis school.

"The schoolhouse was brick and large enough to accommodate about one hundred. The stove sat in the center of the room and the benches faced the middle aisle. Any ventilation we had was accidental, for the windows on the north and south walls were never opened. Fresh air came in by way of the door. The playground was large. I remember the hitching rack was on the west side, where the road ran by. Graham had what we call 'drive' and 'punch' today. He drove straight through his long day of teaching like an electrical machine. Not so much for looks, maybe. When you saw him coming, you scarcely knew whether it was a man or not. He wore a shawl and always had a child or two or three riding with him; and sometimes they would creep under the shawl from the weather, or just as a prank. I recall several who attended that school—Barbara McNabb, John Smoot and his sister Mary, Maria Clark, Matilda Fulton—well, not so many, I guess, out of about seventy-five."

William Clark, another who attended the Curtis school, produced a list of names, his fingers busy counting them as he reeled them off—a remarkable feat after eighty years: Acey, Calpurnia, and Jennie Williams; Bill, Ed, Steve, Clarissa, and Minerva Denton; John, Will, Jane, Calvin, and Coleman Crawford; John, Molly, and Eliza Quaintance; Bill, Queen, and John Marquell; Jim and Molly Hornbeck; John and Sam Terhune; Paris Mosher; Burn Goldsby; and John Fulton.

Both Clark and Terhune remembered a fist fight Paris Mosher had with John Fulton; but they disagreed as to its details. In fact, perhaps it was Bill Clark and Jim Crawford who fought. At any rate, one of the boys pulled a Jimson weed and pounded his adversary with the frozen root "until he raised a lump on his head as big as a goose egg." Brought to justice, the Jimson-weed wielder lay across Graham's knee, "his pants all tightened for the first lick," when Mary Smoot began to cry, begging: "Don't whip him, Uncle Mentor! He won't do it any more! I know he won't!" The lucky lad was released. With alacrity he repeated the formula, "I'm sorry I struck you," to the beaten adversary. He was required to feel the knob, to promise never to fight again.

Curtis had its bucket and tin dipper, and it was a glorious privilege to carry the water down a country lane from Smoot's farm, half a mile off. Thickly sliced meat sandwiches and apple pie now filled dinner buckets. Bull pen had grown up into town ball, and crack-the-whip had arrived, along with the old familiar "Geography Song":

> Rhode Island has two capitals,
> Providence and New Port. . . . .

The girl with the best lessons was privileged to give out the words at spelldown.

The day's routine began with roll call. Then they sang. A favorite song began

> There came to my window one morning in May
> A dear little robin, that came back to stay.
> The tune that she sang was sweeter by far
> Than ever was played on flute or guitar.

Then Graham talked on morals and manners and reminded the school of his rules, after which there were lessons, play-spell, and lunch, then lessons again.

For his money-salary—every dollar of which had to be discounted down to twenty-five cents—Graham taught reading, writing, spelling, geography, arithmetic, and grammar—and Shakespeare's poetry—to seventy-five children, while he anxiously waited for letters from his sons at the front. The few Copperheads among his pupils seem to have been silenced by the effectiveness of Graham's logic, or, it may have been, by his hickory switch in a hand toughened by fifty years of farming. He kept his contract to "keep the school under control."

Thus it happened that the next year, 1863, directors of the Tick Ridge school, who had had their school broken up by Copperheads, offered Graham better wages if he would take Tick Ridge and teach a whole term through. He accepted, this soldier of sixty-three, riding horseback the four miles morning and night. Henry Pollock, one of the Tick Ridge boys, gives a graphic picture of Graham this year. First published in the *Decatur Herald*, in June, 1906, the story is prefaced thus:

> I don't think I am able to do justice to this man who had such a great part in influencing the Emancipator. No one, in my opinion, had such influence over him as did Graham during Lincoln's stay in New Salem.

Pollock, the son of an abolitionist, lived in the midst of a new settlement of southern sympathizers. His is perhaps the most vivid picture of Graham produced by anyone:

> The first day Graham kept me in. He came back to where I was quaking in my hide.
>
> "Aren't you the son of Pollock, up east, the black Abolitionist?" he asked me.
>
> "My father is a *white* Abolitionist," I answered.
>
> "Well, he's a Lincoln man, is he not?"
>
> "Yes he is and so am I," I said pugnaciously.
>
> He had been looking very sternly at me all this time. When I began to get angry he began to smile. Putting his hand on my shoulder he said, "You are *my* boy. You and your father are right. I am for Lincoln, too, first, last, and all the time. Lincoln I have known for thirty years, and in the future I will tell you about my experiences with Abe Lincoln when he was a boy at New Salem. But what I want to know is this. You know that this school has been in a great deal of trouble the last few years and that the directors got me by promising to stand by me to bring this school under control—you heard what they said at your house the other evening. As you know, most of the people around here are opposed to me on account of my politics. Now I want you to be my trusty boy. If I need the directors, I want you to take my horse and go after them. There will, perhaps, be other things which I shall need you for. This must be a profound secret. Will you?"

The next morning the gangsters barred the door and Graham broke it in with a fence rail. This so nonplused them that they subsided for the rest of that day. But on the third morning they charged Graham in the woods, dragged him from his horse, and bumped and rolled him down the creek bank, prodding him with sticks toward the hole they had cut in the ice. Henry Pollock, coming up, yelled: "You stop that! The law will get you if you kill him!"

When he got nothing but loud guffaws, Henry, without waiting for the high sign from the helpless schoolmaster, caught the horse and rode off at a gallop for the directors. The school-busters dragged Graham across the ice to the edge of the hole, where their courage failed them and they turned him loose. He washed off the blood in the creek water, straightened his clothing, smoothed the dents from his hat, and walked, very rapidly and very erectly, to the schoolhouse and rang the bell.

The directors arrived almost at once and a double trial ensued. Finding the schoolhouse door demolished, they asked: "Who broke that door, Henry?"

"Go ahead, tell the truth, no matter who's hurt," Graham prompted.

"Well, then, Mister Graham did."

The trial was short and crisp. Ringleaders of the barring-out party and the ducking party were identified and sentenced to "heavy trashing to be administered before the school and the directors." We have Pollock's word for it that Graham did a magnificent job that settled the school for that day.

Next morning the same boys climbed trees and crowed like roosters when Graham rang the bell. But, seeing Henry about to start for the directors, they changed their minds, came down, and came into the schoolhouse. After that the school had no further trouble, and the boys Graham had thrashed gave him, at the end of the term, the hearty compliment of being a "damned good teacher." Possibly the boys' thrashings had an educational effect upon their parents.

Like many farmers, Graham sold most of his farm horses, wagons, and cattle to the army. He also kept a supply of potatoes, molasses, a sizable amount of money for medicine and bandages, and letters to his boys moving out every week from his farm. Though his apples brought only forty cents a bushel and his chickens a dollar and a quarter a dozen, his large school paid promptly and he had some money. With calico, which had never been more than fifteen cents a yard, soaring to forty cents, Sarah had to spin and weave ceaselessly. She sent many a bolt to the army. With all his shorthanded and short-equipment farming, Graham managed to teach a summer term at the Hog Corner school.

Mrs. Laura Lott, of Petersburg, said in 1941: "Graham's eyebrows were so bushy the bright spots in his eyes appeared to be playing hide and seek. I do not remember that he wore glasses, or carried a cane. Certainly he did not limp. He was slender, erect, very freckled, and keen-eyed, with bushy, whitening hair. He would ride up at a brisk trot, jump from his horse, unsaddle it and tie it to the hitching rack, walk briskly up to the schoolhouse door and rap upon the door casing for order and the beginning of another day of lessons. We had a good time eating together, for Mr. Graham set us the example of bringing raw bacon or beef in our lunches. At play-spell we would build a big fire and roast our meat over it."

Mrs. Abbie Walker, of Redford, Iowa, another Hog Corner pupil, agrees with this. She added in 1942:

"Mr. Graham must have been my first teacher. Naturally I was timid, and one thing I distinctly remember. He lifted me down to the front yard of the school and told me to go to the rail fence, climb it, and read my lesson loud enough for him to hear.

"I can see the little old red brick schoolhouse and the yard where we girls played drop the handkerchief and sheep and wolf. We ate our lunches there when the weather was fine.

"The boys had a separate playground, and Mr. Graham frequently played ball with them. I recall just how *Sander's Speller* looked and how we sang

> "I wandered to the village, Tom,
> And sat beneath the tree
> Upon the schoolhouse play-ground
> That sheltered you and me.
> But none was left to greet me, Tom,
> And few were left to know
> Who played with us upon the green,
> Some forty years ago.

"That song is true, for I do not remember much about the children. Mr. Graham asked us to call him "Uncle Mentor," since he was our uncle, at heart, and would always follow us, proud if we succeeded, and ashamed if we did wrong."

Graham had long since exchanged his hope for more learners of a high capacity for a more commonplace philosophy: smaller minds should be developed so that they would work to their full capacity. No one could tell when the little mind, standing firm, might start a pendulum swinging the right way. Looking back at Graham, as we now can from a vantage point of nearly a century, we can honor that philosophy; he himself was its eloquent argument.

Back from the war, two of his sons married twin sisters. That joy was dulled by news of the death of Aunt Cassandra, the wife of Uncle Johnson Graham, whose influence had been so great in making Graham the humble exponent of right. Local pride in Dr. Stephenson, of Petersburg, a surgeon at the front who had been made an emissary to England, replacing Beecher, kept Graham's faith strong. But, with the president of the United States his best friend, with a cousin of the president of the Southern Confederacy his sister Nancy's second husband, with his brothers and sisters so divided by war that letters from the South ceased coming—Graham's was a troubled world, as this excerpt from a letter which he wrote to his brother Robert at Crab Orchard, Kentucky, in November, 1864, gives poignant witness:

"When Sally went out just now she spoke to me about writing to Polly Viniard who has lately written to Parthena Hill [Mrs. Sam Hill], speaking of us. [Polly is a nickname for Mary Owens.]

"She said I had always been her cousin, but that if I voted for Lincoln she would never call me cousin any more. . . . .

"I have not heard from sister Minerva since the war commenced. I wish I could hear something from her. . . . . Brother Ben is living in Logan County. . . . . He is altogether about the strongest Union man I have seen. He is for sustaining the government, and talks very sensibly in a quiet, cool, dispassionate manner.

"James, Brother Simpson's son, is here now. He left home about last July. He is driving the stage from here to Springfield. He tells me he saw a man, when he went up last, from his father's neighborhood who told him that his father was drafted and that he had left and joined the rebel army. He has been one term of three months in it, was in a slight skirmish with the 14th Illinois Regiment [to which Samuel, Graham's son, belonged].

"Sam returned about the fifteenth of July after being gone three years. He was in a number of hard fought battles and never received a hurt or wound. He suffered many privations and hardships. They marched 6,840 miles, 1,600 of it after Price, trying to catch him. At Hatchy River they had a fight with him and he ran. Samuel talks a good deal, narrates minutely their ups and downs.

You would be interested in conversing with him. He tells me that those wealthy planters in the lower country talk more sensibly and reasonably about this war than the secessionists do here.

"Harrison [a son] is teaching school on the Springfield road to Beardstown. He has been in the army three months—was gone when you were here, I believe. Aunt Lizzie Greene has been low a long time. . . . . [William Greene's mother.]

"I would be glad to see you and Lucy and the children again and hope and trust I shall not be denied that privilege. You must write me as soon as you get this. Write of your trials and afflictions, they have been many, I know. I humbly trust and strongly believe that before long there will be some terms of reconcilliation of the great national trouble. That will be when we are all properly humble enough. . . . ."

XXI

THE GOODNESS OF GOD
1864–74

DESPITE HIS age, Graham was now more in demand than ever. When the teacher at the Franklin school was run out, Graham was offered this school at a raise in wages. When it was learned that he had taken the school, the parents of children who had attended at Hog Corner, certain there would be no ructions if Uncle Mentor taught, sent their children to the Franklin school. A man who could handle Tick Ridge and Hog Corner was to be depended upon. This school was much farther from home than any he had ever taught, and Graham had to rise very early in order to ride the seven miles and get the schoolhouse warmed by the time the children arrived. That time was no longer sunup, but the new law-fixed time, nine o'clock. The children now left school at four.

In 1942 Mrs. Laura Lott described the Franklin school as it was when she attended it in 1864. The building was a new frame structure twenty by thirty-six feet, set back from the road in a fine grove of hickory and oak trees. Four of the oaks are still standing.

"I remember best," Mrs. Lott said, "how Mr. Graham took occasion when the stage stopped at the Oak Ridge post office to stop our lessons and let us go to the window to watch it, going by at what we thought marvelous speed, with its two teams of horses. Everything, he said, depended upon being on time, out in the world from which the stage came and to which it was going. It made us feel a part of the whole world, the way he said it.

"We had great fun playing in the stump patch of Seneca Winters and invented all kinds of games, using the stumps for bears, Indians, or circus poles. Mr. Graham kept a ruler, a pile of foolscap, and a brass bell on his desk. He called us in with the bell. I remember my slatefuls of ciphering, parsing, and conjugating: 'If

LINCOLN ONE YEAR BEFORE HE LEFT ILLINOIS

I be; if you be; if he be.' A cedar water bucket sat at one end of a shelf that held dinner buckets, and we hung up our wraps at the back of the room. The quart-size tin dipper was drunk from by several, until emptied. Our double seats ran on each side of the cast-iron stove. At lunch time we had fun sizzling our bacon at the stove or building a fire outside, to heat up our pancakes and pickled pigs' ears. When it grew warm, we picknicked in the woods."

Play ended when Graham rang the bell and pursued as unbending a routine as ever he had at the age of twenty-six—thirty-seven years before. Now that books were common and almost every child had his own, the schoolmaster had a new rule: A book must be respected. It was a fetish with him. The older he grew, the more intent he became about it; and the one certain way to rouse his furious anger was to deface a book. Any page that was torn or smudged had to be accounted for, and its owner was properly lectured and reprimanded. Should a child be so brash as to tear a page willfully, if it took the entire day Graham would find out who did it and use the switch effectively to prevent future sin.

Graham must have controlled the behavior of this school by severity of look alone, however, for no student remembered rowdyism or thrashings for outbreaks. The boys locked Graham out at Christmas and demanded a treat; he good-naturedly walked to Winter's farm and brought back a bushel of red and green apples, walking briskly through the quickly opened door, laughing with the children as he handed out the treat. There couldn't possibly have been more than one apple apiece. The basket of apples on the table, the master handed them out and waited for each "Thank you, Sir"—no snatching or grabbing—as he called their names: Mary Etta, Ann, and Marion Riley; Laura, Druzilla, and John Walters; Marvin and Josie Sampson; Henry, Marion, Luther, and Mary Eliza Wilcox; Mary, George, Tom, and Charles O'Hara; Will and Sarah Martin; Charles and Sylvia Piercell; Ed and Willard Henderson; Marian and Richard Miller; Kate, Jane, and Laura Maltby; Will Sneed; Douglas Sampson. . . . .

The father of the Henderson boys was a school director. It was his big watch, lent for the term until the directors could buy a clock, that lay ticking on the desk, marking the last happy hours before Christmas. Its hands came to four; and the children ran off down the snowy road, calling back, "Merry Christmas, Uncle Mentor! Happy New Year!" between bites of cold, juicy apples.

After Christmas there was much ado at the Franklin school. The children had already heard about Lincoln: how hard he studied, how hard he had to work to get books; how he had had to wait until he was a man for the chance to learn what they now were learning. The schoolmaster, imbued with energy incredible in a man of his years—because Lincoln had signed the Emancipation Proclamation—hustled those children through a course that would have done credit to a college. He told them daily of Lincoln's sense of responsibility and of how he had risen through his power to use words—the right words, convincing words. If lessons grew difficult, he would say: "Well, if you are ever president [or the president's wife], you'll have to try longer than that."

From January until March, 1864, soldiers home on leave precipitated many riots in attempting to make Copperheads and Peace Democrats swear to support the Constitution. The backwash reached the Franklin school, where the children aped their elders' doings. Some of the older boys quit school to go to war. Graham gave them his Godspeed in a speech of praise made before the school, and thrashed Peter Jacoby soundly for yelling "Niggerlovers" after them the day they left. Peter carried resentment all his life and vowed to thrash Graham, but he never did. No reliable account, however, survives of Graham's thrashing all the rest of the school for yodeling on the way home

> Butternut britches and hickory poles,—
> Democrats, Democrats, damn their souls!

School went on as usual in 1865—but not farming. How could a man farm? Graham at first refused to believe the news: *Lincoln shot and killed?* He went about absently, tinkering at this and that, accomplishing nothing, answering in disjointed phrases when spoken to.

A stooped, white-haired man, he stood on the fringe of the crowd, tearless, refusing to join the procession past the bier. He was an old, old man, his hands trembling together in nervous writhing, his legs shaking under him, as he walked at the end of the procession to the tomb; who saw, but could not afterward tell, how Springfield was draped in mourning and evergreens and flags.

GRAHAM, ABOUT 1865, AFTER THE DEATH OF LINCOLN

When the crowd had gone, he stood alone beside the Doric columns until long after nightfall, walked home, and without rest went into his fields. He walked in the woods for days and days. *Rather than betray these principles, I had rather be assassinated.* . . . . It was with Graham as it was with the freed Negroes:

> Massa Linkum he be ebry whar,
> He walkin' de earf lak de Lawd.

Dooryard flowers bloomed, children romped and laughed; but the glory had gone out of life for Graham. The Cause was won; but Graham, teaching between April and August, left books strictly alone outside the schoolroom. His own sons were back, safe, though only 480 of the 1,980 who left Menard County returned. He could not rejoice over even that, nor that the Union was saved. At noon he walked alone in the woods; and the children, coming upon him sitting bowed, his face in his hands, would slip away again, awed by his groans. *How could God let* . . . .

But his life was still to be lived, was to stretch on nearly three decades, was to hold yet further spiritual examinations which the man could not pass. Lincoln, become immortal, only sharpened the edge of the grief and doubled the weight of the burden for Graham, remaining mortal. For the Great Weaving goes on after one design is completed, even using the selfsame, unbroken threads of the warp, while the brilliant finished figures are turned from sight to give place to the monotonous beginnings of another unknowable design. Graham's drab warp-thread held. He taught on: tomorrow's children might have even worse battles, griefs, disappointments, to face.

If Graham saddened the twenty-eight boys and fifty-five girls who sat in his school that summer, it was by his look, not his words. They progressed better than any school he had ever had except one. They responded to his deepened tenderness toward them, the lowered tone of his voice, his never frayed patience. That a teacher could be so stricken over the death of someone to whom he had once taught grammar and surveying proved what he often said: "I shall always follow you, proud of your successes, ashamed if you do wrong." They called him "Uncle Mentor," with their own voices lowered in sympathy; they vied with each other for the honor of unsaddling and feeding his pony, and no reminder was

needed to keep the water bucket filled. Thus, befriended by the
kindness of his children at school and heartened by Sarah's best
cooking at home, and her silence, Graham got through that summer. He drew the highest salary of his life, $360 for a three-month
term.

The two sons, married during the war, had been living at home.
Now they proposed to leave, but Graham would not hear to it. He
pled with them to stay, build onto the house, buy more land, so
that all of them could farm together. They were both teachers; and
as their father's earnings were now at a thousand dollars a year,
they soon had a fine layout of land and equipment, livestock and
crops. Graham had always been generous in lending; now he collected several long-due notes to help finance the project.[1] After a
few years some of his old vim returned, but this time not via
Euclid. He had grandchildren to cuddle, to rock in the old hooded
cradle, to try to teach from his knee before they could toddle. And
he taught a Sunday school in Wolf District (originally called this
because of timber wolves in the area) and gave New Testaments
as prizes for well-learned texts.

But, after Lincoln's death, he himself did not read or farm—he
only taught. In 1866 he had the Bunker Hill school, on Rock
Creek, within easy riding distance of the farm. Rock Creek was a
less progressive neighborhood than the Franklin school district.
The old log schoolhouse was half-smothered in thick, high timber.
Pigs, cows, mules, and geese had the run of the woods; and the
pigs often came, rooting through the open schoolhouse door. It
was too far to the nearest well to carry water in cold weather; so
Graham brought the same old black kettle from home and melted
snow over the fireplace. Again he took the smallest on his knee to
hear their lispings and folded his old gray shawl for their naps on
the front bench before the fire. There were no desks. Crude ten-
foot benches had troughs underneath to hold books. Except for
the slates, it could have been forty years before.

A good many thrashings took place at the Bunker Hill school
in 1866. The big boys soon found out that they couldn't make fun
of the bushel basket in which one family of eight children brought
their lunch. They had to forego their custom of binding every new
boy, hand and foot, and rolling him down hill into the creek as a
sort of initiation. But once the school "found out who was boss,"

things proceeded amicably. A picture of the "last day" at the Bunker Hill school has been sketched by one of the students:

"The boys had been snowballing in the cleared space before the schoolhouse where the road ran through. Graham, in the act of opening the door to ring the bell for us to come in, was hit squarely by Joe Dickinson, who, as the target for the snowballers, had thought to dodge in quickly. Graham took his spill with a laugh, scrambled up with the agility of a man of twenty, not sixty-six; and he and Joe swept up the snow that had volleyed over the room. Then he rang the bell.

"When the ten benches full had quieted down, he made us a speech. His mood produced a complete hush. He talked about ourselves, what we would be like when we were old men and women. 'Learn something every day as long as you live,' he told us. 'The supply will never give out. Never go to sleep at night without having done this. Now, lessons!' "

On this last day of school there was not time to hear any but the most timid. Little Miss Primm couldn't get up courage to use her face muscles when she read, so Graham chose her to "mount the stump." She pulled on her warm coat and hood and trudged out obediently across the snow, ten, fifteen, twenty, yards down the well-beaten path to the "reading stump." Graham stood in the doorway, and she mounted the stump.

"Say, seven times: 'A sow with seven pigs came by.' " This sort of thing was preliminary to reading, a kind of limbering-up exercise. Graham, so they tell, gave out these warming-up exercises in any sentences or subjects that chanced to come into his mind.

As the sentence was repeated for the third time, a sow (without the pigs) did indeed come by, sending poor Miss Primm screaming to the shelter of Graham's arms. So she read indoors from his knee, and did so well that she was rewarded by being asked to lead the singing. Joe Dickinson and Bill Gruber soon took it away from her: "There came to my window one morning in May. . . . ."

Thus it happened that nobody heard the "madders" coming. The squealing sow should have warned them. A pandemonium of shrieks and howls arose outside, accompanied by solid whacks against the schoolhouse door and the din of pan-beating. In this school those who had "got mad and quit" were privileged to charivari the others, on the last day.

Graham opened the door and dashed the snow water from the iron pot over the madders. It froze where it fell, mostly on their faces; and they beat a squealing retreat, much as the sow had done. The song finished, the school was ready for the last-day spelldown which would establish the best speller until next term. They did not have to hurry, for on the last day parents did their children's chores— splitting wood, carrying water, feeding livestock, milking. It was nearly dark when the last pupil took his seat before the invincibility of William Barker. With a brisk "Christmas gift!" Graham went out to his buggy and brought in a box of candy apples—apples that had cost five cents apiece! After many an "Oh thank you, Uncle Mentor" and many a "Goodbye, Uncle Mentor," the older children finally started for home. Graham bundled the babies, stowed them in his buggy, and started down the long, snowy, rutted road, a brave old man with peace in his heart, setting the children down at their own doors and driving on after dark to the comfort of Sarah's warm supper and the joy of his grandchild-blessed hearth.

When in the next term Tandy Holman hit Pres Cogdel and knocked him down and kicked him, the trial lasted from morning till noon, with Bud Primm getting the job of cutting the stick. This is the school from which comes the classic tale of Joe Dickinson's swallowing a tack. In notes signed "P. W. H.," written by an unidentified person who attended this school this year, the tack story is told much as the books relate it, except that P. W. H. says that Graham did not *spank* Joe. Instead, when Joe howled out the frightening news that "a tack's gone clean down to my stumick," Graham hung him in the air by his heels and pounded him on the back to make the tack come out. As he pounded, he repeated anxiously: "It might kill you and it might not. It might kill you and it might not. Puke, boy, puke!"

This P. W. H. also tells of being sent by Graham for a quilt to cover his horse, shivering in a blizzard; that Graham smoked a pipe[2] in school and the pupils vied for the honor of filling it and lighting it at the fireplace; and that Graham once took him home in his buggy when the boy "took terrible sick."

At this school the "rag-doll" incident is also said to have happened. Graham ruled that no dolls might be brought to school, and punished the first girl who disobeyed by standing her on the floor with the doll in her mouth. The doll's dress, acting as a trough, caught the child's tears and dripped them to the floor. The children began to laugh. The first one to laugh, a boy, was made to stand beside the girl with a paper doll, which Graham manufactured, in his mouth. Graham was kept busy making more paper dolls. When everybody standing began to laugh, Graham laughed too. But no more dolls were brought to school.

Graham no longer needed to seek a school, the school sought him. He taught at Tonica again, and at the Shipley and Sampson schools; but now he refused private tutoring. He spent the time thus gained in taking Sarah to all the lectures in Springfield, Jacksonville, Decatur. He began to sit longer with his book, reading, while the boys did the farm work he delegated to them. Illinois towns of this section ran quite an intellectual competition. Quincy and other towns had literary circles that read Plato, Hegel, Locke, Darwin, and Spenser. Emerson lectured in Quincy in February, 1867, and Graham went up to hear him. The newspaper account of the lecture dismissed the lecturer with the scathing remark that he had read more than he had thought, that his lecture was merely a rehash of what he had read. It was a telling line, in Graham's estimation: "Read more than he had thought." Graham from then on spent more time thinking, less time reading.

And now rose the furor of a second coming of Christ, preached at a new form of the old camp meeting, now more elegant with tent and sawdust and called a "protracted meeting." Graham took the family down to hear a Reverend Spears from Indiana, for protracted-meeting preachers were traveling preachers, going from town to town, pitching their tents and staying as long as it was profitable. The Reverend Spears had been invited by Sugar Grove Church. He was soon joined by an Elder Lynn, also from Indiana, and the two of them worked such havoc in the routine of peoples' lives that nothing prospered because of neglect. They baptized nearly the entire countryside into the one and only sure salvation: a public statement of belief that a second resurrection was at hand. "Folks actually expected to see the Lord, right down there on Sugar Creek," it was said. But when summer passed and the Lord did not appear, the protracted-meeting preachers were turned out of their comfortable best-room beds and away from their free-food

tables, and the two disappeared into more considerate fields. "Fal-
derol and fiddlesticks!" was Graham's comment.

A new organization, however, was much more enthusiastically
accepted. B. F. Stephenson wrote out a ritual for an organization
which he proposed to call "The Grand Army of the Republic."
Post No. 1 enlisted Graham's two sons when it encamped at Decatur. Post No. 2 soon followed, camping near Springfield. By
midsummer the organization had swept the nation. To have a
cause, to meet together out of doors to acclaim that cause—this
was and has remained the human pattern for enthusiasms.

And the basic pattern of frontier life remained the same—with
long, arduous journeys west to a "better country." Graham, sitting on his porch, reading, paused to tell his grandchildren the
stories of how he had come to Illinois from Kentucky, how his
father had come to Kentucky from North Carolina and his grandfather from Virginia to Carolina. Now a new chapter was being
added. Always there had been that backwash of folks who
stayed behind—and this time Graham was in that backwash when
his sister Nancy had left the others and with her husband and two
sons had struck out for California years before. Content to recall
his own pioneering, Graham went on with the established routine
—schoolroom and field, reading and thinking. An aging man, he
watched the pioneering of younger men and women—a spectator,
not a participant. No better picture of him at this time exists than
the one supplied by the late Agnes Rourke Garretson, of Lincoln,
Illinois, as she remembered him as he was in 1867, when he was
sixty-seven years old:

"One cold winter afternoon my brother, running home ahead
of the other children, slammed the kitchen door, shrilling at the
top of his voice, 'Mother, mother! Teacher's coming!'

"I, a child of four, playing with my younger sister on the floor,
was thrown into a panic of fear. I had never seen a teacher. I
abandoned my sister to her fate and hid behind the roller towel.
The knock came, the invitation to enter. I saw merely another old
man. His picture is engraved on my memory: a tall stiff hat, a
heavy woolen shawl pinned with what looked like a horse-blanket
pin, trousers thrust into knee-high boots, a cane, a carpetbag.

"He began telling of the children's progress at school. I wanted
to talk. 'What do you do when you go to school?' I asked,

" 'Hush,' said my father.

"Mr. Graham led me by the hand to the fire, took off his shawl, folded it, laid it across the chair back, and took me on his knee. He took a sugar apple from his carpetbag and put it on the mantel, in my sight but out of my reach. 'If you will keep still for an hour,' he said, 'that candy is yours.' He showed me the hour and the minute hand on the clock and said I should watch the minute hand run all the way round and then the hour would be up. Just before supper, with a smile, he put the apple into my hand.

"The evening meal over, Mr. Graham put each child through his paces. When my parents announced themselves well satisfied, Mr. Graham climbed up the ladder to his bed in the loft. He paraded the children every night that week and complimented my mother on her cooking when he left, Friday morning."

In 1869 Graham taught three three-month terms. In history class he now included the Civil War, and in closing he was fond of referring to the freedom of the Negro by a song. No one those days was timid about singing before others, any more than speaking spontaneously. Little was known of the trained voice; and singing, as natural as speech, was still found a more effective method of expression. So Graham sang, in his high, even emotional voice—sang with considerable effect as a part of the lesson, such songs as

> I'se gwine from de cotton field,
> I'se gwine from de cane,
> I'se gwine from de ole log hut
> Dat stands down in de lane.
> De boat am on de ribber
> Dat am gwine ter take me off,
> I'se gwine ter join de exodus
> Dat's making' for de norf.
> Fo' de colored folks in Kansas,
> A way up dere, dey say,
> De colored fulks am flockin'
> Case dey's gettin' better pay:
> I'se bound to help my chillun some
> Afore I comes ter die,
> So when de sun's goes down tonight
> I'se gwine ter say good-bye.

Graham's old gray shawl, bulging with children he was bringing to school on his horse, was too familiar a sight to cause comment. Slender, wiry, his whitish hair bushed out on either side of the high hat, he was a man who simply would not endure having a child or a book abused, a man who rocked his grandchildren to sleep as tenderly as a mother. He continued to systematize his reading, giving himself two weeks between books to digest each thoroughly. He still polished his shoes and brushed his coat every time he wore them, studied the book catalogues with a trained eye, walked round the country thirty or forty miles to see his married children or to hear a lecture. His appetite for learning was undiminished, his desire to hear the answers of others to the enigmas of life was still sharp. Between terms he walked all over Menard County, selling Bibles. At this time he is reported to have been dismissed from a school in the middle of his third term because he insisted upon the boys and girls playing separately.

So, again, he took pupils to tutor privately. Kitty Purkapile was one of these. In the autumn of 1942 Mrs. Kitty Purkapile Miles told what she could remember of her old schoolmaster. Her husband, Jimmy, as a boy had also gone to school under Mentor in that interrupted third term. "Yes," she said, "we both knew Mr. Graham, back as far as maybe '68 or '69. I remember him as a tall, slender gentleman, very freckled, and with a long almost running stride that covered the ground quickly. I used to watch him coming up our road, his coattails flying out, his hat pushed far back on his head. When he came to our house to tutor us children, he often stayed overnight, and he and father sat up talking. We always sat around the fire with him when we studied, and after lessons he told us stories and sang songs to us. He always made us memorize poetry. I have the little book yet that he gave to me."

James Miles had come in from milking, twinkle-eyed and hearty—at eight-four. "Why I could tell you a bookful about that man," he said. "Different from the common run of us, always with his head up in the clouds. I used to run and hide from him when I saw him coming to our house because he always collared me and put me through my spelling paces before my parents—and my paces were considerable slow. One time he stayed all night, and next morning I was hitching from door to door—getting behind the doors, you understand—to keep out of sight, when he peeked through the crack and dragged me out. 'Spell flocks, Jimmy,' he said. 'Might as well put in the time to some purpose till breakfast's ready.' Now my mother had let me have her flower-seed catalogue to look at and she had been planting *Phlox drummondii*, so I ups and spells, *p-h-l-o-x*. Well, sir, do you know he never cornered me again.

"He had a way of looking cross and cranky and turrible serious and all the time not be meaning a bit of it. He was at our house a good deal, visitin', but never with his wife, as far as I recollect. She was ailing a good deal in her last years and took to staying close at home. He used to sit and talk, or go out to the barn with my father, and they'd sometimes forget what they went out to do and just stand, talkin'. He was a great hand for that."

In 1869 Sarah died. As a child of thirteen she had promised to be a faithful wife, and she had kept her promise. Her tongue may have had a sharp edge, but beneath her Irish temper beat a heart too loyal to fail its pledge of devotion to her husband. Sarah, in her last years, was too weak to work much, and lived in the past, knitting by the fire or telling tales to her grandchildren. As a mother she had told her children stories of their life in Kentucky and their journey to Illinois; as a grandmother she told her grandchildren of New Salem. Thus, ironically, she preserved the story of Mentor Graham's life, while his own painstakingly written-out narrative was destroyed by fire. She who bore fifteen children and gave a home and a mother's care to four other children, two of them orphans, rests beneath the fine white-marble monument Mentor placed above her grave. Its inscription mystifies:

> Whatsoever thy hand findeth to do, do it with thy might, for there is no device, no knowledge, nor no wisdom, in the grave where thou goest.

It was Graham's favorite text.

When his son Harry decided to move into town, Graham bought for $3,600 his share of the farm and continued to live at the farmhouse with Samuel and his family. Mary, Sam's wife, petted him and kept warmed, dry shoes waiting by the best chair before the fire. Still he found teaching—for he had another school—harder than ever, and home-coming not an event. Though he taught and read and studied as of old, and could still lose himself utterly in the grand-children, his habits of half a century were disrupted; and he found himself, in his seventieth year, planning to leave the old farm he had so long called home.

The month they sold the farm Samuel died. Graham, left now to provide for Sam's wife Mary and the three little children, followed Harry into town—the village of Greenview. In this community he was known as a kind old gentleman who gathered the children about him and told them stories. When the town drunkard died, he was the only one who could be persuaded to "lay out the corpse and sit up with it." When Mary remarried, Graham kept on teaching. Now he was living with his children, Harry and Elizabeth and Minerva, in Greenview, Petersburg, Tallula; boarding round when his school took him too far away to ride out to it every day, coming home if the weather was not too bad on Friday nights.

In 1870 he made a last trip to Kentucky, and drew much comfort from it. But his itinerary did not include Green County or the site of the tulip-poplar cabin. Instead he attended the centennial celebration of the Long Hunters and heard his boyhood anathema, Christopher Columbus Graham, now Kentucky's boasted centenarian, address a throng on the subject of early Kentucky. The men in that audience, their fathers, and their grandfathers had experienced all of American history. Graham's old fervor of responsibility for little children who must drive on alone into an unknown future swept back with its pristine fieriness. That future might demand more steadfastness than the past.

Returning to Menard County, Graham obtained a school near Chandlerville and there, with McGuffey readers, Ray's arithmetics, and several geographies, grammars, and histories, started teaching more than a hundred boys and girls. He did not need to teach, for the tax report of this year shows that he owned $12,000 in real estate and $11,000 in personal property. As a preliminary he was obliged to pass an examination, which he did, winning a first-grade certificate. While in town on this errand he heard of the proposed Petersburg Seminary, and that news set him to teaching, as elated, excited, eager as in his youthful days.

With clocklike precision he taught Dick's school and other schools, getting such results that town teachers, hearing of his methods, invited him to speak at their conventions. It was the elixir he needed—his first recognition, at seventy-two. He told them about exercising the mind, of complete meanings, of lazy tongues, face muscles, of mush-mouthings. He was so completely unique, with his exaggerated impersonations, gestures, and facial gymnastics, that many of his hearers went away calling him a very excitable, eccentric old man. But the proof of his sanity lay in the timbre of the pupils who studied under him. They understood completely what they read and could say, clearly and pointedly, just what they thought.

Teachers were not wearing flowered vests and high hats in 1872 —but in Graham's mind these things stood for the profession and he clung to them. Teachers in modern clothing smiled at him, but nevertheless gave strict heed to his methods and profited by them. Certainly, few could have accounted for odd moments as well as he. In a two- or three- or five-minute wait, the latest book was whipped from a pocket, a page read, the gist of the thought underscored—a new idea to ponder upon. Few, facing their pupils the next Monday morning, could attempt in opening exercises what he was past master of: talking to children out of his own experience. As always, he spoke in the same exact, rapid-clip way, in the same low-pitched voice, emotionally vibrant, spinning a key or coin between finger and thumb as he walked back and forth. And, as ever, if a pupil betrayed trust or disobeyed rules, that voice rumbled, dangerously throaty with indignation. But nobody whipped miscreants any more.

When he was with his daughter Elizabeth, in Petersburg, he spent much time at Crawford's hardware store on the north side of the square. Crawford was an ardent Republican and temperance advocate. In summer Graham "did considerable chinning under the shade of the trees on the courthouse lawn." He had a way of summarizing his opinion on the subject at hand and then listening intently to negative speakers. Nothing disgusted him as much as a drunken man. Elizabeth was a rabid temperance worker; and when the frost gathered on her glasses one morning and she mistook the saloon for the drug store, Graham was not long in chiding those who were laughing about it. They couldn't stand up to his cutting remarks. But they loved to pass on the opposite side of the street singing

> Ha! Ha! Ha! You and me
> Little brown jug, don't I love thee!

Tad Lincoln's death in 1871 had "unstrung" Graham. It opened anew the old, never healed wound. But the growing peace with which he had been blessed in the last few years returned. The toil and grief of seventy-three years had taken their toll of him, but he still bundled his babies, and looked the bully and the liar out of countenance with his steel-point blue eyes, confident of the goodness of God.

XXII

FINAL EXAMINATION

1874–86

*A*T SEVENTY-FOUR Graham was still teaching—as he was at seventy-five, seventy-six, and seventy-seven. At seventy-eight he taught his last school, thus rounding out fifty-two years of service to Illinois, which, added to the Kentucky terms, totals six decades. Though he had not been quite the same man since April, 1865—when an assassin's bullet had taken something of his starch and enthusiasm, along with the life of Lincoln—he had struggled on, buoyed by Sarah's growing pride in him, by her heartening welcome at home, by his unshakable faith in a God of goodness.

He was now being given the same respect by his grandchildren as he had required of his children for his old mother and father. The whole of Menard County welcomed him to its family circles as if he were one of them; he had taught most of these householders. Since Sarah's death, the habits of introspection, weighing, debating, had grown upon him. He had only scorn for those who now and then referred to his long tails, satin vest, and high hat as ridiculous. The ridiculers were yokels who measured him by themselves, by their idea of what life was for; or town gossips who rarely rise above the insignificant in their talk.[1] Meticulous in dress, prompt in courtesy, Graham stayed with his children. But he paid his way.

Edgar Lee Masters first related a trivial but most illuminating incident during Graham's last year in Menard County. Edgar's father borrowed his son's rubber spider on the end of an elastic cord and dangled it before the old schoolmaster's eyes as he stood under the trees in the Petersburg square—"just to hear him talk." Mr. Masters wanted to hear that perfection of grammar and exaggerated enunciation. And he heard it. "Did anyone see something, with legs, dangling before my face?" Graham asked.

That sentence may have been only a schoolteachery sentence-to-parse. Yet, if we know our Mentor Graham, he was administering a rebuke, even though the prankster did not realize it and found the sentence only very amusing. The younger Masters once sought to entertain the readers of a New York daily with the incident and recently unearthed it as bearing upon the history of the Sangamon River.

That Graham, as old records show, sued his son on a note for $270 when he did not need the money is right in line with the man's doctrine of responsibility. Suing for payment of notes, judging from the Petersburg records, was about as common as giving notes. Those who dismiss Graham as "an eccentric, tending to become involved in litigation," were themselves well acquainted with the condition of suing and being sued. If Harry Graham had borrowed, and put off returning because the lender was his father, Graham was not the man to let it pass. The world would not let such conduct pass, and the boy would suffer for his laxity. To pay honorable debts was a part of Mentor Graham's life-creed. He put it into a maxim: "A country is no more honest than its least honest young man." He sued and Harry paid.

And now, after all those heartbreaking years, after all that unfulfilled longing somehow to lessen the infamy and agony of the assassin's bullet, somehow to free the memory of his dearest friend from the "infidel" stain—Mentor Graham had his chance. B. F. Irwin, writing a biography of Lincoln, referred to Graham as the one man who could settle the infidel charge. He appealed to Graham because, he said, he knew him to have been Lincoln's most intimate associate at the time of the inception of the scandal. Here is Graham's answer:

PETERSBURG, ILLINOIS
March 17, 1874

Mr. B. F. IRWIN,
Pleasant Plains, Illinois

In reply to your inquiries, Abraham Lincoln was living at my house at New Salem, going to school, studying English grammar in the year 1833. One morning he said to me, "Graham, what do you think about the anger of the Lord?" I replied, "I believe the Lord never was angry or mad and never would be; that his loving-kindness endureth forever; that he never changes." Said Lincoln, "I have a little manuscript written which I will show you," and stated that he thought of having it published. The size of the manuscript was about one-half quire of foolscap, written in a very plain hand, on the subject of Christianity and a defense of universal salvation. The commencement of it was something respecting the God of the universe never being excited, mad, or angry. I had the manuscript in my possession some week or ten days. I have read many books upon the subject of theology, but I don't think, in point of perspicuity and plainness of reasoning, I ever read one to surpass it. I remember well his argument. He took the passage, "As in Adam all die, so in Christ shall all be made alive," and followed with the proposition that whatever the breach or injury of Adam's transgression, which no doubt was very great, was made just and right by the atonement of Christ. As to Major Hill burning the manuscript, I don't believe he did, nor do I think he would have done such a thing. About the burning of the paper by Hill, I have some recollection of his snatching a letter from Lincoln and putting it into the fire. It was a letter written by Hill to McNemar. His real name was Neil. Some of the school children had picked up the letter and handed it to Lincoln. Neil and Lincoln were talking about it when Hill snatched the letter from Lincoln and put it into the fire. The letter was respecting Miss Ann Rutledge for whom all three of these gentlemen seemed to have respect.

MENTOR GRAHAM

This is a calm, unbiased piece of writing, just to all persons mentioned. Mentor Graham, a man of seventy-four when he wrote these words, could, indeed, "remember well his argument." There is no sign of eccentricity or testy meticulousness here; it sounds as though a very dispassionate and clear-minded man had written it. He had obeyed his own principle: to "say the best of everyone." Of the few documents extant that bear the signature of Graham, this one alone could verify the faithfulness, sincerity, and keen-mindedness of the man. He was remembering back forty-one years.

The following winter, of 1875, brought the bleak news of the death of Graham's brother Robert. Yet the elder brother's shoulders straightened as he read the obituary in the Danville paper; for Robert had been to the legislature, had founded a bank and a home for the deaf. He had won his fellows' respect, honor, and praise. Robert had fulfilled his brother's favorite maxim: "No man can do more or better than to live so that his chief legacy is a bettered world."

As late as October, 1878, Graham is still riding his pony out of Petersburg to his rural school. His eyebrows and his once-red mop of upstanding hair are white and grizzled; and though his blue eyes are still keen, his thin shoulders have lost most of their do-or-die set, and the high hat looks a bit rakish, far back on his head, topping the trailing gray shawl. He jogs contentedly, not forgetting to stop by for the smallest child, for he still remembers that short legs tire on long, rutted roads. His friends, the flaming trees, the sumac and the sassafras are still both true and dear. God is good.

When Christmas released the children from their lessons—and released the master who would never return, he continued to sell Bibles. People usually bought the big brown family Bible he offered. To him all other books now seemed less valuable: they were filled with glib answers to the humanly unanswerable. At eighty, Mentor Graham, an alert old gentleman, walked from farm to farm, and doors were swung wide for him. People loved to hear him talk.

When he visited his children, he slipped back into the habits of sixty years, took his grandchildren upon his knee, and taught them for the pure love of teaching. In his pocket rested that little book which, when lessons came off well, was laid in a rapturous little hand. Two of those grandchildren grew up to be teachers and are remembered to this day as "cranks on reading." If little Mary or Kitty or Flora would ask, upon opening the book, "Who is that man, grandfather?" he helped her read beneath the picture, "Gen-er-al Hook-er." If the child asked, "But where are his horns?" he had his teaching chance. "Just a name, child, like yours is Graham. That doesn't mean that you are a gray ham, does it? I'll look it up and see where it came from." And on next visit the child would get the whole story of the Hookers.

When grandchildren were sick, he came to sit at their bedside and read to them or tell stories. Or sing to them—and he had not forgotten how to pantomime—some of the funny songs he knew, which numbered well over half a hundred. There were songs from his own childhood, from the Civil War, and love songs—doubtless "Barbara Allen." First it would be that slave song:

> Run, nigger, run, the patter-roller'll kotch ya!
> Run, nigger, run, it's nearin' de brake ob day!

And that would call for the juba patter song:

> Juba dis an' juba dat
> And juba skin the yaller cat,
> Juba! Juba!

Or he would take both parts in some such nursery yarn as

> Auntie, will your dog bite, dog bite, dog bite?
> Auntie, will your dog bite?
>
> No, child, no.

GRAHAM AT THE AGE OF SEVENTY-FIVE

But he sang only the gay parts of some songs:

> Dey called him "Ole Uncle Ned"
> A bery long time ago:
> He had no wool on the top of his head
> In the place whar de wool orter grow:
> He had no eyes for to see
> He had no yeahs for to heah
> He had no toofs for to eat a hoe-cake
> So he had to let a hoe-cake be.

He enjoyed them as much as the children and always waited for the expected request for the "Marsa Fat Man Song":

> Marsa's six feet one way and free feet tother
> An' he weighs five hundred pounds:
> His coat so big he can't pay de tailor
> An' it don't reach half around.

When one child was helpless with rheumatism, he bundled her up and carried her to a cousin's party, where the children all ran squealing with delight to meet them and to drag him by the coat-tails to the best chair. He told them horses couldn't stay at parties but that he'd be back to carry his missus home when the party was over, like a good horse should. They didn't want him to go. So he made a very funny face at himself in the mirror and said, "Well, I don't like this phiz, but as I've used it all these years, I reckon I could hardly do without it," and ducked out the door while they were still laughing. But when he came back for his missus they wouldn't let him go until he had imitated a steamboat coming down the river and sung the juba song from the start to finish of its seventeen verses.

By late 1878 Graham had gone to live with his son, Harry L., at a McLean Street address in Lincoln, "across from the old Latham place." He reveled in the lyceum lecture course and the newspapers and his daughter-in-law's salt-rising bread—and his numerous grandchildren. Who knows why he at last decided to join the Cumberland Presbyterian Church in Lincoln? Undoubtedly there was much more behind the simple entry than the old register relates:

> Name—Mentor Graham
> Date of Admission—January 15, 1883
> How received—By recommendation

Among those received the year before were his granddaughters, Flora and Kitty.

After he had helped Harry purchase a new and larger house on Eighth Street, he read the placid hours away, sitting under the trees in summer, by the Franklin stove in winter, until Harry's business took a turn for the worse. Still Graham did not worry; he had his life's savings in a safe bank. He enjoyed a visit from a nephew who had come up to Lincoln especially to visit him. A few days after this young man had gone, Harry found that Graham had unwittingly signed away all his life's savings to the young fellow, who was going into business in Kansas City.[2]

When a granddaughter, Flora, came in from high school that Friday afternoon, her distracted father, Harry, ordered her to take the teacher's examination the next day and told her he had arranged for her to teach at Sigg school. Without knowing the cause of such an order, Mentor promised to help Flora, telling her she was but little younger than he had been when he began teaching and that she had had twice his advantages.

Graham sent for his granddaughter Mary at Greenview, whose birthday was near in date to his own, that they might celebrate together. They had a fine party with cake and candles and ices. As a fitting climax he bundled the child in a new coat with a fur hood and muff and sent her home *on the train*, hugging the best present of all, a live puppy. Little wonder that this granddaughter almost certainly settles the question of the date of Graham's birth. What little girl would ever forget such a birthday celebration?

The death of Graham's brother Simpson James, on May 28, 1882, at Paris, Missouri, was the event which disclosed to Graham his state of dependence. He prepared to go to the funeral; but his banker told him he had no deposit. He had signed away thousands of dollars under the impression that he was signing a note for fifty. Thus Mentor, at eighty-two, became dependent upon a son whose business had gone to pot.

Harry was all for going West. Graham, true to his promise to help Flora with her teaching, decided to go along. Flora, who was not quite sixteen, was supporting the family. Though his old eyes sometimes played tricks on him, and his stride sometimes crumpled and he sometimes had to sit down upon the curb before he could walk the rest of the way to church, Mentor Graham nevertheless left Illinois and the Lincoln Eighth Street house, to go on a last, long trek.

Fifty-one families boarded the long passenger train at the Lincoln station one cold, rainy morning late in March. The Youngbergs, Wrights, Hirtmans, Keys, Duffs, Buckles, Petersons, and Grahams planned to settle on claims near each other. They were going to the promised land of Blunt, South Dakota, where every man of them, in dreams, had already become wealthy by growing wheat on government land. *A new country!* Again the West-infatuation was in all eyes, even those of the old men.

But Blunt turned out to be only a wind-swept siding of new plank shacks where thousands of free-land seekers had been disgorged, to overflow the one hotel and the lean-to boarding-houses. Many sought shelter from driving snow in empty boxcars, in tents, in dugouts, or dens made by topping stacked sacks of corn and bales of hay with planking. Harry paid down his earnest money on a boarding-house, arguing that profit would come more quickly that way. Every train brought more settlers, and he was sure of the patronage of those other fifty families from Illinois. As Flora and her mother were remaining in Illinois a few weeks longer, until Flora's school was out, little Kitty faced alone the job of cooking for a crowd of rough men, grunting Indians, and bewildered women and children.

The old grandfather shivers at the little stove in the big room and is scarcely noticed as he goes about, supported by a cane. The boys from Illinois beg him for stories: "Tell us about the New Salem and Clary's Grove goings-on, Uncle Mentor." In the hopeful atmosphere of a new boom-town, Mentor paints, out of the love he bore them, the trees and hills of the Sangamon, the unruly escapades of Clary's Grove boys, and the boys of Wolf Creek and Rock Creek and New Salem at Peter Cartwright's camp meetings. He tells of his log church-house school and, with a ghost of a prided smile, of his most advanced learner. Albert Peterson and Charles Hirtman are two of the boys listening. From them and from Flora and Kitty we have the story of the migration to South Dakota.

When arriving settlers had dwindled to a few a day, Harry Graham sold the boarding-house, loaded his goods upon mule-drawn wagons, and drove through the high, cold wind to the claim where he had thrown up a planking shack. The wagons bumped along over the unbroken trail, the course being determined by dead reckoning and by the help of occasional shingles, still stuck in some pre-empted and abandoned claim. Times were more than pinching, and as the old grandfather still had some little income from Illinois property, he staked it in Harry's venture. In September, 1883, he received $1,600 from the sale of Lincoln, Illinois, real estate. The money was stretched and stretched while the "Illinosians" broke the short-grass prairie sod and brought down a few deer and antelope.

The *Blunt Advocate* carried a tale explaining that the haze off along the horizon line was dust raised by buffalo herds, but the Grahams never saw a buffalo. Their wheat did not grow, and stomachs would have been empty if Harry and his wife and daughter had not all taught, so that with their combined low wages they might meet the high food bills. Flora and her mother rode muleback to their schools, and Harry loaded his small children into a cart and took them with him to his school, over in the next county.

Kitty and her grandfather remained at home together, and of these days she told at home in Mount Pulaski, Illinois, in 1942. Of course Graham taught her while she cooked and kept up the fire. If the family did not get home by sundown, they were given up for the night, since they were probably staying with the pupils in the schoolhouse and keeping the fire up all night so that no one would freeze to death in the blizzard. When they did get home, it was often with a pack of wolves at their heels.

Here, in this dismal land, at eighty-four, Mentor Graham set his still firm signature to file upon 160 acres of "wheat land" and 160 acres of "tree claim," six miles to the northeast of Blunt. He never proved up. His land "went back." But he enjoyed the prick of life, justified, which is strong enough to stay despair in the heart of the true pioneer, who goes out prepared to weather whatever storm breaks, in the name of a new country. Like his father and grandfather before him, Mentor forgot his age. No longer in the backwash, he breathed the challenging air of pioneering, kept his face cleanly shaven, his cravat tied evenly, and his frock coat and tall hat well brushed.

In fair weather he rode muleback to visit his claims and watch the Indians. Now and then he was encouraged by news of the opening of another school. He took immense pride in Flora, who was cheerfully enduring more hardships than Nancy Elizabeth Lynn. She was jolly and filled with courage, laughing at the job of fire-making in the early gray morning in her lonely little cold schoolhouse. Incidentally, her pupils learned to read with comprehension, as Mentor knew to his great satisfaction. True to his promise, he constantly tutored her on the hows of teaching and once rode with her to visit her school to make sure she was doing the job right.

After wheat failed a second year, many settlers turned to freighting as a livelihood. Kitty married one of the Duff boys and accompanied her husband from Pierre to the Black Hills, camping out in a lean-to on the mule wagon, crossing the Missouri over a pontoon bridge, and being a farmer's wife between trips. Her reports of "on farther West," together with letters from relatives in Kentucky, California, Texas, Georgia, and Illinois, kept Mentor busy with speculation and letter-writing. On his good days he read to the children or marshaled them to toe the cracks in the kitchen floor close to the stove while he gave out spelling words and taught them seven times nine and things out of his own experience, with Helen, the youngest grandchild, on his knee.

At Blunt they had lived in sight of the flats and could see the one giant cottonwood that stood above Medicine River, for which the Indians had named the spot Lone Tree. But on the claim there was no tree, no water in sight, nothing but the level circle of grass topped with a hemisphere of brassy hot or coldly stinging sky— a monotonous, treeless horizon line. How Graham, the tree-lover, fared in this treelessness we can only guess. But he walked out over the flat land, hopefully, no doubt, leaning on his cane. And he kept his interest in people, so that on July 4, 1884, he could bounce and bang into town in a wagon with the rest, to take in the Indian celebration.

Town sheriffs locked the saloons and kept the keys, to prevent the usual trouble, and the celebration turned out to be largely a mild milling-around all day and a banging and bouncing home again at night—but not before a purse of two hundred dollars had been raised. When the Sioux chief received the money, he ordered his two hundred and fifty warriors to execute a war dance, which they did, accompanied by tom-toms, buffalo horns, and yells. Blunt had given the Indians a small herd of fattened steers, which the Indians now slaughtered and cooked and ate while the whites looked on—a brand-new kind of Fourth of July celebration, strange to experience when one was remembering the times in old Kentucky and the Illinois barbecues.

On the Grahams' claim, Indians were often on hand to beg provender or trade skins for such goods as the shiny brass kettle. On Independence Day, 1886, they came trooping up to the Graham homestead offering, this time, a very fat papoose for the polished brass kettle. When they could not strike a bargain, they substituted the piano for the pot; then the violin. Angered by refusals to all their propositions, they began to yell and threaten. Flora sat down at the piano and began to sing. The Indians were so dumbfounded at the white squaw's indifference to their threats and so charmed with her singing that they stopped their noise and went off, Flora singing them out of sight. Grandfather Graham was proud of his girls with good reason.

Unashamed, he spoke with tears of his granddaughter Laura Edith, "dead at fourteen, out there in the barren churchyard." In each of the last four years wheat—the nightmare and not the dream come true—had failed; hot winds shriveled the fields and the unbroken drought all but took the lives of the farmers. And one dusty, windy day in April, 1886, Laura Edith was buried at Blunt.

"Back home," as they now called Illinois, the fine brick house that Mentor had built for Sarah had been repaired during the previous year. It was at this time that the workmen found the iron wedge inscribed "A. L." under the room in which Lincoln had slept. It was a good letter that brought that news. It gave the old grandfather material for happy and proud musings. The old house still stood!

Graham's silk stovepipe hat had at last given way before the harsh Dakota winters, and he now covered his thinned white hair with a fur cap. At the age of eighty-five he still went out for walks, a rather rotund old gentleman whose language made everybody stare—for thought, and the words that couch it, guarded his spirit to the end. He would shut his eyes in order to see the wooded Sangamon and the cabin on Brush Creek, and he would describe them until his listeners saw them too. He talked of pawpaws and sweet nuts on the bottoms—in this land of skin-and-pit wild plums.

He talked of red haws, wood violets, May apples, lady-slippers, and dogwood—in a land that had no shade.

When in October, 1886, news came of the dedication of the Statue of Liberty, Mentor, who had been feeble and ailing, brightened. He rose at the table, straightened his shoulders, gave his family a speech upon liberty—its perpetuation and its cost. It was, he said, the only wealth anyone should try to obtain, or should want to obtain, in the world. Its price, forever, must be eternal vigilance.

On the cold fifteenth of November, Mentor Graham, who had been trying to read with eyes that failed to make out the words, put the book in his pocket and went out for a walk. Walking had always cleared his mind, his eyes. But he did not return. He had gone to meet the final examination.[3]

They found him where he had fallen, a little way from the house, a finger still keeping his place between the pages of his book.[4] Like a leaf in the frost, he drifted down on the sere short grass of the Dakota prairie when the last sugar-maple leaves were drifting down along the Sangamon and along the wooded coves of Brush Creek. In that bleak, treeless land they buried him, beside Laura Edith's grave on the barren hillslope south of Blunt, in the little Presbyterian cemetery. Above his grave they had only a wooden slab to place; but it was inscribed: *The Teacher of Abraham Lincoln.*

EPILOGUE

1886-1944

*F*OR NEARLY half a century Mentor Graham's body lay in South Dakota, while the wooden panel above it rotted and sifted down. A man who had had a vastly productive life, he lay in a barren alien land in a half-forgotten grave. Harry Graham and his family had gone back to Illinois in 1894.

When, in 1897, fire destroyed the fine brick house Mentor Graham had built for Sarah, a few people then living remembered that a Scotch schoolmaster had built it before the New Salem days. Most of his books had been auctioned when the family went to Blunt. At that time his great stacks of laboriously penned papers and his array of scrapbooks had been burned. He was mentioned, in a sentence or two by men eulogizing Lincoln, as the "old schoolmaster who helped Lincoln with grammar and surveying."

But other men and women with their fingers between the pages of books began to understand something of the devoted labor and the complete unselfishness of this all-but-forgotten man. In 1933 that granddaughter Mary who had grown up to be a teacher (and who later became a great grandmother herself) decided: "We must and we shall bring him home." She went with her children and searched out the spot;[1] and they brought him back—back to his beloved wooded hills where he had given his perfect gift to a world—and they laid his dust beside the dust of Sarah. The Episcopal rector who said the final prayer was Jerry Wallace, greatgrandson of Mentor's sister Minerva, who married Ed Goldsby after the War of 1812.

Teachers of Illinois, understanding at last,[2] came there with tribute and blessing and eulogy to plant the spiring juniper and the living green of arbor vitae. Upon the monument they raised above his grave is etched a Grecian lamp; and beneath it is inscribed, "Abraham Lincoln's Tutor at New Salem"—a man who never guessed that he was lighting a lamp to burn through the ages.

Now in the dim sanctuary of the timber along the Sangamon, at the edge of the recently restored village of New Salem—which has its post office back—stands a log Baptist church, a replica of Mentor Graham's first Illinois schoolhouse. New Salem Park officials relate on the placard upon the church door, not that it is a Baptist church, but that it is the schoolhouse of Mentor Graham.

The pilgrim to New Salem today finds on the flat top of the high bluff overlooking the Sangamon the little village complete to the last weight-pole and roof-shake. It so completely transports back more than a hundred years in time that surely you will meet Dr. Allen or the stern schoolmaster, or catch a half-glimpse of rowdies taking hastily to the woods to escape being caught in some devil-try. Candy and calico are to be had at Hill's store; but there are no buyers. Yet a booming voice from Hill's covered stoop will ever threaten the absent storekeeper with hell-fire, and a lean young man will ever sort a rich little handful of letters at the counter. The carding machine stands ready to buzz and whir with fleeces that are never brought in; but, walking down the one grassy little street, the heart restores the whir of wheel, the distant whine of the mill round the turn of the road by the dam, and the voices of the villagers bringing in their pumpkins in October.

Half-doors stand open. The pilgrim faces spinning wheel and rag rug and patchwork quilt and gate-leg table draped with red checkered cloth and laden with heavy platters, plates, and jugs and pitchers of pewter. The wide hearths are blackened, and the once-used pots hang empty above cold andirons; but the heart restores the fire and the hearty folk in their everydays, baking and brewing, churning and chaffing, singing hymns, throwing on the great back-log against the whirling snows of winter.

Little children play about the street. There is the rattle of oxcart and the brave tooting of stage horn, the rat-tat of the cooper's hammer finishing a barrel, and of the cobbler's fitting in a goose quill that will lend a holy Sabbath squeak to the wearer's arrival at church and a two-bit piece to the cobbler's pocket. The lye hopper is wet down, and the iron pot of soft soap bubbles and boils above the back dooryard fire; and, bent above his leathern lap, the hatter concocts rich marvels of rabbit fur and beaver. Lullabys from cabin doors fall softly with evening as the older children come up the hill from school.

Wander down there. In the hush of the friendly woods the thrown-up log church stands, its unhewn logs pig-penned at the corners, its holy pulpit in place within. As of old, the door is unlatched. Slowly you push it open, half expecting the hubbub of a blab school. But the place is empty, silent. The schoolmaster has gone away. *The responsibility of a teacher. . . . . Fed according to mental capacity. . . . . Carefully enunciated and articulated. . . . . The FULL sense. . . . . The power of convincingly worded constructive thought to guide the world. . . . . Lazy minds make a dying nation. . . . . To raise the world, not glorify the self. . . . . A God of kindness. . . . .* The air rings with it, though you close the heavy door upon silence.

Scarcely visible in the dusk, a flat old headstone confronts you . . . . a few long, unmarked graves besides. But there is no sign now of those little mounds heaped long ago in the snowy winter and the droughty summer when the little sons of Mentor Graham were lowered in coffins he had made and Sarah had lined—lowered into the earth by Preacher Berry's kind hands and the aching arms of a lank young man, weeping for his friend's sorrow, ashes to ashes.

The whippoorwill sounds through the woods, and the cry of the nightjar. Back through the gathering dusk you catch a glimpse of a log chimney where, nestled among its sweet wild crabs, stands the rude shrine of the man who taught Lincoln.

APPENDIX

ACKNOWLEDGMENTS

$\mathcal{S}$PECIAL acknowledgment and deepest gratitude go to those completely generous persons who turned over to us the research of a lifetime: Mrs. Mary Graham Bradley, of Greenview, Illinois, granddaughter of Graham, not only relinquished her partially planned biography of her grandfather but also entertained the writer more than once in her home. Here, she and her children, Mr. and Mrs. Elton D. Ennis, drove me about the Graham country, introduced me to his old pupils and helped gather many details. Other grandchildren—Mrs. Kitty Graham Duff, of Mount Pulaski, Illinois, Mrs. Flora Graham Seller, of Lincoln, Illinois, and Arthur E. Graham, of Los Angeles, California—submitted graciously to interminable interviews by Mr. Nickols and myself and made available Graham's old books and many photographs.

Mr. and Mrs. C. E. Graham, of Greensburg, Kentucky, though belonging to another branch of the clan, invited me more than once to be their house guest while I grubbed away at the old Green County records. They aided me in finding new sources of information, drove me to interviews, and took many pictures. They own the original Brush Creek church record. Like Mrs. Bradley, Mrs. Graham kept up a live interest during all the long months while the work was in progress. My file shows more than a hundred letters written by each of these women, each letter telling of some new find or clue or inclosing valuable books, papers, or data.

Then there is Robert E. Goldsby, of Elizabeth, New Jersey, a family-history faddist, who had collected documents and records concerning his forebears, one of whom was Graham's sister. All this material was lent me with unparalleled graciousness, as was also

241

the scholarly research of a lifetime on the Lynn family by Mr. and Mrs. G. W. Beattie, of California.

Certainly the battery of attorneys who have untangled records and criticized and corrected many details have added substantially to the dependability of this volume. One of the most generous of them was Thomas P. Reep, of Petersburg, Illinois, an authority on Lincoln, whose verifying ability is without equal, unless it is to be met in the person of Judge Otis M. Mather, of Hodgenville, Kentucky, who not only aided in supplying information, as did Mr. Reep, but also was kind enough to read and correct the Kentucky chapters. Walter Milby, a lawyer of Greensburg, Kentucky, a lifetime student of his native Green County, drew from his data to answer my questions and to locate points on the maps of Graham's boyhood environs. The late Judge Lawrence B. Stringer, of Lincoln, Illinois, never lost interest in the projected biography and up to the last week of his life contributed much appreciated criticism and highly dependable material.

Impossible to name them all, thanks are due to all of those interested editors who supplied information and clippings, who helped locate sources, often publishing letters of quest with sometimes remarkable harvests; and to all of those librarians and researchers who thumbed old books and records and painstakingly copied the capping bit that was the missing link in the chain of the story. Especial acknowledgment goes to Dr. Harry Pratt, recently of the Abraham Lincoln Association of Springfield, Illinois, whose untiring efforts and warm interest, whose long hours of research, and whose complete generosity in lending books, papers, and records has had no little part in the Illinois chapters. And, likewise, thanks to that researcher extraordinary, the late Miss Louise Phelps Kellogg, of the Wisconsin Historical Society; and to all the others: Miss Sereta Morris, Mrs. Ethelyn Keese, Paul Angle, Clarence Fox, Downing O'Hara. . . . .

K. D.

A full list of all who contributed follows:

*Abell, Joseph E., Springfield, Ill.
Adair County News, Columbia, Ky.
Adams, E. E., attorney, Taylorville, Ill.
Alexander, Mrs. Eliza A., Loami, Ill.

* Denotes relatives of Graham.

Altsheller, Brent, Louisville, Ky.
American-Irish Historical Society, New York City
Angle, Paul M., secretary, Illinois State Historical Library, Springfield, Ill.
Arnold, Mrs. I. W., Bardstown, Ky.
Arnold, Joseph, Petersburg, Ill.
Atkins, Ethel, Lincoln, Ill.
Atlanta Argus, Atlanta, Ill.
Augspurger, Edmund M., school superintendent, Menard County, Petersburg, Ill.

Baker, Miss Clara, librarian, Decatur, Ill.
†Bale, Miss Alice, Petersburg, Ill.
†Bale, Harris, Petersburg, Ill.
†Bale, Miss Ida, Petersburg, Ill.
Beach, Miss Alice, librarian, Friends University, Wichita, Kan.
Bear, Mrs. Mary Evans, Chicago, Ill.
*Beattie, G. W., Highland, Calif.
*Beattie, Mrs. Helen, Highland, Calif.
†Beekman, Colby, Petersburg, Ill.
Beverlin, Mrs. Rosalie, Wichita, Kan.
*Black, Mrs. S. M., Red Bluff, Calif.
Black, W. C., Veterans Administration, Washington, D.C.
Blane, Mrs. F. E., Petersburg, Ill.
Blaylock, J. B., register of deeds, Yanceyville, N.C.
Bodenhammer, C. E., editor, *Redding Record*, Redding, Calif.
Bone, H. D., editor, *Anderson Valley News*, Anderson, Calif.
*Boswell, Frank, Mebane, N.C.
*Bradley, Mrs. Mary Graham, granddaughter of Mentor Graham, Greenview, Ill.
Brigham, Clarence S., American Antiquarian Society, Worcester, Mass.
Brown, Mabel, Illinois Historical Society, Decatur, Ill.
Burry, Miss Alice, librarian, Lincoln National Life Foundation, Fort Wayne, Ind.
Burt County Historical Society, Tekamah, Neb.
Bushing, T. G., editor, *Madison County Eagle*, Madison, Va.

Caldwell, S.D., president, Peoples Bank, Cave City, Ky.
Cannon, Mrs. Jouett Taylor, State Historical Society, Frankfort, Ky.
Capt, J. C., director, Bureau of the Census, Washington, D.C.
Carter, Wesley E., editor, *Hardin County Enterprise*, Elizabethtown, Ky.
Caton, L. G., secretary, Library of Congress, Washington, D.C.
Cheaney, Margaret M., Petersburg, Ill.
†Clark, Charles, Petersburg, Ill.
†Clark, Harley, Petersburg, Ill.
†Clark, Miss Lou, Petersburg, Ill.
†Clark, William, Petersburg, Ill.
Clift, J. Glen, Lexington Public Library, Lexington, Ky.
Cooch, Mrs. Eleanor B., registrar-general, Daughters of the American Revolution, Washington, D.C.
Coombs, Miss Elizabeth, librarian, Kentucky Building, Bowling Green, Ky.

† Denotes pupils of Graham, or those who knew him personally.

Craig, Mrs. Ella, Petersburg, Ill.
†Crawford, Miss Sally, Petersburg, Ill.
Creal, E. W., editor, *Herald-News*, Hodgenville, Ky.
Crihfield Brothers, editors, *Atlanta Argus*, Atlanta, Ill.
Crismon, Leo T., librarian, Southern Baptist Theological Seminary, Louisville, Ky.
Crittenden, C. C., secretary, North Carolina Historical Commission, Raleigh, N.C.

Dabney, Virginius, editor, *Times-Dispatch*, Richmond, Va.
Daniels, Jonathan, editor, *News and Observer*, Raleigh, N.C.
Dawson, Miss Bertha, Petersburg, Ill.
Decatur Historical Society, Decatur, Ill.
Demorest, Miss Rose, Public Library, Pittsburgh, Pa.
†Dowell, Mrs. Tom, Petersburg, Ill.
*Duff, Mrs. Kitty, granddaughter of Mentor Graham, Mount Pulaski, Ill.
Duncan, Miss Nell, Wichita, Kan.
Durham, Mrs. Lee, Greensburg, Ky.

Edinburgh University, Edinburgh, Scotland
*Elmore, Mrs. Cora, Columbia, Ky.
*Elmore, Robert, Springfield, Ill.
*Elmore, Silas, Springfield, Ill.
*Ennis, Elton D., Greenview, Ill.
*Ennis, Mrs. Marie, Greenview, Ill.
*Evans, Robert Graham, Claverhouse, Perryville Road, Danville, Ky.

Felts, Homer, Campbellsville Junior College, Campbellsville, Ky.
Ford, Mrs. Bettie, Allendale, Ky.
Fox, Lawrence K., secretary, South Dakota State Historical Society, Pierre, S.D.
Freeman, D. S., editor, *Richmond News-Leader*, Richmond, Va.

Garretson, Mrs. Agnes, Lincoln, Ill.
Gellerman, John W., postmaster, Lincoln's New Salem, Ill.
Gifford, H. E., Springfield, Ill.
Gifford, Henry E., Petersburg, Ill.
Gifford, Mrs. Lena May Tiel, Petersburg, Ill.
Gilbert, W. M., Carnegie Institute, Washington, D.C.
*Glenn, Mrs. Cynthia Elmore, Springfield, Ill.
*Goldsby, Edgar B., Springfield, Ill.
*Goldsby, Mrs. Ellen, Springfield, Ill.
*Goldsby, Mrs. Maggie, Springfield, Ill.
*Goldsby, Robert E., Elizabeth, N.J.
*Goldsby, Robert E., Fulton, Ky.
*Graham, A. L., Mebane, N.C.
*Graham, Arthur F., grandson of Mentor Graham, Los Angeles, Calif.
*Graham, Miss Bonita, Greenview, Ill.
*Graham, C. E., Greensburg, Ky.
*Graham, Mrs. C. E., Greensburg, Ky.
*Graham, David, Brush Creek, Green County, Ky.
*Graham, Mrs. David, Brush Creek, Green County, Ky.
*Graham, Miss Dorothea, Brush Creek, Green County, Ky.
*Graham, Miss Elizabeth, Greensburg, Ky.

*Graham, Evans, Claverhouse, Perryville Road, Danville, Ky.
*Graham, Mrs. Evelyn Elmore, Greenview, Ill.
*Graham, Fielding Vaughn, Brush Creek, Green County, Ky.
*Graham, Frank, Athens, Ill.
*Graham, George R., Burlington, N.C.
*Graham, H. T., attorney, Louisville, Ky.
*Graham, James, Brush Creek, Green County, Ky.
*Graham, Mrs. James, Brush Creek, Green County, Ky.
*Graham, John E., Kileen, Tex.
*Graham, Joseph, Iron Station, N.C.
*Graham, Joseph, Wichita, Kan.
*Graham, Miss Shirley, Greenview, Ill.
*Graham, Miss Virginia, Mebane, N.C.
*Graham, Walter, Greenview, Ill.
*Graham, Walter, Jr., Greenview, Ill.
*Graham, Dr. William, Greensburg, Ky.
Grauman, Miss Edna J., Louisville Public Library, Louisville, Ky.
Grohlman, Mrs. Ida, granddaughter of Bowling Green, Blanca, Colo.

*Halleck, Mrs. Evelyn Lynn, Hollywood, Calif.
Hamer, P. M., chief, Reference Division, National Archives, Washington, D.C.
Hamilton, Miss Jean Stuart, genealogist, Wichita, Kan.
Hamlett, E. C., editor, *Adair County News*, Columbia, Ky.
Hammond, Miss Ruth, librarian, Public Library, Wichita, Kan.
Hardin, Bayless, State Historical Society, Frankfort, Ky.
Harkness, R. E. E., president, American Baptist Historical Association, Chester, Pa.
*Harlenski, Mrs. E. F., Wichita, Kan.
Harms, Miss Ruth, Lincoln, Ill.
Harrison, Miss Bess, archivist, Charleston, W.Va.
Hellman, Miss Florence, chief bibliographer, Library of Congress, Washington, D.C.
†Henderson, Mrs. Marcia, Petersburg, Ill.
†Henderson, Willard, Petersburg, Ill.
Henkel, Rev. Leo, St. Mary's Church, Lincoln, Ill.
Heustead, Miss Elsie, Lincoln, Ill.
†Hinds, H. C., Salisbury, Ill.
Hipple, R. B., editor, *Daily Capital Journal*, Pierre, S.D.
†Hirtman, Charles, Lincoln, Ill.
Hoke, Mrs. L. B., Hardin County Historical Society, Elizabethtown, Ky.
Holbert, George K., judge, Circuit Court, Elizabethtown, Ky.
Horner, Mrs. Josephene C., Petersburg, Ill.
Houghton, Mrs. Ellen La Mar, Petersburg, Ill.
*Houghton, Mrs. Mary Lynn, Springfield, Ill.
Howard, Miss Bess, Barrens County Historical Society, Glasgow, Ky.
Hughes, Fred, editor, *Leitchfield Gazette*, Leitchfield, Ky.
Hunt, Miss Carrie, Public Library, Lexington, Ky.
Hutton, D. M., editor, *Harrodsburg Herald*, Harrodsburg, Ky.

Illinois State Journal, Springfield, Ill.
Institute of American Genealogy, Chicago, Ill.

Irwin, Emery, Petersburg, Ill.
Irwin, Kenneth, Springfield, Ill.
Isely, Bliss, Wichita, Kan.
Isely, Mary Blair, Washington, D.C.

Jacoby, John, Salisbury, Ill.
*Johnson, Mrs. Ellen Goldsby, Springfield, Ill.
Johnson, R. N., inspector, Illinois Public Works, Springfield, Ill.
Johnson, Miss Rebecca, secretary, Virginia Historical Society, Richmond, Va.
Jones, Mrs. H. C., New Market, Ala.
Juhl, Mrs. Leonard, Lincoln, Ill.

Keese, Mrs. Ethelyn D., Lackawanna Historical Society, Scranton, Pa.
*Keller, Mrs. W. E., Clarkson, Ky.
Kellogg, Miss Louise, reference librarian, State Historical Society, Madison, Wis.
Kendall, W. Fred, pastor, Severn's Valley Church, Elizabethtown, Ky.
Kennedy, Mrs. Louisa, Atlanta, Ill.
Kerr, Rev. Daniel E., Lincoln, Ill.
King, Mrs. W. E., granddaughter of Bowling Green, Springfield, Ill.
Kinkead, Miss Ludie J., curator, Filson Club, Louisville, Ky.
*Kirby, Mrs. Mary Goldsby, Rochester, Ill.

Lackey, Miss Katherine, secretary to Dr. Graham, president, University of North Carolina, Chapel Hill, N.C.
Laffoon, Miss Grace, Library, University of Wichita, Wichita, Kan.
Larson, A. H., Lincoln, Ill.
Lee, Miss Alice, Lincoln National Life Foundation, Fort Wayne, Ind.
Lincoln Evening Courier, Lincoln, Ill.
†Littner, Arthur, Petersburg, Ill.
†Lott, Mrs. Laura, Athens, Ill.
Louisville Courier Journal, Louisville, Ky.
†Lozer, William, Decatur, Ill.
Lukenbill, E. H., county superintendent of schools, Lincoln, Ill.
Lundeen, Miss Dorothy, Western Pennsylvania Historical Society, Pittsburgh, Pa.
*Lynn, A. W., Wellington, Kan.

*McArthur, Dr. S. W., Chicago, Ill.
*McComb, Mrs. Mary Rafferty, Glasgow, Ky.
McKetchnie, S. W., editor, *Times-Sentinel*, Red Bluff, Calif.
McLaughlin, Mrs. R. W., Wellington, Kan.
McLean County, Ill.
†Marbold, Mrs. Jude, Petersburg, Ill.
*Marlette, Miss Ruth, Graham, N.C.
*Martin, Mrs. Josie, Columbia, Ky.
*Masterson, Mrs. Lelia Elmore, Chico, Calif.
Mather, Judge Otis, Hodgenville, Ky.
Milby, Walter, attorney, Greensburg, Ky.
†Miles, James S., Petersburg, Ill.
†Miles, Mrs. Kitty Purkapile, Petersburg, Ill.
*Miles, Mrs. Olive B., Pueblo, Colo.

†Miller, Gus, Salisbury, Ill.
Miller, Mrs. Gus, Salisbury, Ill.
*Miller, Mrs. I. L., Campbellsville, Ky.
Miller, J. G., editor, *The News*, Red Bluff, Calif.
*Miller, Miss Nancy, Lexington, Ky.
Miller, William, Petersburg, Ill.
Moomaw, Leda, Lincoln, Ill.
Moore, Mrs. Mary T., State Teachers College, Bowling Green, Ky.
Morris, Miss Sereta, reference librarian, Wichita Public Library, Wichita, Kan.
Munns, Mrs. Annie, State Historical Society, Madison, Wis.
Murray, Sara, clerk, Supreme Court, Alamance, N.C.

Nance, Ross A., clerk, Circuit Court, Menard County, Petersburg, Ill.
Neisser, Rittenhouse, librarian, American Baptist Historical Association, Chester, Pa.
Nickols, Mrs. D. F., Lincoln, Ill.
Nickols, Franklin, Jr., Lincoln, Ill.
Noficer, Miss Lena, Library, Old Capitol, Frankfort, Ky.
Noggle, C. H., attorney, Greensburg, Ky.
Norton, Mrs. Charles F., librarian, Transylvania College, Lexington, Ky.

Ogden, Maurice E., clerk, County Court, Menard County, Petersburg, Ill.
O'Hara, Downing P., librarian, University of Wichita, Wichita, Kan.
Oliver, M. M., editor, *Alamance County News*, Graham, N.C.
*O'Neil, Mrs. Ethel Lynn, Hollywood, Calif.
†Onstot, Mr. and Mrs. John N., Sheridan Road, Petersburg, Ill.
Onstot, John K., Mishawaka, Ind.
Owens, John K., editor, *News-Record*, Harrisburg, Va.
*Owings, Mrs. Margaret B., Tekamah, Neb.

Paddock, Mrs. Beatrice, City Library, Wichita, Kan.
Parks, S. C., Jr., Cody, Wyo.
*Perdue, Mrs. John A., New Orleans, La.
Peterson, Albert, Mason City, Ill.
Pickett, Ray, Greensburg, Ky.
Placer County Historical Association, Red Bluff, Calif.
†Pollard, Mrs. Julia Beekman, Petersburg, Ill.
†Pollock, Rev. Henry, Decatur, Ill.
Pond, Mrs. Fern Nance, Petersburg, Ill.
Pratt, Dr. Harry, secretary, Abraham Lincoln Memorial Association, Springfield, Ill.
Presbyterian church, Lincoln, Ill.
*Price, William. J., Harvard University, Cambridge, Mass.
Primm, J. Q., Lincoln, Ill.

*Rafferty, Homer, Buffalo, Ky.
*Rafferty, William, Magnolia, Ky.
Reep, Thomas P., attorney, Petersburg, Ill.
Richardson, Abe, Lincoln, Ill.
Richmond, Miss Mabel, secretary, Macon County Historical Society, Decatur, Ill.

†Robertson, Mrs. Lucy Beekman, Tallula, Ill.
Robinson, H. S., attorney, Campbellsville, Ky.
Rogers, Walter, editor, *Burt County Herald*, Tekamah, Neb.
Rorke, Alexander I., American-Irish Historical Society, New York City
Rosenfield, W. A., director of parks and memorials, Springfield, Ill.
Rosseau, V. T., editor, *The News*, Glasgow, Ky.
†Rothschild, Albert, Petersburg, Ill.

Sampson, Mrs. Lulu Graham, Petersburg, Ill.
Sampson, Luther, Petersburg, Ill.
Sanders, Miss Gladys, Lincoln Library, University of Chicago, Chicago, Ill.
Schaff, Miss Gertrude, Wichita, Kan.
Schwegmann, Geo. A., director, Union Catalog, Library of Congress, Washington, D.C.
*Seller, Mrs. Flora Graham, granddaughter of Mentor Graham, Lincoln, Ill.
Seller, Frank, Lincoln, Ill.
Settle, S. D., Bowling Green, Ky.
Shaw, Sidney, editor, *Petersburg Observer*, Petersburg, Ill.
*Sinton, Mrs. W. K., Colorado Springs, Colo.
Sioussat, St. George L., chief, Division of Manuscripts, Library of Congress, Washington, D.C.
Small, Robert, Petersburg, Ill.
Small, William, Petersburg, Ill.
Smith, Miss Alice, manuscript curator, Wisconsin Historical Society, Madison, Wis.
Smith, Allen, clerk, County Court, Menard County, Petersburg, Ill.
Smith, J. Emil, editor, *Illinois State Journal*, Springfield, Ill.
Smith, M. M., photoduplicator, Library of Congress, Washington, D.C.
Smith, Miss Nell, librarian, Petersburg, Ill.
Steger, Mrs. Gertrude, president, Shasta County Historical Society, Anderson, Calif.
Stephens, Irwin D., editor, *Caswell Messenger*, Yanceyville, N.C.
Stout, Miss Marietta B., Historical Society, Tekamah, Neb.
†Stringer, Lawrence B., judge, Lincoln, Ill.
Sutton, Mrs. George, Chicago, Ill.

Taylor, E. V., editor, *Greensburg Record*, Greensburg, Ky.
†Terhune, John, Sweetwater, Ill.
Thompson, H. R., clerk, Superior Court, Yanceyville, N.C.
Trent, Fred E., Petersburg, Ill.
Trinity College, Dublin, Ireland

Ulio, J. A., brigadier general, War Department, Washington, D.C.

Vance, Miss Marie, secretary, Illinois Historical Survey, University of Illinois, Urbana, Ill.
*Victor, Miss Mary, Larned, Kan.

*Wallace, Rev. Jerry, Springfield, Ill.
Wallace, Miss Louise, Nashville, Tenn.
†Walker, Mrs. Abbie, Redford, Iowa
Walker, Miss Nellie, sculptor, Chicago, Ill.

Walton, E. C., editor, *Interior Journal*, Stanford, Ky.
*Ward, Ellen E., Los Molinos, Calif.
Warren, Lewis A., director, Lincoln National Foundation, Fort Wayne, Ind.
Wathen, A. S., editor, *Kentucky Standard*, Bardstown, Ky.
Watkins, Lyle, Petersburg, Ill.
Webster, Miss Ida, Public Library, Lincoln, Ill.
Wells, Gabriel, collector of rare books, New York City
*Wilcox, Mrs. V. C., Manton, Calif.
Williams, C. T., editor, *Somerset Journal*, Somerset, Ky.
Williams, Mrs. D. H., Springfield, Ill.
Williams, F. L., clerk, Superior Court, Alamance, N.C.
Williams, George W., director of parks and memorials, Springfield, Ill.
Wilson, Miss Fannie, librarian, Yanceyville, N.C.
Wilson, Rev. G. A., Tallula, Ill.
Withrow, W. O., superintendent of Sangamon County schools, Springfield, Ill.
Woods, Mrs. C. H., Lincoln, Ill.
Wright, Dr. D. S., president, Campbellsville Junior College, Campbellsville, Ky.
Wright, Edith A., United States Office of Education, Washington, D.C.

Young, William C., custodian, New Salem Park, Ill.
†Youngberg, Frank, Lincoln, Ill.

GRAHAM'S LETTERS TO WILLIAM HERNDON
FOR HIS BIOGRAPHY OF LINCOLN

PETERSBURG, July 15th, 1865

Mr. Wm. Herndon

DEAR SIR:

In reply to your inquiries in regard to our much lamented Lincoln: he was good, and great as he was good,—*as he was good*. Great not like Caesar stained in blood; but only great *as he was good*.

I said to you in your first inquiry that the first time I saw him was at the election in New Salem in 1830; but I saw him frequently when a lad about twelve years of age though was not personally acquainted with him. This was at his residence at his place of birth in the winter of 1819 & 20. I went to school in the county of Hardin, Ky. adjoining Green County where I was raised. During my attendance at this school I often passed by old Mr Lincoln's house and often saw his son, Abraham, out about the premises with his father. This was near No Linn river on the little stream Barren Run. It was then a barren though picturesque country. The house was a rude cabin. I never had any conversation with either of them during my stay in that section. I remember thinking as I would pass by the place and see them out that they had the appearance of a dignified man and boy as they truly were.

In regard to what Lincoln read and studied in Kentucky and Indiana, it was principally the Bible. He has spoken to me often of his employment in Indiana after his father moved over the Ohio river. He devoted his time principally in assisting to clear a little farm and make a subsistence for the family and that every leisure moment was employed in writing for some of the neighbors back to Kentucky or in reading such books as he could obtain, but they were limited—except the Bible.

In New Salem he devoted more time to reading the scriptures, books on science and comments on law and to the acquisition of knowledge of men and things than any man I ever knew and it has been my lot to teach in the primary school forty-five years and I must say that Abraham Lincoln was the most studious, straight-forward young man in the pursuit of a knowledge of literature than any among the five thousand I have taught in the schools. The time I allude to is his studiousness in Salem from 1832 to 1836, He was regular in his habits. punctual in doing anything that he promised or agreed to do. His method of doing *any*thing was very systematic. He discharged all his obligations and duties to his God, his fellow men, himself and his country with more fidelity than is common to humanity.

You ask what gave him the title of "honest Abe." That is answered in these few words. He was strictly *honest, truthful* and *industrious* and in addition to this he was one of the most companionable persons you will ever meet in this world.

He was well calculated to be President of such a nation as ours and it may be a *long, long* time before we have another to be his equal. I have no idea that this or any other country has ever had his superior. He is now and always will be first in the hearts of his countrymen. How much, how deep, how feelingly have we grieved his loss.

I have been harvesting two weeks and it is difficult for me to write.

Yours respectfully,

M. GRAHAM

Mr. W. H. Herndon

DEAR SIR,

In answer to your various inquiries let me say—I came to Illinois in the year A D 1826 and settled in Sangamon County near the Sangamon river close to the village of New Salem and was at that time 26 years of age.

In the month of August, 1830, I first saw Mr. Lincoln. He came down the Sangamon river from Decatur, Macon County, Ill. to New Salem in old Sangamon—Menard now being a part of old Sangamon. The next time I saw him was on election day—we were deficient a clerk for the polls. Mr. Lincoln was about the sheets, looking around, and was asked by one of us if he could write. He said, "Yes, a little." "Will you act as clerk of the election today?" asked one of the judges. "I will try and do the best I can, if you so request."

He was then sworn in and acted as clerk of the August election. There were 49 candidates, it being a general state election. He performed the duties with great facility, much fairness and honesty and dependability. I clerked with him that day and at the same polls. This was the first official public act in his life. The election books are now at the city of Springfield, Ill. where they can be seen and inspected any day.

The next work he did was clerking for Denton Offut which was in the fall and winter of 1830 and 31. He was among the best clerks I ever saw: he was attentive to his business and kind and considerate to his customers and friends and always treated them with great ——— kindness and honesty. He in fact superintended and managed Offut's store himself. Offut was an unsteady, noisy, fussy and rather brutal man, wild and unprovidential. Offut rented the water mill at the foot of Salem hill of Cameron and Rutledge. Mr. Lincoln frequently had to attend to store and mill. Offut broke up in the spring and summer of 1831, leaving Lincoln out of business again. But before Mr. Lincoln came to New Salem, he had gone down the river with Offut and got off at Beardstown in Cass County and walked back afoot to New Salem. Then it was that he commenced clerking for Offut. After clerking for Offut and now being out of business, he turned his attention to the law. He read Blackstone in the fall and winter of 1831 & 2. One word here: During the time he was working for Offut and hands being scarce Lincoln turned in and cut down trees and split enough rails for Offut to build a pen sufficiently large to contain 1,000 hogs. The pen was built under New Salem hill, close to the mill. Offut had purchased a great deal of corn and had it in and about the mill. The hogs were purchased to eat the corn so he would have good well-fattened hogs for market. I know where those rails are now, are found today.

He went, in 1830, about the month of May or June, to the Black Hawk War. He volunteered as private and was, without his knowledge, elected Captain. He went through the war and was well spoken of by all of his company and respected—especially his own company—as being a gentleman—kind-hearted noble man—who did his duty well, without fear, gold, favor or affectation. He had a somewhat good eye for military affairs as said by competent judges. I have no doubt of this. His heart and head were large and comprehensive enough to command a company, or regiment, or other core of men at any time or under any circumstances.

When he returned from the Black Hawk War he became a candidate for the legislature and in his first, or among his first public speeches in that canvass which was in 1832, he addressed the people of Petersburg—the old town. From the time of this speech and during that canvas he read attentively the Louisville

Journal, the Missouri Republican and other papers. His text book was the Louisville Journal. He was a regular subscriber to the Journal. Mr. Lincoln was defeated in the election of 1832. He was a Whig. After the election of 1832 Mr. Lincoln turned his attention exclusively to the law, surveying, history, geography and general newspaper reading. Mr. Lincoln drew up deeds, contracts and other papers for the people, never charging them for it—not a cent.

In the month of February A D 1833 Mr. Lincoln came to live with me. and continued with me about six months. It was here that he commenced the study of English grammar with me. I then was teaching school. I taught him the rules of surveying. I do not think that Mr. Lincoln was anything of an arithmetician—especially so of geometry and trigonometry—before he came to my house and I think I may say that he was my scholar and I was his teacher. His assistantship under Calhoun was long after this—say one or two years.

Mr. Lincoln spoke to me one day and said, "I have a notion of studying grammar." I replied to him thus, "If you expect to be before the public in any capacity I think it is the best thing you can do." He said to me, "If I had a grammar, I would commence now." There was none in the village and I said to him, "I know of a grammar at one Vance's about six miles," which I thought he could get. He was then at breakfast—ate, got up and went on foot to Vance's to get the book. He soon came back and said he had it. He then turned his inordinate and almost undivided attention to the subject of grammar. The book was Kirkham's grammar—an old volume which I suppose—so I have heard—is in the Rutledge family today.

During the spring, summer and fall he read law, studied, practiced surveying and the grammar and would recite to me in the evening. I have taught in my life four to six thousand pupils as schoolmaster and no one ever surpassed him in rapidly, quickly and well acquiring the rudiments and rules of English grammar. This I repeat was in the spring, summer and fall of 1833. As before stated he was writing deeds, contracts and other papers for the people. His playful hour for the year was pitching quoits, jumping, skipping, swimming, shooting, telling stories—anecdotes—and not infrequently as we ——— ——— ——— ———, "sitting up to the fair girls of Illinois."

In the summer of 1834 he was again a candidate for the legislature and was elected. He went to Vandalia the capital of Illinois and there became a good legislator and became then and there as I am informed with the great men in Illinois ——— ——— ———. In 1836 he was again a candidate for the legislature and was elected and was one of what is called "the long nine"—two tall senators and seven tall representatives from Sangamon who moved the capital of the state of Illinois from Vandalia to Springfield.

He then moved to the city of Springfield in 1836 or 7 since which time I have seen him only occasionally. I wish to say one or two words about his character. It was this—he was a very simple, open-souled man; he was a ——— man, a man of purpose, very frank and ingenuous; he was kind, humorous and always honest, never deviating from the exact truth; he was studious, so much so that he somewhat injured his health and constitution. The continuous study of the man caused—with the death of one he dearly and ardently loved a momentary—only partial and momentary circumplacement. Mr. Lincoln's character at once seized the observation and that only led to respect, love and confidence in Abraham Lincoln.

Your friend

Mentor Graham

GRAHAM'S ANSWERS TO HERNDON'S QUESTIONNAIRES

ANN RUTLEDGE

I know Miss Ann Rutledge took sick while going to school. Lincoln and she both were studying at my house. Miss Rutledge died about 1834. She was about 20 years old, blue eyes, large and expressive, fair complexion—sandy or light auburn hair—not flaxen. About 5 feet 4, face rather round—outlines beautiful—nervous element predominated. She had good teeth—mouth well made—beautiful. Nervous chin. Weight about 120–30. Beautiful and ingenious—amiable—kind—exceptionally good scholar in all the common branches including grammar. She was beloved of everybody and she loved everybody. Lincoln and she were engaged—Lincoln told me so—she intimated to me the same. He—Lincoln—told me he felt like committing suicide after her death but I told him of God's higher purpose. He told me he thought so too—somehow—couldn't tell how. He said my remarks and others' had often done him good. The Rutledges came from White County. Rutledge and Cameron built Salem Mill about 1828. I saw the same commenced.

MARY OWENS

I knew Miss Owens always—my cousin. Knew her in Ill. about 1834 or 6. Knew her from a child in Kentucky.

She was about 28 when in Ill. Black eyes—medium sized, about 5/5 feet 6. Black hair, weighed about 150. Symmetrical face with roundish features, unusually fresh. Good natured—excellent disposition. She was a very intellectual woman, well educated and well raised—Free and social—Beautiful even teeth. She was gay and lively, mirthfulness prominent. Her mind was better cultivated than Miss Rutledge's. She now says that though opposed to Abe and his advances still he was one of the best and most honest men that she ever knew. She dressed neatly—grandly, never—though she could well have afforded it.

MENTOR GRAHAM'S SCHOOLS

KENTUCKY

1817–20	Brush Creek, Green County	1822–24	Friendship, (now) Taylor County
1820–22	Otter Creek, (now) La Rue County	1824–26	Greensburg, Kentucky, Green County

ILLINOIS

1826–38	Baptist church school, Sangamon County (at New Salem, but before the town existed)	1858	Honeyhart Tick Ridge
		1859	Concord Partridge
1839–40	"Salem School," a new brick building	1860	Concord Farmer's Point
1841	Hickory Grove Little Grove	1861	Curtis Farmer's Point
1842	Walnut Ridge Tonica	1862	Curtis (Smoot) Farmer's Point
1843	Walnut Ridge Peel	1863	Tice, near Oakridge post office
1844	Pleasant Hill		Tick Ridge
1845	Indian Point		Hog Corners
1846	Walnut Ridge Pancake Little Grove	1864	Tice
		1865	Tice
		1866	Sampson
1847	Walnut Grove Shipley No. 8		Partridge Rock Creek
		1867	Rock Creek (Bunker Hill)
1848	Walnut Ridge Hog Corner No. 8	1868	Rock Creek
		1869	Rock Creek
		1870	Dick's school near Chandlerville
1849	Pleasant Hill Barclay Peel	1871	Pleasant Plains
		1872	Pleasant Plains
1850	Pleasant Hill Concord Barclay	1873	Virginia
		1874	Private tutor to Petersburg's young people Virginia
1851–55	Pancake Tonica Concord	1875	Private tutor and at No. 8
1856	Partridge Rock Creek	1876	Liberty No. 8
1857	Farmer's Point Tick Ridge	1877–78	Liberty

This list is incomplete in that Graham taught many short terms each year in the early days. The schools listed were obtained from school-money reports, old school records kept by Graham, and from pupils who attended his schools.

Available records, which are scattered, show Graham obtaining teacher's certificates, by examination, on March 22, 1862; October 17, 1866; October 2, 1869; April 13, 1872; and December 18, 1874.

ITEMIZED DEBT OWED BY BALE TO GRAHAM IN CASE OF
GREEN VS. *GRAHAM*, NOVEMBER, 1845[1]

	Copy (FIRST SHEET)		
1818	Jacob Bale Dr to Mentor Graham		
	To 3 days cutting briers & sprouts		
not admitted	in Kentucky.................................	$ 1.50	.....
1833	To balance of tuition of 6		
	children (school 12 mo) sub		
admitted	3 scholars (balance term 3 yrs).....................	18.00	.....
	# To 107 days over subscription.......................	5.35	.....
	To int on $18. as above 6 years.....................	6.48	.....
1834	To tuition of 5 children for		
admitted	1 scholar subscription 6 mo........................	4.50	.....
	# To 65 days over subscription.......................	3.25	.....
	To int on $4.50 5 years............................	1.35	.....
1834 & 5	To tuition 7 children term		
admitted	3 mo sub 2 scholars...............................	5.00	$5.00
	# To 87 over subscriptions...........................	4.35	4.35
	To int on $5. 4 years..............................	1.20	1.30
1835	To tuition of 7 children		
admit	sub. 3 scholars term 9 mo..........................	18.00	18.00
	# To 153 days over subscription......................	7.65	7.65
	To int. on $18. 4 years............................	4.32	4.32
1836	To tuition of 3 children		
Adm	term 9 mo. sub. 1 scholar..........................	7.50	7.50
	# To 97 days over sub..............................	4.85	4.85
	int on $7.50 4 years..............................	1.80	.....
1837—	To balance on tuition 10.00........................	10.10¼	10.00
	int on same 4 years...............................	2.64	1.80
left	To 200 ft studing.................................	5.00	2.50
admit	½ doz fowls & 2 doz eggs...........................	.75	.75
1839	tuition 3 children 65 days..........................	3.25	3.25
admit			
		117.80¼	71.17

[1] Exhibit in case *Mrs. Bowling Green* vs. *Mentor Graham*, November, 1845.

(SECOND SHEET)

Amount brought over............................ $117.80¼   71.17

37'1840   To teaching scholar $\begin{Bmatrix} 37 & \text{By H Bale} \\ 66 & \text{days} \end{Bmatrix}$ 3.30   1.42

Amount...................... $121.10¼   72.59
Credit
By your book account

1834   Dr order from A. Lincoln.........................   10.00

$131.10¼
32.00

$99.10¼

72.59   Jacob Bales
38.51¼   ac
────   Mentor Graham
34.08¼

NOTES

PROLOGUE

1. Boone went little farther west than the Kentucky River, by December, 1769 (John Bakeless, *Daniel Boone* [Rahway, N.J.: Quinn & Boden, 1939], p. 939). The Long Hunters, in August, 1769, had reached the Barrens, eighty miles farther west.

2. "Benjamin Lynn was a wandering hunter in the Green River Valley before its settlement. His name is connected with the traditions and in some cases with the earliest records of the oldest churches in Southern Kentucky, near the Tennessee line. His name is preserved in No-Lynn (now written Nolin) River, Lynn Camp Creek, Nolin Church, Lynn Association and other localities and religious bodies" (William Cathcart's *Baptist Encyclopedia*, II, 729).

3. The Camp Knox in Green County, not the one near Louisville. Lyman Copeland Draper says: "James Knox was an Irishman of pretty good talents and education. When war broke out he went into the back part of Virginia as a peddler. He met an Indian, named Dick, who took him on an exploring expedition until they came to what is now Boyle. He came to Kentucky in 1768 and named Dick's River. He lived to the age of eighty and died in the neighborhood of Shelbyville, Ky."

4. The No-Lynn story is a tale told in Kentucky, especially the Green River country, today. Historians say Lynn and others were exploring Nolyn valley and camped on the knoll near the present site of Hodgenville and that the No-Lynn incident occurred then, in 1777.

The church records attach the incident to the founding of Severns' Valley Church.

The *Christian Repository*, October 26, 1856, says: "Early in 1871 Ben. Lynn, John La Rue, John Garrard and others went out from Bear-grass to found a settlement. Selecting a knoll they made preparations for the approaching winter." This statement is copied by Draper, who tacks the No-Lynn story to it.

However, I am led to believe that the naming of No-Lynn River happened as I relate. I base my opinion upon a report made by Ben Lynn himself to his son-in-law, John Chisholm, who says: "Ben. Lynn told me that he and ten other men were hunting in the Barrens, and exploring, each separately, but coming into camp together, at night. On the first day Lynn came on an Indian trail and followed it out of curiosity so far he could not make it back into camp. When the hunters began to come in the second night they would say, 'No Lynn yet?' They gave the creek where the camp was, that name." If it had been as late as 1777 or 1781, Lynn would have known all the Indian trails thereabout. Green River country was all explored and all trails in it were known by 1777 and 1781. The story he told his son-in-law had to do with hunting, not church-founding or settlement-founding. Exploring and hunting are exactly what the Long Hunters did and what church-founders and settlement-makers were not doing. The very fact that the story is told in so many versions attests, in my opinion, to the antiquity of its origin.—K. D.

5. According to Draper, Ben, flushed with success, married Hannah Sovereigns (Severns) "amid much merriment" at the fort in July. But a year later they had gone; for Ben had his "tomahawk rights" to land on Beech Fork, not far from the Falls. Hannah, like all

frontier women, was soon awaiting the return of her husband. He had gone to the Monongahela with war messages and to help raise troops. What further part he played in American independence is unknwon except for a glimpse of him at Vincennes, in June, 1779.

6. James Alton, *Illinois Historical Collection* (1934), p. 42, says: "A plan to secure gunpowder from New Orleans was conceived by Captain George Gibson of the Virginia line. Bearer of the letter from General Lee, accompanied by Lieut. William Linn and fifteen other men in guise of traders, he arrived at New Orelans in early August, 1776. Powder and arms had heretofore been purchased in England and the West Indies, but with the opening of hostilities, these sources of supply had been cut off. . . . . With forty-three men Lieutenant Linn set out from New Orleans, Sept. 22, 1776, with a cargo of 98 kegs of gunpowder— 9,000 pounds in barges. They passed the winter at Arkansas Post and resumed the voyage in the spring of 1777. Linn was met at Kaskaskia by Thomas Bentley. They arrived at Wheeling and Fort Pitt in May where the ammunition was sorely needed."

7. Draper reports a settler who came to Kentucky in 1781 as saying: "There were 180 of us, when we came out. Lewis Craig came then, it was his church that moved out. They prayed and sung, every night. Lewis Craig had not a very great talent for preaching, but was not to be beat at exhortation. We were sometimes in a string of three miles, but never saw an Indian. Providence seemed to order that there should be none, so many came out that fall. More, I suppose, than in any other year. The road seemed always full." Craig's "traveling church" settled near the site of Lancaster, Kentucky, forty miles east of Lynn's cabin on Beech Fork.

8. John Bradford arrived at Lexington from Farquier County, Virginia, in 1785. In 1787 he was given a free lot upon which to build a "printing house." He whittled his own woodcuts and printed by the light of a tallow candle. The first *Gazette* appeared in 1787.

CHAPTER I

1. The little settlement of Crab Orchard was the crossroads clearing house for settlers when the Grahams came that way. Men without means of transportation might get service with pack trains, either farther west or back "to the settlements." Here oral and written messages were intrusted to strangers, people going in the general direction in which the addressee had gone. Such messages might be changed over from one stranger to another several times before they reached their destination, but settlers were trustworthy and few messages miscarried. All the news of Kentucky could be learned here, at the junction of America's future. The *Kentucky Gazette* carried many such notices as this: "Olihu Pinkstaff wants passage from Crab Orchard to the Holsten, come summer, for service with pack animals." The route traveled by the Grahams was nearly the same as that taken by the Long Hunters of eighteen years before.

2. J. H. Spencer, *History of Kentucky Baptists*, I, 251, says: "Johnson Graham was the fourth pastor of Brush Creek church. . . . . He was born in South Carolina, October 2, 1772, and came with his father to Kentucky in his youth. In 1798, he married Miss Casandria Stone. He was probably converted during the great revival of 1800–3 under the ministry of his uncle, Benjamin Lynn, by whom he was baptized into the fellowship of Brush Creek church. . . . . He did not enter fully into the work of the ministry until about 1812, he being at that period, forty years old. He was called to the pastoral care of Otter Creek church, in La Rue County, Greensburg and Brush Creek, in Green County, and Friendship, in what is now Taylor county. 'I do not remember,' says his daughter, 'but one change in his pastoral relation during a period of about twenty-five years. . . . . His success was fair, in all his churches. He was twice Moderator of Russell's Creek Association. . . . . He united with a temperance society that was organized in Green County, and was a zealous advocate of total abstinence from the use of intoxicating drinks. He was a very skillful peacemaker. When two members of his charge would have a disagreement he would go at once to see them, and labor affectionately with them till the difficulty was adjusted. He . . . . died October 26, 1840.' "

Spencer (*ibid.*, p. 251) also says: "William Graham, the father of Johnson Graham, was a native of North Carolina, and an old Revolutionary soldier. He served seven years in the continental army. He married Nancy Lynn, a sister of the famous old Kentucky pioneer,

Benjamin Lynn. This marriage was blessed with two daughters and three sons. William Graham was an early settler on Brush Creek in Green County, Kentucky. Whether, as some have suggested, he came with his brother-in-law to Kentucky and settled first on Nolyn (now spelled Nolin) River, or whether he followed him at a later period, and settled first on Brush Creek, may not now be determined."

CHAPTER II

1. Destruction of family records by fire makes it impossible to name the exact day of November, 1800. Mrs. Mary Graham Bradley, a granddaughter, now living at Greenview, Illinois, recalls that she and her grandfather used to celebrate their birthdays together, because they were so near in date. Hers occurs upon the fourth of November, the day before Guy Fawkes's Day. Her grandfather used to twit her about that, saying his was a much better day to be born, as it was the same date upon which Lincoln was elected president. That would make it November 6. We are, however, certain of such details as the mother of Mentor Graham herself related. She spent her last days in her son's home; and it was here that she, recounting her youth, left us the story of his nativity. The author has taken occasion to restore the drama in the language of the times and to enrich it with background bits culled from old records, letters, papers, tradition, and history.

2. It is definitely known that Mary Graham was not educated; few frontier women were. They were hurried from young girlhood into marriage and usually had from ten to a dozen children. By the verdict of their day, learning was not needed for such tasks as turning cakes, sewing seams, and bearing children. Mary was a faithful wife and therefore, by the standards of her time, a "noble woman." Judging from the children who went forth from her hearth, she must indeed have been a noble woman.

CHAPTER III

1. Biographers treat of Tom Lincoln as a ne'er-do-well, a rolling stone. This characterization misinterprets the times. Tom Lincoln was no poorer than most; he was twenty-nine when his son Abraham was born, and he owned land, farm horses, and carpenter tools. He was a trusted guard for prisoners, an honest, hard-working cabinetmaker, a sober man, a religious one, and a respected one. He remained in one location about as long as most and longer than many.

CHAPTER IV

1. Children and grownups danced a kind of reel to an interminably versed nonsense song, "Cl'ar de Kitchen," which began:

> "In old Kaintuck in the afternoon
> Sweep de kitchen with a bran new broom,
> After that form in a ring
> And everybody begin to sing:
>   Oh, cl'ar de kitchen, young folks, old folks,
>   Cl'ar de kitchen, young folks, old folks,
>   Old Virginny never tire.
> A little old man comes riding by,
> Says I, 'Old man your horse will die.'
> Says he, 'If he dies I'll tan his skin,
> And if he lives I'll ride him agin .... OH!'
>   Cl'ar de kitchen, etc."

CHAPTER V

1. Stone-collecting was a common interest. Lexington papers carried descriptions of rocks that had been sent to the editors.

2. There were four first cousins named William Graham. Mentor's Uncle Nat called him William M. to distinguish him from the others; everyone else called him Mentor.

CHAPTER VI

1. Broadsides were argumentative handbills, usually very abusive. "Pusillanimous liar" and "culminating coward" are sample epithets. Duels caused by broadsides were common.

CHAPTER VII

1. Graham ricked his hay on a center pole after the manner of northern England. In the 1940's Green County farmers were still using that method.

CHAPTER IX

1. Mrs. Bradley says: "The homemade pages of lesson and song were among my grandfather's papers, and I have always supposed they were a part of his school work, probably valued by him on account of the pupil for whom it was prepared—Lincoln—though I have no proof of this. Books were hard to get, and he prepared much of the lesson material."

2. The game of bull pen was the grandfather of baseball. As many bases as there were players to a side outlined the "pen." One side took positions as basemen and threw the ball, trying to hit one of the other side, who were the bulls in the pen. In back-and-forth order basemen threw the ball, the bulls' skill in dodging heightened by the memory of the sting of a hit. Bulls hit must then hit as many basemen, and the first half ended when all the basemen were "out" because they had been hit. In the second half, teams exchanged positions.

CHAPTER XI

1. The Pottawatomie chiefs, Shick-Shack and Shambolee, still camped on the bluffs above the Sangamon with their thinning followers. They came to trade peltries for calico, candy, and iron pots at McNeil and Hill's store. The Indians' day was waning, and their saddening faces mirrored their recognition of the fact. We catch a glimpse of them, proudly erect, returning down the village street like actors in a tragic drama, going out courageously to extinction.

2. Mrs. Mary Graham Bradley says: "This table was one of Mentor and Sarah's dearest possessions, both because it was a fine handmade walnut piece and because it had belonged to their good friend, Dr. Allen. It is one of their possessions which I inherited." When Mrs. Bradley stopped keeping house, she sold the table to D. F. Nickols.

CHAPTER XII

1. James R. Herndon, of Green County, Kentucky (who married Graham's sister Elizabeth), was a cousin of the William Henry Herndon (also from Kentucky), who was Lincoln's law partner for a term and who questioned Graham concerning Lincoln for material for his biography of Lincoln. James R. Herndon was known as Rowan Herndon, in New Salem. Like Graham he dropped his first name and used his middle name.

CHAPTER XIII

1. In early days the Rutledge Tavern was rarely lacking guests: It housed drovers, itinerant preachers and doctors, settlers from near and far, and the mail-carrier. There were several dozens of books on the shelf in the sitting-room, where, on a Sabbath, preaching was always in order as long as the Rutledges ran the inn.

2. While Lincoln worked for Offutt he cut trees and split enough logs to pen one thousand hogs. He helped around the village with odd jobs, after store hours or while Billy Green kept store. He tended the mill and waited on grist customers.

3. The settlers had a song for everything. Out of pure exuberance everybody whistled or went around humming. The children were only imitating their elders and adding pantomime to the song:

"The engine bust,
The biler flew,—
It hain't gonna rain no more!

Cut that—shoofly!—
Pie in two,—
Hain't gonna rain no more!"

4. Graham at this time was elated by the news that James Burney was back in Kentucky again, had freed his slaves, and was heading an antislavery association. Graham probably had the slavery question up for debate in one guise or another.

5. Solving blackberry problems for urchins who brought him wild berries to buy led to parents' bringing him their more difficult problems. Sometimes Lincoln was stuck and had to relay the solution to Graham for confirmation and correction.

CHAPTER XIV

1. When Lincoln recounted the story of his life, he described himself as "a piece of floating driftwood" when he arrived at New Salem to clerk for Offutt. After he had studied a few weeks in Graham's school, he was still without compass, for he said, "I can go it alone, now: I can read and write and cipher"—a statement that shows he was at least not actively ambitious for public life then, that he had no crystallized objective. This crystallization Graham indubitably produced, or at least activated and made positive to the point of working toward a goal. The nearest Lincoln ever came to acknowledging his debt to Graham was his saying that Graham had more information and knew better how to tell what he knew than anyone he had known. But, as far as I am able to learn, Lincoln never did give Graham any specific credit for his (Lincoln's) achievements. This raises the question, Why? The answer can be only speculative: he may not have recognized or realized it; or he may have overprided himself on being self-made or have been unwilling to permit another to have part in his successes; or he may have discounted, after it was mastered, the very learning and writing skill and mastery of words to which Graham directed and urged him. The path of mastery is forgotten at its consummation by almost all learners, great and small. Lincoln was, after all, a most ambitious man; and ambition does not love partnerships. But I prefer to conclude that Lincoln's personal love for Graham outweighed so much his student indebtedness that he was forever expressing the one and omitting the other. I do not know of any other old New Salem friend whom Lincoln invited to sit on the platform at his inauguration; nor any other man's little child that Lincoln helped to bury; or, as far as that goes, any other man whom Lincoln ever embraced. It is not impossible that his intense gratitude for Graham's aid paced his personal love for his teacher.

2. Rock Creek—and probably New Salem—was debating: "Is it necessary for the good of the community and future prosperity of society that females receive equal education with males?"

CHAPTER XV

1. It was customary for a suitor to help out his girl's family at rail-splitting, husking, reaping, etc., even as, back in 1790, a suitor had to kill and dress a deer to prove his ability to support a wife.

CHAPTER XVI

1. The first meeting of the society took place on October 28, 1837. The *Sangamon Journal* of November 4, 1837, reported the proceedings in part as follows: "A committee of five was then appointed to recommend a uniform series of school books for the county consisting of Messrs. Sill, Hatch, Rogers, Trotter and Graham. Adjournment to meet at the school room of Messrs. Sill and Town two weeks from today."

2. This year Graham also served on a grand-jury committee to inspect the jail.

3. Lincoln was entranced with plays. When Springfield put up posters prohibiting them, Lincoln took the case of Joseph Jefferson, the actor, when he arrived in Springfield with his cast. The town council had to tear down its big posters. Mentor, hearing about it, couldn't say—plays might be educational.

4. Another "river-rat" song went:

> "OH . . . . .
> De schoonahs an' de linahs
> An' de li'l tuggin' boats
> Be chuggin' fru de watah
> Like a bunch ob frisky shoats . . . . OH . . . . ."

5. Ida Bale, of New Salem, said in 1939: "My father, Abram Bale, was eight years old when his family came to the deserted village. They lived in the house that stood last on Salem hill. I have stood beneath its old roof, after the partition was gone and the brick chimney had crumbled down." This house was Rutledge Tavern.

CHAPTER XVII

1. The despondent tone of poetry and song quoted by Lincoln was not, however, unique with him. The era was one of dolorous verse, endemic sadness. All papers carried verse, most of it memorial, such as this:

> "Toll not the death-knell for me,
> When I am dead
> Strew not the flowery wreath
> On my cold bed."

Lincoln, like everyone else, tried his hand at writing verse. Indeed, the trial is still in vogue in the Lincoln country of Illinois, which has produced two worthy poets.

But a new vein was creeping in—the parody. Everybody made parodies on no notice at all, especially temperance folks and the abolitionists. Usually they were parodies on hymns and were sung to hymn tunes.

2. Graham's granddaughter, Flora Graham, was later teaching at this same Tonica school when Henry Coffee, then an old man and her janitor, told her this story.

CHAPTER XVIII

1. This was not a law—it was a subscription school agreement (1848, Sangamon County).

State of Ill ⎱
Sangamon Co ⎰ SS

This article of an agreement made and entered into this............................day of............................in the year of our Lord A.D.   between   of the first part and the undersigned sub-scribers of the second part,—witnesses
that the said............................agrees to teach a common English school in the............................school-house dist.—in Range............................in the county and state mentioned above, a term of three months, five days in each week. He agrees to teach in said school Orthography, Reading, Penmanship, Arithmetic and English Grammar; also to use all proper means to advance them placed under his care in their respective studies, and to keep good order in the school. The subscribers on their part agree to furnish a comfortable school house, fuel, and all necessary implements for the accommodation of the scholars and to pay to the said............................
the sum of $2.50 per scholar, to $1.50, according to their respective assignments. School to commence on the
                    inst.,   provided 25 scholars are subscribed.

CHAPTER XIX

1. On August 22, 1853, the new Illinois "center" was named Lincoln. Judge Stringer of that city reports the christening in detail: The proprietors consisted of Virgil Hickox, Robert C. Latham, John G. Gillett, and Abraham Lincoln. Lincoln had drawn up the papers for the new town.

"Well, gentlemen," he asked, "have you decided upon the name?"

One spoke up: "We have. We have decided to call it Lincoln, for Abraham Lincoln, the lawyer."

"I don't believe I'd do that thing, gentlemen," Lincoln said quickly, "for I never knew anything that Lincoln ever did that amounted to much."

But the others insisted and instructed Lincoln to carve a watermelon, which he did with his jackknife; he gave each one a piece, kept one for himself, and handed the rest around to the knot of men looking on. Letting a few drops of the melon juice fall upon the ground, he said: "We christen thee Lincoln, Illinois"; and they ate the melon and buried the rinds.

CHAPTER XXI

1. A case brought by Tracy Bancroft, in July, 1865, accused Graham of ejecting Bancroft from land. It was settled out of court and the land given to Graham. In 1866 Bancroft ejected Graham from the same quarter-section.

2. Mary Graham Bradley says: "I never knew Grandfather to smoke a pipe; but one of his former pupils said he smoked a little clay pipe on the road to school, but broke it and threw it away before entering the schoolhouse. I do not think this is true. He was strictly temperate in all things."

A second granddaughter, Mrs. Kitty Graham Diff, at whose parents' home Graham spent his last years, said: "He was always clean-shaven and wore his hair long. It was white, slightly tinged with red. He was very clean about himself. He did not smoke, chew, or drink."

A third granddaughter, Mrs. Flora Graham Sellars, said: "Grandfather, like most people, liked to go to the barbecues. That was the way they celebrated the Fourth of July. He usually gave a shoat, and sometimes there were as many as twenty animals cooking over the trench fire at once. Watchers turned them on the spits and basted them with butter. Grandfather told us children how much was eaten and how good it was; and I remember he was what they called a hearty eater, himself. But that was his one indulgence. He worked hard and needed a lot of food. They always read the Declaration of Independence and honored the soldiers at the barbecues, and the young fry ran races and wrestled and swam horses in the creek."

3. The following is an excerpt from an article written by W. W. Elmore, published near Red Bluff, California, about 1927, and supplied by his granddaughter from her scrapbook. The name of the newspaper is not given, and the date was deduced from an article on the back telling of the construction of the Akron dirigible. Mr. Elmore lived in Anderson, California, at the time he wrote this article.

"My father, William Harrison Elmore, and my mother, Nancy Ellen Graham, were married in 1841. My mother went to school with Abraham Lincoln.

"She became a widow after her first marriage and later married A. G. Davis, a cousin of Jeff Davis.

"I was born in Missouri in 1845. In 1854 the Elmore family started from Sullivan County, Missouri, in a company of 40 wagons for California. We drove 100 head of cattle across the plains. I was nine years old and was in the saddle all day helping the men drive the cattle the entire way. When the wagons camped at night they drew up in a circle for protection against Indian raids. The stock was turned out to pasture in care of a herder. . . . . ."

CHAPTER XXII

1. Mary Graham Bradley says: "If he met with insolence—which he did—he put it down as an exhibition of bad manners. He was too conscious of his own integrity to be affected by silly antics."

2. Mary Bradley, Ida Bale, and others agree that a nephew, wheedled Graham into signing a paper and absconded with the money obtained on it.

3. Mrs. Duff relates: "Grandfather came to live with us in 1878 and when he was eighty-three years old went with us to Blunt. He was well and up and around until he died—very active, and walked with a cane. We had no warning of his death. He just walked out and fell—a stroke, I guess. He was eighty-six when he died."

4. According to Mrs. Bradley, "Most of grandfather's books and papers were auctioned in Lincoln. While he lived with us our house burned, and many books and papers of his were destroyed. He had caches of books at every one of his children's houses and had given literally hundreds of books to his children and grandchildren. But his own life-saved library was auctioned before they left for Dakota."

In Harry Graham's possession at the time of his death were these schoolbooks, bearing his father's name: Gray's botany; *Home Book of Wonders;* Louis Pujot's *French Grammar* (1860); John S. Jenkin's *Heroines of History* (Auburn and Rochester, New York, 1855); Asa Gray's *Botany for Young People* (1872); Wells's *New English Grammar* (Portland, Me.: Sanborne & Carter, 1849); Barnes's *Fourteen Weeks in Chemistry* (1875); Reed and Kellogg's grammar; Hemans' *Poems;* Butler's *Pronouncing Speller;* Robert Kidd's *Elocution;* Edward's *Fifth Reader;* Phillips and Sampson's *The Presidents of the United States;* Sanders *Speller;* Weed's *English Grammar;* Robin's algebra; Fish's *Intellectual Arithmetic; Introduc-*

tion to English (backless); another backless book, a grammar (1840); Greene's *English Grammar*; and Weed's *Rational Philosophy*.

EPILOGUE

1. Before Harry Graham and his family had left South Dakota, Mrs. Bradley had visited them there. "They took me to the cemetery where grandfather was buried in a metal lined casket," she says. "Some day they hoped to bring him back to Illinois. I knew right then. I made up my mind that some day he would be brought back. The only marker was a pine board with his name on it and the statement that he was the teacher of Abraham Lincoln."

2. Edmund M. Augspurger, school superintendent of Menard County, said at this service on July 23, 1933: "We honor a man who realized the sacredness of public trust and the responsibility of teacher to pupil."

On behalf of the Illinois State Teachers' Association, D. F. Nickols on this occasion delivered the following address, emphasizing the great contribution made by Graham to Lincoln's preparation for future tasks:

"Abraham Lincoln rightly described himself as 'a piece of floating driftwood' when he came to New Salem in the early spring of 1831. This was literally and figuratively true, for he had but recently left the humble parental cabin near Decatur to begin life for himself, to embark upon that rugged, fateful journey which eventually led to and ended at the White House.

"It must have been a dark day for the emotional Lincoln when he and his cousin, John Hanks, and his stepbrother, John Johnston, left their home by canoe to float down the Sangamon River to Springfield, where Denton Offutt had promised them employment.

"Upon arriving at Sangamo Town, no flatboat was to be found; and they set to work to build one from the forest trees. When completed, this craft, eighty feet by eighteen feet, loaded with corn and pork and hogs, pushed off on the narrow waters of the Sangamon for New Orleans, only to lodge within a few hours on the Rutledge milldam at New Salem. The inventive mind of Lincoln saved the day, and he became a local hero. How he shifted the cargo, bored a hole in the bottom of the boat to let the bilge water out, thus lightening the load and permitting it to slip over the obstruction to safety, is a well-known story.

"The remainder of the journey was made without mishap; and Lincoln returned to St. Louis by steamer, walking across the prairies of southern Illinois to visit his parents in Coles County, thence on to New Salem. Without doubt, the impelling force which lured him back to this settlement was the fact that its inhabitants had applauded his skill and appreciated him personally as no other community had ever done before. Even the enthusiastic Offutt had been so delighted that he engaged the young inventor on the spot to clerk for him in a store. It is human nature to gravitate toward those who treat us best.

"When Abraham Lincoln first entered New Salem in the spring of 1831, he was a hired man on a flatboat. When he left the village in 1837, to reside in Springfield, he was an attorney and a member of the state legislature. According to his own statement, he had not had more than one year in the public schools in his early life. Therefore his achievement during the six years spent in New Salem corresponds to the training now obtained in the high school, college, and university. New Salem was Lincoln's alma mater.

"It is interesting to turn the searchlight on this particular period of Lincoln's life. We find that Mentor Graham, the village schoolmaster, played an important role in this unusual drama. It was he who gave Lincoln a chance to serve as election clerk when the regular clerk, John McNamara, failed to arrive; and, while in the performance of this duty, the discerning mind of Graham discovered that the young backwoodsman possessed mental powers exceptionally keen and strong. What followed rivals, if not excels, the historic story of 'Mark Hopkins on one end of a log and James Garfield on the other.' In my judgment, the human appeal is greater when we visualize the log-cabin scene with Mentor Graham on one side of a crude table and Abraham Lincoln on the other side, poring over principles of grammar or problems in surveying well beyond the midnight hour. Therefore, to Mentor Graham belongs the credit of being the tutor, counselor, and inspirer of Lincoln when he was at the crossroads of that long, fateful journey from the lowly cabin to the White House. It was he who advised Lincoln 'to brush up in his grammar,' upon learning his ambition to enter political life; that a thorough knowledge of grammar was necessary if he wished to 'advance politically or appear well in society.' Upon being asked where such a treasure could be found, the schoolteacher, according to Beveridge's *Lincoln*, told him that a farmer by the name of John Vance, who lived six miles distant, owned a copy of Kirkham's *Grammar*. Thereupon, Lincoln, who was then boarding with Graham, rose from the breakfast table, walked to Vance's cabin, and returned with the book.

"Under Graham's guidance he studied so hard and well that in an incredibly short time he knew Kirkham's rules by heart and observed them. Three decades afterward, Graham declared that, having then taught for forty-five years, he had never seen anyone 'so apt and quick in learning grammar as Lincoln was.'

"After filling various positions in New Salem, all of which ended in failure, Lincoln was recommended by a friend to John Calhoun, surveyor of Sangamon County, who needed a deputy; and he was appointed. Lincoln again went to board in the cabin of Graham, who helped him at night to master a volume on surveying given him by his employer. Beveridge tells us that, although Lincoln had no aptitude for figures and had to labor hard and long to understand the intricacies of surveying, yet after six weeks he succeeded well enough to begin his work with Calhoun.

"A few years ago, Dr. O. T. Corson, former State Superintendent of Public Instruction of Ohio and president of the National Education Association, came to our city to give the commencement address for the Lincoln Community High School. While he was there, I took him out to see the old Postville Courthouse in which Abraham Lincoln practiced law from 1840 to 1846. Dr. Corson had written a splendid life of Lincoln, in which his traits of character were skilfully analyzed, and as a consequence he revered the historic place more than most visitors. While we were in the old courtroom, Dr. Corson told me of an interesting incident that occurred when he was in England. It happened while he was visiting at Oxford with the chancellor of that historic old university. Upon asking what the English people regarded as the best short selection of literature, Dr. Corson was conducted to the end of the corridor, quite naturally expecting to see something written by Shakespeare, Dickens, Thackeray, or some other distinguished English writer; but, to his very great surprise, he found hanging upon the wall a framed copy of Abraham Lincoln's letter to Mrs. Bixby. This letter, as you well know, was the outpouring of one broken heart to another, and in penning it Lincoln reached the heights of the literary world; and we must not forget his famous Gettysburg speech, which is rated as one of the greatest orations, and the first and second inaugural addresses, which are studied as classics in high school and college.

"It is a far cry from that day back in New Salem when Mentor Graham asked Lincoln if he could write and Lincoln replied, 'I can make a few chicken tracks, I reckon,' and from the day when he was advised to 'brush up in his grammar,' to that time when he was proclaimed author of the finest and purest short sketch ever written in the English language.

"And in the light of all that transpired, we must not lose sight of the great teacher, Mentor Graham, whose guidance and instruction so materially aided Lincoln in laying the foundations on which he built eternal fame.

"Senator Beveridge tersely summarizes it all by quoting R. B. Rutledge: 'I know of my own knowledge that Graham did more than all others to educate Lincoln.'

"As a teacher and as a member of the Illinois State Teachers Association, I count it an honor to participate in this memorial service for Mentor Graham. I am sure the members of this great organization, now and in years to come, will be profoundly grateful to his descendants for removing his remains from that unmarked grave in South Dakota to this cemetery, where he buried his wife and children.

"And if, by the providence of God, those who have crossed the Great Divide are permitted to know what happens here on earth, I am sure that Mentor Graham and his good wife are looking down from the battlements of heaven now and are rejoicing with us in this hour."

INDEX

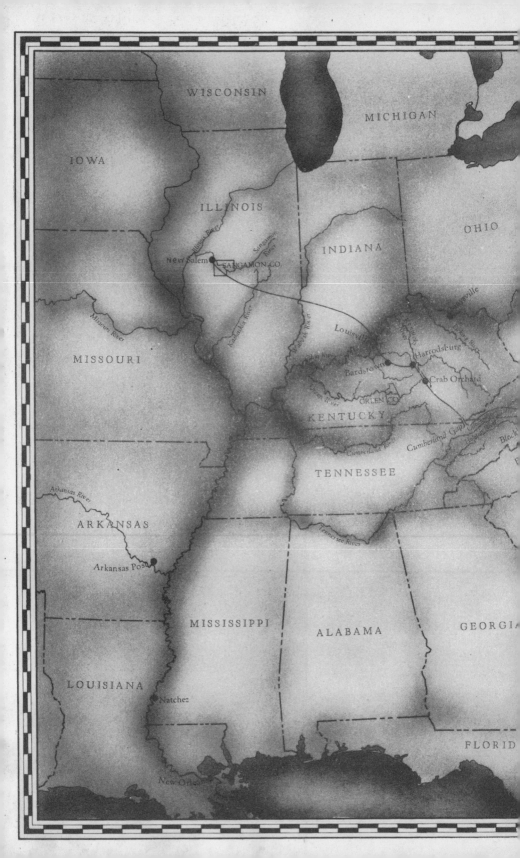